892

# THE MULTINATIONAL MISSION

# The
# MULTINATIONAL
# MISSION

*Balancing*
*Local Demands*
*and*
*Global Vision*

C. K. Prahalad
Yves L. Doz

THE FREE PRESS
*A Division of Macmillan, Inc.*
NEW YORK

Collier Macmillan Publishers
LONDON

The Free Press
A Division of Macmillan, Inc.
866 Third Avenue, New York, N.Y. 10022

Collier Macmillan Canada, Inc.

Printed in the United States of America

printing number

1  2  3  4  5  6  7  8  9  10

**Library of Congress Cataloging-in-Publication Data**

Prahalad, C. K.
    The multinational mission.

    Includes index.
    1. International business enterprises—Management.
I. Doz, Yves L.    II. Title.
HD62.4.P69     1987          658′ .049          87–11970
ISBN 0–02–925050–1

# Contents

*v*

# Preface and Acknowledgments

This book represents an important milestone in our intellectual effort. For more than ten years, starting with our doctoral research effort at the Harvard Business School, both of us have been concerned with the work of senior management in managing large, diversified multinational corporations. The processes of controlling and coordinating operations, and changing strategic direction, as well as providing for flexibility, in a variety of businesses in a diverse set of national markets are the basic themes in the book. Such a demanding task, we believe, forces managers to be both analytically sophisticated and organizationally savvy. In this book we present the essence of the managerial task—its conceptual and administrative dimensions—based on more than ten years of detailed, in-depth research in more than twenty United States–based, European, and Japanese multinationals.

The ideas presented in the book are derived from detailed clinical studies of actual business situations faced by managers in multinational firms. We have integrated those ideas into our teaching both at the MBA level and in executive programs. While our research revealed the richness and complexity of the managerial task, our effort to teach disciplined us to articulate the complexity and capture the excitement of our research territory. It also provided us with an invaluable opportunity to test the usefulness of the ideas to managers—all the way from divisional managers to CEOs of some of the largest U.S. and European firms.

This book is written primarily for practitioners. Our focus therefore has been on developing a framework for managerial action. The building blocks of the overall framework are illustrated with examples to help the reader readily grasp the concepts. While our focus is on managerial action, we believe the overall framework adds to the academic literature on managing the multinational corporation.

The point of view in this book represents not only research efforts spanning a decade but the active involvement and support of a large number of practitioners and academics. Our work would not have progressed without the cooperation of a large number of multinational firms and managers who generously gave their time and shared their perspective on issues. The clinical work demanded a high level of trust, as often we were researching issues on a "real time" basis, as events unfolded. We owe a substantial debt of gratitude to those managers.

Our effort began when we were doctoral students at Harvard. We were introduced to the excitement of both the methodology of research and the substantive issues of management by our mentor, Professor Joseph L. Bower. Joe has remained a powerful influence in our efforts to gain greater clarity. We owe our intellectual appetite for complex managerial problems to Joe.

The Division of Research funded our initial doctoral research. Dean McArthur supported the research both in his institutional role and through his personal enthusiasm. He believed in the value of this research effort.

Of all the researchers who have worked in our field of inquiry, two have greatly contributed to the development of the overall framework. Chris Bartlett at Harvard and Gary Hamel at Michigan helped elaborate aspects of the argument. Chris focused on the administrative dimensions of the managerial task. The series of cases he developed are invaluable in illustrating the basic logic presented in the book. Gary has focused on the emerging patterns of competition and how they influence the need for change in both the analytical and organizational demands in a multinational.

Both our schools—the University of Michigan and INSEAD— have been very sympathetic to our ambitious undertaking. Dean Gil Whitaker at Michigan and Dean Heinz Thanheiser at INSEAD gave us opportunities to create new executive programs to test our ideas and helped to free our time to write and continue the research. Our colleagues, especially Rich Bettis (SMU), Dominque Héau, José de la

Torre, and Sumantra Ghoshal (all at INSEAD), helped us with insights and provided opportunities for improving the text. Mr. Hariharan provided valuable editorial assistance.

Debie Chadwick, Joann Ripple, and Alison James worked through many drafts, under time pressure, with great efficiency and cheerfulness.

Gayatri and Nicole, our wives, ensured that we had the best of working conditions by taking on an unreasonable load of parenting. Without their constant encouragement and immense patience, this would have been impossible.

While many have contributed, the final product is ours, for which we take total responsibility.

April 1987                                                C. K. PRAHALAD
Ann Arbor,                                                YVES L. DOZ
Michigan

# 1

---

# Introduction

During the past decade, managers in businesses as diverse as semiconductors, automobiles, copiers, television sets, machine tools, foundry products, telecommunications, and financial services have come to accept a new reality: global competitors and global competition. Coincident with that awakening has been a realization that developing and implementing global strategies require more than a good analysis of cost and of the technological advantages of competitors. The ability to compete in the global market place requires not only the skills to foresee the shifting patterns of competitive advantage in a given business but in equal measure the ability to redeploy resources to maintain and in some cases regain competitiveness. It also requires the ability to motivate people at different levels in the organization and to keep them alert and focused on competition. That is the overall task of senior management—analysis and identification of competitive opportunities and threats, redeployment of corporate resources, and motivation of the entire organization—and it forms the central theme of this book.

We are concerned in this book with the processes by which top management of large, diversified (multibusiness) multinationals (DMNCs) provide direction to businesses in the pursuit of strategic goals. The task inevitably demands both analytical sophistication and organizational savvy. We shall provide the tools for analyzing global competition and a method for top management to translate that understanding into organizational action. This book provides for top management an *explicit logic* and a basis on which to act.

Top management's analytical and organizational problems are unfolded in the context of a DMNC, which encompasses both a *diversity of businesses* and a *diversity of national markets*. Top managers must comprehend the strategic characteristics of a wide variety of businesses as well as the differences and similarities in the multiple national markets in which those businesses compete. This represents the task in its most difficult and complex form. While firms may, through explicit choice, reduce the diversity of businesses in their portfolios, we shall argue that they will have to cope with global competitors and global competition even if left with such businesses as footwear, apparel, and mushrooms. Top management's general framework for action, developed in the context of a DMNC, is therefore just as valid in firms that are not significantly diversified geographically.

We start with simple premises. Competitive posture for a business results from a stream of resource commitments, made over a period of time, by several organizational subunits within the firm. The business unit managers at corporate headquarters, the researchers in the laboratory, and the managers in organizations of various countries all contribute to building an overall competitive posture. They all allocate resources—financial, technical, and managerial. The coherence with which a wide network of managers responsible for various activities make decisions to commit or not to commit resources is the basis for developing a sustainable competitive advantage. The actions of those managers are influenced by the decision-making process in the organization—the analytical sophistication, the types of data used, and the quality of the mechanisms through which conflicts are recognized and resolved. *Competitive advantage is the end result* of a series of actions, taken over time in the organization, all of which are influenced by the decision-making processes. Top management's work, therefore, is to ensure that the quality of the decision-making process is carefully monitored and improved. Top managers must focus their energies and attention on issues like the following: How do middle- and upper-middle-level managers within the organization perceive and analyze the economic, technological, and political forces that shape the businesses we are involved in? What internal organizational processes and competitive forces shape their perceptions? What is the process by which differences in perspectives between subunits (e.g., national managers and business managers) are resolved and a consensus is developed? What are the management processes that I, as a top manager, can use to shape the motivations of middle and upper-middle managers? Their analytical sophistication? Their actions? How do I improve the strategic capability of my organization—its ability to conceive and execute a wide variety of strategies? In a nutshell, this book's basic thesis is that strategy is concerned with action, and top management is concerned with managing the processes by which action, or the commitment of resources, is taken in the organization.

Academic attention on strategic management has so far focused either on the analytical tools for strategy formulation or on the organizational processes. One aspect of top management's work tends to get emphasis to the exclusion of the other. While either aspect, taken by itself, is critical and deserves attention, neither by itself reflects the reality of that work. We provide a framework to consider simultaneously the analytical and the organizational aspects as well as the linkages between the two.

## THE RESEARCH FOR THE BOOK

The research program on which this book is based was initiated in 1974. A pilot study of resource allocation in a global business in a U.S.-based diversified materials and chemicals MNC was the starting point. A detailed study of two additional firms—a European DMNC and a Japanese DMNC—trying to cope with the conflict between subsidiary autonomy and central control in strategy formulation followed. Those initial efforts led to research, involving several DMNCs, concerned with the shifting role of subsidiaries, more specifically the extent of autonomy of subsidiaries, in strategy, in the context of a fast-changing competitive milieu. The list of DMNCs studied included L. M. Ericsson, Brown Boveri, & Cie, General Telephone and Electronics, General Motors, Ford, Gamma (a disguised European DMNC), Nippon (a disguised Japanese DMNC), Corning Glass Works, IVECO, Alcan, Massey Ferguson, Philips, and IBM.[1] The research project in each DMNC consisted of an in-depth study of the process by which senior managers were realigning the strategy of one or more businesses. The project was based on interviews with executives, both at subsidiaries and at product divisions, and was supported by an examination of documentary evidence. Interviews numbered between twenty and fifty in each case. In some cases, research was conducted as events unfolded. Some firms were studied in depth by the authors, and others by doctoral students who followed the authors' basic research agenda and framework. Detailed descriptions of the process by which firms made strategic shifts were written, and some have been published as cases. In all firms, we checked our perceptions and data regarding the process of change for completeness and accuracy by sending detailed descriptions back to the managers whom we interviewed.[2]

We tested our findings in a variety of ways. First, we presented our framework to the top managers of DMNCs as diverse as IBM, ICI, Philips, GTE, Akzo, and Unilever. That gave us an opportunity to test the managerial validity of our thesis. Further, we presented our findings in many international academic conferences and to discriminating groups of academics to test the academic rigor of our study. We published aspects of our work in a variety of managerial and academic journals. What is presented in this book is a comprehensive framework, based on extensive clinical research in large DMNCs and tested for validity before a discriminating group of top managers and academics.

## THE FRAMEWORK

The work of top management in gaining and sustaining global competitive advantage depends on an understanding of the often conflicting forces that affect a business. For example, the shifting patterns of competitive advantage, based on changes in technology, economies of scale, factor cost advantages, and global distribution, impose a set of requirements on businesses if they are to remain competitive. In a business such as the production of television sets, it would be difficult to be a large-volume competitor without manufacturing in some low-wage countries or without mastering new manufacturing technologies. The preconditions of minimum volume, technology, and global distribution imposed by the dynamics of global competition on various businesses are the *economic imperatives.* In an ideal world of pure competition, winners and losers would be determined by the firms' ability to adapt and to manage the blend of economic forces.

Managers of DMNCs do not live in the ideal world of pure competition. As they prepare their firms to cope with the demands imposed by economic imperatives, they have to recognize that policies of host and home governments tend to distort competitive dynamics. Government policies either restrict managers' freedom to respond to the economic imperatives (e.g. to transfer work to low-wage countries), or enhance the options open to them (e.g. selective subsidies or protection of home market). Restrictions imposed on U.S.-based DMNCs like General Electric, Caterpillar, and IBM on the sale of their defense-related products to the Soviet Union and the Eastern bloc are examples of how home government policies distort competitive dynamics. Restrictions on Caterpillar allow Komatsu an unchallenged opportunity in the Soviet Union. On the other hand, subsidies and special privileges (such as access to public sector markets) provided to European and Japanese information technology firms can enhance some firms' competitive muscle and staying power. We may label the intervention of governments in the competitive process *the political imperative.* It is important to realize that the political imperative does not always restrict a firm's strategic choices. Instead, it is appropriate to think of governments as modifiers of competitive conditions. Governments have the ability to create as well as to restrict opportunities open to a firm in a specific set of businesses.

While the interplay of economic and political imperatives allows managers to identify a feasible set of strategic options for a business, the ability to implement that strategy depends on the quality of the organization. The ability of the organization to redeploy resources, to redirect the energies of its people, and to adapt to new competitive conditions limits the feasibility of strategic change. In other words, organizations can be differentiated by their capacity to conceive and implement complex strategies. Top managers in DMNCs must be sensitive to that very real, but often overlooked, limit to their freedom to execute complex strategies. We may label that aspect of competitive dynamics *the organizational imperative.*

In considering an implementable strategy for a business, top managers must recognize the simultaneous interplay of economic, political, and organizational imperatives. We may capture that interplay schematically, as in Figure 1.1. We believe that the work of top management is concerned with increasing the subset that encompasses the three imperatives—sometimes in conflict and sometimes in reinforcement. Stated in another way, top management should be sensitive to the external forces—competitive and political—and at

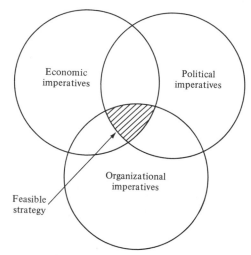

**Figure 1.1.** A Framework for the Work of Top Management

the same time be aware of the state of their organization and its capacity to analyze environmental trends, to identify opportunities, and to mobilize resources to exploit those opportunities.

## Road Map for the Reader

This book is organized in two parts. Part I deals primarily with the analytical tools required to understand strategic choices. Part II deals primarily with the organizational capabilities required to exploit strategic choices.[3] Each chapter provides a building block to the overall argument. The overall scheme is shown in Figure 1.2.

### Part I: Analysis for Strategy Development

We start with the analysis of the strategic options of a single discrete business (in a diversified MNC). Chapter 2 deals with the fact that each business, in a global setting, is subject to the twin pressures of central coordination and integration of activities across borders and autonomous subsidiary responsiveness to local demands based on the nature of economic, competitive, and market forces. This chapter provides a framework for analyzing the unique characteristics of

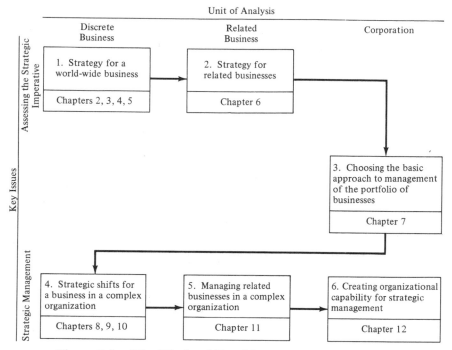

*Figure 1.2.*    The Work of Top Management in DMNCS

a business in its global setting. It deals with the question: What is a global business?

In Chapter 3, we develop the distinction between global business and global competition. This chapter provides a fuller description of the dynamics of competition. We argue that global competition is likely in all global businesses as defined in Chapter 2 and that even in some "local and regional businesses" global competition can take place; therefore, businesses that are essentially local may still need to be strategically coordinated.

Some businesses by their nature are subject to host and home government intervention. Businesses that are defense-related, business that form the basis for the national industrial infrastructure (e.g., telecommunications) or national development priorities, and industries requiring restructuring may belong to this category. In Chapter 4 we outline a methodology for assessing the impact of government intervention on the strategic options open to a firm in a specific business. We argue that it may be desirable for a firm to treat certain businesses as locally responsive even when their underlying economic and technological conditions would favor global integration.

Governments are not alone in intervening and modifying the underlying competitive imperative. Labor unions have wielded significant power in determining the strategic choices open to the firm, especially in Europe. Chapter 5 is devoted to an analysis of the influence of unions and organized labor in changing the strategic options.

So far we have assumed, for the sake of narrative simplicity, that businesses are discrete and stand alone. We assumed that strategy for a business can be developed without explicit attention to the impact of that strategy on other businesses within the portfolio of the DMNC. In a DMNC, businesses are often related and interdependent. Strategies cannot be developed for businesses in isolation, and one cannot assume, for purposes of strategy development, that businesses are discrete. In Chapter 6 we outline various types of interdependencies among businesses and suggest that not all types of interdependencies are "critical." We provide a framework to assess how critical the interdependencies among businesses in the portfolio are.

In Chapter 7 we move on to the analysis of the total corporation, which may have several businesses, some of which may be related. We suggest top management approaches to coping with "variety" in a DMNC's portfolio.

### Part II: Management Responsibilities and Techniques

Part II allows us to shift gears and focus on managing rather than on understanding and analyzing options. We start with the framework developed in the first seven chapters and ask the question: How do I, as a top manager, provide strategic orientation to a set of businesses?

The task of top managers is best understood when they are involved in managing strategic change and creating strategic flexibility. In Chapter 8, we start with strategic change as it involves a discrete business in the DMNC. We develop a methodology for understanding strategic flexibility and change and suggest that the building blocks for developing such a capability may be the individual middle- and upper-middle-level managers—that strategic change takes place only when their world views are changed and refocused.

In Chapter 9 we identify the management mechanisms that top managers can use to influence and motivate other managers, resolve conflicts, and manage the distribution of information in the organization. We develop protocols for change based on extensive chronologies of successful and unsuccessful strategic change in a wide variety of DMNCs.

In developing an agenda for change, top managers must be sensitive to the impediments to strategic change within their own organizations. Those impediments may relate to the nature of head office subsidiary relations or to external forces like government influence or labor unions. We suggest in Chapter 10 that the success rate can be considerably enhanced in strategic change efforts if a detailed analysis of the impediments to change is undertaken prior to initiating the process.

In considering strategic change in Chapters 8, 9, and 10 we assumed a discrete, stand-alone business setting. In Chapter 11 we evaluate the difficulties in making strategic change in related businesses. Often in such settings the various constituents of the interrelated set have differing strategic priorities. We shall examine different approaches to handling that problem.

Finally, in Chapter 12 we develop the notion of strategic capability, or the ability of a top management to create conditions within the DMNC that allows it to conceive and execute a wide variety of strategies in different businesses, an organization that can cope with "variety." We also develop the concept of an "ideal organization," one that can cope with the multitude of pressures that are the result of global competition.

**What We Don't Do**

While we are concerned with the work of top management in DMNCs, we have consciously left out several aspects of the top management task. For example, we say very little about top management's role as a spokesman for the company in public and government forums. We say nothing about top management's role in managing relationships with the external board or with the investment community. We are concerned primarily with the *executive role of the top managers*—their role and work in managing the strategic direction of various businesses. We believe that to be the most important part of the top manager's task.

# PART I

# ANALYSIS FOR STRATEGY DEVELOPMENT

# 2

# Mapping the Characteristics
# of a Business

As the emerging patterns of competition in a wide variety of businesses become of increasing concern, especially the intense competition brought about by overseas competitors, the words "global business" and "global competition" have entered the lexicon of most managers. However, the distinction between the intrinsic characteristics of a business*—its cost structure, technology, and customers, for example, at a given point in time—and the characteristics of competition in that business is not always well understood.[1] Further, labeling businesses as "global" or "multidomestic" may hide broad variations in the underlying managerial tasks. In this chapter, we shall develop a methodology for capturing, in a managerially meaningful scheme, the characteristics of a wide range of businesses or for understanding the "existing rules of the game" in a business. In the next chapter, we shall go beyond the analysis of "existing rules" and examine how determined competitors often change those rules.

---

*In this chapter, as in the rest of the book, the word "business" refers to a set of related product markets and tasks, not to a company. Our use of the word "business" thus covers more than a product line but typically less than a whole industry.

## THE BUILDING BLOCKS

The building blocks of the methodology for mapping the characteristics of a business start with the managerial demands that it imposes on senior management.

### Global Integration of Activities

Integration refers to the centralized management of geographically dispersed activities on an ongoing basis. Managing shipments of parts and subassemblies across a network of manufacturing facilities in various countries is an example of integration of activities.

The need for integration arises in response to pressures to reduce costs and optimize investment. Pressures to reduce cost may force location of plants in countries with low labor costs, such as South Korea, Taiwan, and Malaysia. Products are then shipped from those plants to the established markets of the United States and Europe. The same pressures may also lead to building large-scale, highly specialized plants, to realize economies of scale. Ford's European operations and IBM's worldwide manufacturing operations are examples of the phenomenon. In either case, the goal is leveraging the advantages of low manufacturing cost. Managerially, that translates into a need for ongoing management of logistics that cut across multiple national boundaries.

### Global Strategic Coordination

Strategic coordination refers to the central management of resource commitments across national boundaries in the pursuit of a strategy. It is distinct from the integration of ongoing activities across national borders. Typical examples would involve coordinating R&D priorities across several laboratories, coordinating pricing to global customers, and facilitating transfers of technology from headquarters to subsidiaries and across subsidiaries. Unlike activity integration, strategic coordination can be selective and nonroutine.

Strategic coordination is often essential to provide competitive and strategic coherence to resource commitments made over time by headquarters and various subsidiaries in multiple countries. The goal of strategic coordination is to recognize, build, and defend long-term competitive advantages. For example, headquarters may assign highly differentiated goals to various subsidiaries in the same business in order to develop a coherent response to competition.

Strategic coordination, like integration of activities, often involves headquarters and one or several subsidiaries. Coordination decisions transcend a single subsidiary.

### Local Responsiveness

Local responsiveness refers to resource commitment decisions taken autonomously by a subsidiary in response to primarily local competitive or customer demands. In a wide variety of businesses, there may be no competitive advantage to be gained by coordinating actions across subsidiaries; in fact, that may prove to be detrimental.

Typically, businesses where there are no meaningful economies of scale or proprietary technology (e.g. processed foods) fall into this category. The need for significant local adaptation of products or differences in distribution across national markets may also indicate a need for local responsiveness.

## CHARACTERISTICS OF A BUSINESS AND MANAGERIAL DEMANDS

The three building blocks described above—global integration of activities, global strategic coordination, and local responsiveness— refer to the nature of relationships between headquarters and subsidiaries, as well as among subsidiaries in a multinational setting. However, those relationships are *dependent* on the nature of the businesses in the DMNC. The economic, technological, and competitive characteristics of a business enable us to define the pressures for global integration of activities and local responsiveness. The need for strategic coordination is harder to focus on. Typically, businesses that need significant global integration of activities also require strategic coordination. However, given active global competition, which we shall discuss in Chapter 3, locally responsive businesses may demand strategic coordination as well. In Chapter 4, we shall identify situations where businesses that would require integration and coordination in conditions of free competition are forced to be locally responsive, at least in part. At this stage it is useful to recognize two essential demands—global integration and local responsiveness—and assume that the extent of strategic coordination is related to the need for integration. We shall identify those linkages by examining one DMNC in detail.

## Mapping the Characteristics of a Business

Let us take the case of Corning Glass.* As of 1975 it operated internationally in six business categories with more than 60,000 line items. The businesses were:

• *Television products,* which included supplying TV bulbs to original equipment manufacturers (OEM) like RCA, Philips, and Sylvania. The technology was mature, and competition was based on costs, delivery, product development, and ability to meet bulb specifications, which differed according to transmission standards in different countries. Corning had few competitors around the world in this business and had an identifiable, small set of relatively large OEM customers.

• *Electronic products,* which consisted of components like resistors and capacitors used by computer, communication, and military equipment manufacturers. Most of the products were mature, and the business was extremely price sensitive. Customers shopped around worldwide for the best prices and technical specifications.

• *Consumer products,* chiefly Corningware, the leading cookware product in the United States. The mass market for cookware was reached through retailers. Distribution channels varied by country. While some large, global competitors like Noritake of Japan existed, most competitors were regional and local.

• *Medical products,* consisting of scientific instruments such as blood gas analyzers and diagnostic reagents. The instruments were high-value-added products, manufactured in small quantities, using a highly technical process. Product development was a key task in this business, and product life cycles were short. A direct sales force

---

*The Corning Glass Works example relies on data made public in the case series from Michael Y. Yoshino and Christopher A. Bartlett, "Corning Glass Works International (B1)," Case 9-381-161. Boston: Harvard Business School, 1981. Reprinted by permission.*

was used. Differences existed between various country markets, which made product development difficult.

• *Science products,* specifically laboratory glassware, an old, mature product line. Competition was primarily based on price. This business category also included chemical systems like heat exchangers and process piping designed for specific applications.

• *Technical products,* mostly ophthalmic products, which consisted of photochromatic eyeglass blanks, produced in a variety of thicknesses, curvatures, and so forth. Because of the variety of shapes, sizes, colors, and materials in which the product had to be delivered, sourcing decisions were critical. This business group also contained technical materials, which involved supplying specialty subassemblies to governments and OEMs.

Corning's overseas activities comprised fourteen major foreign manufacturing operations and a host of licensees. Its products were produced abroad, and the overseas sales volume was significant. Its overseas manufacturing and sales involvement in the six broad business categories is shown in Table 2.1.

**TABLE 2.1**   Corning's Overseas Involvement, 1974

| Business Group | Overseas Manufacturing Plants in | Approximate Overseas Sales as a % of Total Sales for That Business |
|---|---|---|
| Television products | France, Brazil, Mexico, Taiwan, and Canada; licensees in Europe and Japan | 30% |
| Electronics products | France, U.K. | 35% |
| Consumer products | France, U.K., Argentina, Australia, Holland | 35% |
| Medical products | U.K. | 25% |
| Science products; lab ware | France, U.K., Argentina, Mexico, Brazil, Japan, India, Australia | 40% |
| Chemical systems | France, U.K. | 65% |
| Technical products; ophthalmic products | France, Brazil | 33% |
| Technical products | — | 15% |

With such a spread of overseas activities in both manufacturing and marketing, should Corning treat all its businesses as global? Are there differences among those businesses that transcend the location of plants and the distribution of markets around the world?

It is a great temptation to categorize businesses as diverse as Corningware and electronic products as either global (meaning their activities can and should be integrated across borders) or multidomestic (meaning that they are local businesses in multiple countries). However, each business is subject to varying degrees of economic, competitive, and technological pressures that push it toward becoming global or toward remaining locally responsive. Some of the Corning businesses have to accommodate both pressures simultaneously.

## The Integration–Responsiveness Grid

The Integration–Responsiveness (IR) grid provides us with a way of capturing the pressures on a given business—pressures that make *strategic coordination* and *global integration of activities* critical, as well as the pressures that make being sensitive to the diverse demands of various national markets and achieving *local responsiveness* critical.

We can use the following criteria for evaluating the pressures for global coordination and integration, as well as local responsiveness.

### Pressures for Global Strategic Coordination

*Importance of multinational customers.*    The dependence of a business on multinational OEM customers imposes a need for global strategic coordination. For example, in the TV bulbs business, a significant portion of the total sales went to multinational OEM customers like Philips and Sylvania. Multinational customers can, and often do, compare prices charged them by their suppliers around the world, demand the same level of service and product support, and have centralized vendor certification. The product is often sold at the center, say to the OEM's product division, and delivered around the world—wherever the multinational customer may need it. The percentage of sales to multinational OEM customers and their importance to the business can thus dictate the need for global coordination. In the case of Corningware, the opposite was true. Its customers were mostly local, and it was primarily a mass-marketed item.

*Presence of multinational competitors.*    The presence of competitors who operate in multiple markets indicates the potential for global competition. Consequently, it is crucial to gather intelligence on competitors across national markets, to understand their strategic intent, and to be ready to respond to their actions wherever most appropriate. The presence of multinational competitors calls for global strategic coordination. Competitors for Corning's various businesses ranged from global competitors in electronic products, to regional competitors in TV products, to local competitors in lab ware and Corning cookware.

*Investment intensity.*    If an aspect of the business is investment-intensive (e.g. R&D, manufacturing), the need to leverage that investment increases the need for global coordination. Worldwide product strategies have to be developed and implemented quickly to make the large initial investments profitable.

At Corning, the intensity of the R&D effort in the medical products business and the intensity of investment in manufacturing and product development in the electronics business indicated that a high level of global coordination and integration was required in those two businesses. In the lab ware business, the pressure for international strategic coordination was not felt.

*Technology intensity.*    Technology intensity and the extent of proprietary technology often encourage firms to manufacture in only a few selected locations. Having fewer manufacturing sites allows easier control over quality, cost, and new product introduction. Centralized product development and manufacturing operations in a few locations result in global integration, particularly when the markets are widely dispersed.

Again, at Corning the technological intensity differed from business to business. For example, the lab ware required a very low technology as compared to the medical products business. Medical products had short life cycles, with constantly renewed markets, whereas lab ware had stable products and applications.

*Pressure for cost reduction.*    Global integration is often a response to pressure for cost reduction. Cost reduction requires sourcing the product from low-factor-cost locations (global sourcing), or exploiting economies of scale and experience by building large plants that serve multiple national markets. Either approach to lowering costs imposes a need for global integration.

Some of Corning's businesses, such as electronic products, were subject to severe cost pressures, while others, like Corningware, were less so.

***Universal needs.***   If the product meets a universal need and requires little adaptation across national markets, global integration is obviously facilitated.

Electronic products—capacitors, resistors—are good examples of universal products. They do not vary by country. On the other hand, Corningware is not universal. It must be adapted to suit various market needs. For example, the "oven-to-freezer" feature may be a big hit in the United States but may not be appropriate in France; a soufflé dish popular in France may not have a big market in the Midwest.

***Access to raw materials and energy.***   Access to raw materials and a cheap and plentiful supply of energy can force manufacturing to be located in a specific area. Aluminum smelters, paper mills, and, increasingly, petrochemicals tend to be located where the raw materials are available. That tendency in some businesses suggests global coordination and integration. None of Corning's businesses had to contend with this issue.

### Pressures for Local Responsiveness

***Differences in customer needs.***   Businesses that thrive on satisfying a diverse set of customer needs, most of which is nation- or region-specific, require a locally responsive strategy.

Several businesses within Corning have satisfied country-specific needs. Corningware, technical materials, and to some extent chemical systems were designed with specific customers of individual countries in mind. On the other hand, electronic products met a universal need.

***Differences in distribution channels.***   Differences in distribution channels in various countries and the differences in pricing, product positioning, promotion, and advertising that those differences entail indicate the need for local responsiveness.

In the lab ware business at Corning, the distribution system used to access the school systems in various countries varied; comparable differences in distribution channels characterized Corningware. On the other hand, in the electronic and TV products businesses, which were primarily serving OEM customers, the differences among national markets were only marginal.

*Availability of substitutes and the need to adapt.*   If a product function is being met by local substitutes, with differing price–performance relationships in a given national market, or if the product must be significantly adapted to be locally competitive, then a locally responsive strategy is indicated.

Corningware had a significant number of substitutes—cooking ware made from other materials, as well as cooking ware promoted differently. It also needed to be adapted to suit local conditions. In the case of electronic products, neither condition was important: Products were universal and faced no differentiated local substitutes.

*Market structure.*   Market structure includes the importance of local competitors as compared to multinational ones, as well as the extent of their concentration. If local competitors tend to control a significant portion of the market and/or if the industry is not concentrated, then a locally responsive posture is most usually indicated (unless there are merits to competing globally to make the industry structure evolve in your favor, as will be discussed in Chapter 3). A fragmented industry with local competitors indicates that there may be no inherent advantages to size and scale, unless product and process technology can be changed.

Again, among Corning's businesses, lab ware had to compete in each national market with a large number of local competitors in a fragmented industry, while TV products had to cope with only a handful of large competitors in a globally concentrated industry.

*Host government demands.*   Demands imposed by host governments for local self-sufficiency for a variety of reasons—from concerns of national development to concerns of national security—can force a business to become locally responsive. We shall deal with the impact of the demands imposed by host governments in Chapter 4.

*Mapping Corning's Businesses
in the Integration-Responsiveness Grid*

It is obvious that Corning does not operate in any one type of business—either global or multidomestic. Each of its businesses is subject to a different combination of pressures toward global coordination and integration and toward local responsiveness—pressures that elude a simple "either-or" classification. We can identify the differences using the criteria we have developed, as shown in Table 2.2.

The characteristics of the three businesses can now be captured in an Integration–Responsiveness Grid, as shown in Figure 2.1. From the foregoing analysis, the following generalizations can be drawn:

1. The mapping of the characteristics of the various businesses illustrates the differences among them, even though all six businesses share the same corporate logo and all evolved out of the same broad glass technology. Because of those differences, managers must examine each business individually to develop strategies rather than treat them all alike.

2. Classifying businesses broadly as either global or local can be misleading. There are few businesses that are totally local. If there were no advantages to be gained in that business by an MNC, then it is likely to be very fragmented with no scope for leveraging knowledge, products, financial muscle, or brands across markets. On the other hand, few businesses are totally global. A variety of factors, including the need for a responsive and differentiated local presence in various countries, make it difficult to ignore totally the demands of various national markets.

3. The purpose of the IR framework is to assess the *relative importance* of the two sets of conflicting demands on a business and to determine which of the two provides strategic leverage at a given point in time.

4. In the case of Corning, some businesses tend toward global integration (e.g. electronics, medical products). In those businesses, strategic advantage will accrue to the competitor who is organized to exploit the benefits of strategic coordination in investments, product policy, product development, pricing, monitoring competitors, and so forth. In businesses that tend toward local responsiveness (e.g. Corningware, lab ware), strategic advantage accrues to the firm that is sensitive to the need for decentralized pricing, promotion, and product policy. There may be little benefit in strategic coordination.

**TABLE 2.2**   Comparison of Three Businesses within Corning

| Criteria | Electronics | TV Products | Corningware |
|---|---|---|---|
| **Pressures for Global Strategic Coordination** | | | |
| Importance of multinational customers | high | high | low |
| Importance of multinational competitors | high | medium/high | low |
| Investment intensity | high | high | low/medium |
| **Pressures for Global Operational Integration** | | | |
| Technology intensity | medium | medium | low |
| Pressure for cost reduction | high | high | low |
| Universal needs | high | medium | low |
| Access to raw materials and energy | NA | NA | NA |
| **Need for Global Integration** | *high* | *medium* | *low* |
| **Pressures for Local Responsiveness** | | | |
| Differences in customer needs | low | medium? | high |
| Differences in distribution | low | low | high |
| Need for substitutes and product adaptation | low | low | high |
| Market structure | Concentrated | Concentrated | Fragmented |
| Host government demands | NA | NA | NA |
| **Need for Local Responsiveness** | *low* | *medium* | *high* |

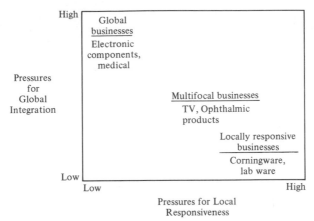

*Figure   2.1.*   Integration-Responsiveness   Grid:
Characteristics of Corning's Business

5.  In Corning's case the real challenge to management is not in
managing the extremes; it is in managing multifocal businesses, which
demand sensitivity to both dimensions *at the same time,* as is the
case with the TV products business. This implies that in such businesses it is unwise to make a one-time tradeoff in favor of either
global integration or local responsiveness. Both demands have to be
managed simultaneously.

**Some Implications**

Several managerial conclusions can be derived from mapping the
characteristics of a business on the IR grid.
   1.  Corning's electronic components, which is high on the need
for global integration and low on the need for local responsiveness,
suggests that managers developing strategies for that business must
pay considerably more attention to leveraging aspects like economies
of scale, product development, global customers, and global competitors than to issues of local responsiveness. This also implies that
resource allocation decisions with respect to key elements of strategy
for that business (such as plant location and investment, pricing,
product development, and key account management) may have to
be centralized. In other words, for the electronic components business, the locus of strategic management is the central worldwide
business management group. On the other hand, for Corningware

or lab ware, the key strategic choices (pricing, promotion, choice of channels) have to be managed in a decentralized mode. The center for strategy making is the regional or the national subsidiary managers, as contrasted with the center for the electronic components business, as shown in Figure 2.2.

2. In both those businesses representing the extremes—electronic components and Corningware—managers can make "clear one-time choices" of what aspects of the business to leverage. Therefore, a clear and simple organizational form—worldwide business management in the case of electronic components and area management in the case of Corningware—is possible. In other words, the relative simplicity of the strategic priorities enables a clear-cut choice of simple organization.

3. In the case of the TV business the strategic choice is not all that clear-cut. Some elements of strategy, like plant size and technology, may have to be managed centrally. On the other hand, deliveries, competitors, and some key customers may have to be managed both regionally and locally. That implies that managers cannot make a "one-time choice" on which of the two dimensions to leverage. They must *simultaneously focus their attention* on aspects of the business that require global integration and aspects that demand local responsiveness, and on varying degrees of strategic coordination. This need for *multiple focal points for managing* suggests that managers must reflect the need for multiple points of view—the

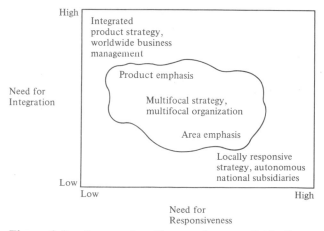

*Figure 2.2.*   Integration-Responsiveness Grid: Strategic Focus and Organizational Adaptation

need to integrate and be responsive at the same time—in the way that business is organized. That requires the organization to be *multifocal* or matrix.

In general, many businesses that have the characteristics of Corning's TV business will need a multifocal or matrix organization, despite all the problems of managing such an organization.

The IR grid is not just a tool for discovering the essential orientation of a business for strategy making. It also enables managers to decide on the appropriate form of organization to manage the strategic orientation desired.

## MAPPING THE DYNAMICS OF A BUSINESS ON THE IR GRID

While taking Corning to illustrate the basic approach to mapping the characteristics on the IR grid, we have assumed our data and have assessed the characteristics of a business at a given point in time, rather than the way it might change over time. For the strategist, the direction of possible change in the characteristics of a business is even more interesting than the situation at a given point in time. Now we shall identify the factors that can change the location of a business in the IR grid over time as well as suggest the type of data that might be useful in understanding such trends early.

### Changes in Underlying Industry Economics

Shifts in the location of a business on the IR grid are often a result of shifts in the underlying economics of the industry. Let us take the example of ethylene oxide. During the early 1970s, most chemical firms operated plants of an annual capacity of 50 million to 75 million pounds. In most markets of the world, especially in the United States and Europe, that meant firms could dedicate a plant (or more) to each important national market. As each market could afford its own manufacturing and marketing facilities, and as ethylene oxide was a commodity product, managers could be very sensitive to local needs. In the early 1970s most firms operated with considerable local responsiveness and a low level of global integration. However, over the period 1972–75, several chemical firms, especially ICI in the United Kingdom, started building plants with a capacity as large as 250 million to 400 million pounds. The cost advantage arising from the economies of scale was around 12 to 15 percent over traditional, smaller plants. Because a single national market could not absorb the output of the large-scale plants, the firm had to coordinate prices, product specifications, logistics, and, most importantly, investments across several, so far autonomous national markets. In a very short time, the center of gravity for strategy making in the ethylene oxide business for several chemical firms had shifted toward high need for integration and low need for responsiveness. Given a 12 to 15 percent cost advantage in a commodity chemical, few competitors could resist the pressure to build large plants in order to remain competitive. On the IR grid, the ethylene oxide business would be depicted as locally responsive until 1972. It moved toward international integration because of changes in industry economics during 1972–75.[2]

Could that have been predicted? Clearly, the technology breakthrough that was required to build large plants was no secret, nor were the cost advantages that would accrue as a result. The nature of the shift in industry economics that would result from a dramatic increase in plant size was obvious. The implications of the trend for the business could have been predicted.

## Impact of Governments

During the same period drug companies also faced a shift in their business. The proprietary drug business, involving significant investment in R&D and requiring strict quality controls in manufacturing, is best managed centrally, from a few locations. However, the politics of health care in many countries around the world force drug firms to manufacture in multiple locations. They are also subject to local clinical testing, registration procedures, and pricing restrictions. As governments and quasi-government agencies control a significant portion of the health care budget in most countries, they are in a position to demand a high level of local responsiveness. That has forced most drug firms into simultaneously facing a high need for global integration and a high need for local responsiveness.[3]

## Shifts in the Competitive Focus of Customers

Supplier industries tend to follow the shifts in the industries they serve. For example, the automobile industry has become global in terms of its sourcing and design, as well as manufacturing. In firms like General Motors, design teams out of the United States, Germany, and Great Britain may be working on a series of "world cars." That trend has had impact on suppliers to the auto industry. For example, paint manufacturers, who manufacture paints for household use as well as car finishes, have typically operated on a locally responsive basis. The trend in the auto industry has forced one segment of their operations, car finishes, to become globally integrated. Product planners and purchasing agents in the auto industry would like to contract with a set of suppliers who can supply the same quality of car finish around the world. Yet the home paint segment is still locally responsive. Paint manufacturers who saw their business as essentially locally responsive had to contend with the realization that the auto industry internationalization was changing the nature of customer relations in a segment of their business; they had to recognize that they could no longer treat both segments of their business—car finishes and home paints—alike.[4]

### Resegmenting a Business

Often resegmenting a business provides an opportunity for reexamining the appropriate location of a business in the IR grid. While we have assumed the business as a unit of analysis, a reexamination of "what constitutes a business" may provide useful insights. For example, if the business is defined as health care products, based on the criteria we have developed, it might occupy a certain location in the IR grid. On the other hand, if we segment the business into its constituent parts—proprietary drugs, ethical drugs, and health care supplies—we may see three distinct trends. Each one of those segments is subject to a distinctly different set of economic and competitive forces.[5] The dynamics of change in a business in the IR grid is shown in Figure 2.3.

### Firms Learn

The way a business is perceived in the IR grid may shift as firms learn about their businesses and see new opportunities and problems. For example, when a processed food firm, Nabisco, went overseas, its management assumed the businesses could be managed centrally and that the benefits of coordinating in advertising and product development outweighed the benefits of local responsiveness. It soon

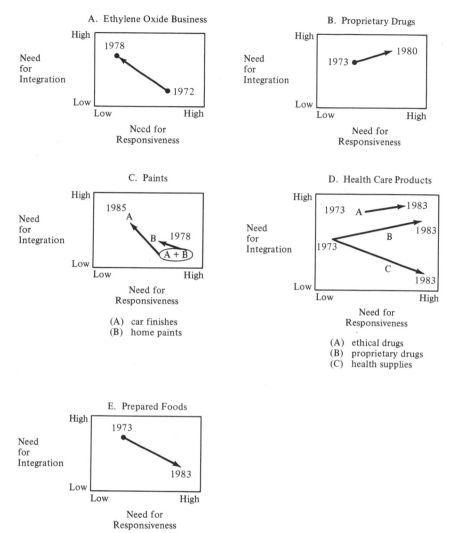

***Figure 2.3.***  Mapping Mobility of Businesses in the IR Grid

became apparent that the habits of consumers were harder to change in some of the businesses than originally thought; a locally responsive strategy made more sense.[6]

## Changing the "Rules of the Game"

Other firms saw opportunities to do exactly the opposite. Otis elevator saw an opportunity in the late 1960s to integrate its operations in the elevator market in Europe. At that time the market was dominated by local firms; most MNCs also operated on a locally responsive mode. Through a process of acquisitions and consolidations, by standardizing elevator design, and by cutting costs, Otis changed the rules of the game. It changed the economics of the industry to a point where regional integration, if not global integration, became the dominant mode. The first company to initiate and exploit that change can gain a considerable advantage over its competitors, who are slower to move toward international integration.

The success of Japanese competitors in a variety of industries can be attributed to their ability to pick primarily locally responsive industries, even those populated by MNCs, and change them to globally integrated businesses. Examples abound. Traditional competitors who were multinational prior to the Japanese competitive thrust in the auto industry (e.g. General Motors), ball bearings (e.g. SKF), and television sets (e.g. Philips) operated on a locally responsive basis. They were caught off guard. Once a determined competitor changes the rules of the game, the degrees of freedom available to others may be limited, as in the case of ethylene oxide or in the auto and elevator industries.

## MAPPING MOBILITY OF BUSINESSES
## IN THE IR GRID

In Figure 2.3, the shifts discussed above are illustrated. It is important to note the mobility of businesses within the IR grid. That mobility requires that managers not only recognize the balance of the forces of global integration and local responsiveness to which a business is subject to at a given point in time, but also assess the pattern of change in that posture over time. A careful analysis of the underlying cost structure of the industry (e.g. ethylene oxide), the political pressures on it (e.g. ethical drugs, computers), shifts in the competitive focus of customers (e.g. paints for the auto industry), opportunities for resegmentation (e.g. health care), and an ability to change the rules of the game (e.g. elevators) are crucial for assessing the opportunities and threats in the industry. In addition to data on the behavior of costs, changes in technology, and shifts in the policies of host governments, managers have to make judgments on how fast those factors will have an impact on the industry. In many cases, managers *can and do change the rules of the game,* proactively, as in the case of elevators or ball bearings. In other words, an analysis and understanding of "objective data" tell us only part of the story.

The movement of a business within the IR grid is very much influenced by the perceptions, judgments, and ambitions of managers on how it can be resegmented or changed. Significant shifts in the location of a business in the IR grid imply that the key success factors in that business have changed dramatically, leading to shifts in strategy. Strategy development is therefore not just an exercise in assessing the "rules of the game" in a given business, at a given point in time (i.e., the location of a business in the IR grid); it is as much developing viable "new rules of the game" (i.e., identifying opportunities for mobility within the IR grid). That calls for marrying analysis of objective data and current industry patterns and managerial perceptions together with judgments on how the business can be changed.[7]

## Capturing Perceptions of Managers

In order to capture the perceptions and judgments of managers regarding the potential for change in a business, we suggest the use of questionnaires similar to the ones in Figure 2.4 (for assessing the extent of local responsiveness) and Figure 2.5 (for assessing the extent of global integration). Each questionnaire captures aspects of a business, like the nature of competiton, evolution of technology, scope for manufacturing economies, and so forth, on a seven-point scale. Managers are asked to:

1. Identify the relative importance of each factor to the business by ranking, the most important being 1 and the least important 6, in the questionnaire on local responsiveness.

2. Identify where the business was three years ago, where it is now, and where it is likely to be, in his or her judgment, in the next three years, on the seven-point scale for each dimension. This provides a method for capturing his or her perception of the changes that have taken place in that business, in each dimension, (the difference between now and three years ago), as well as the extent of change that he or she expects in that dimension in the near future (the difference between the score now and three years from now). By consolidating the weighted scores for the dimensions representing the forces of local responsiveness and global integration, we can represent the extent of change in that business as well as the expectation for change in the perception of each manager. We can also develop a score for the management group as a whole.

O = Three years ago
X = At present
√ = Three years from now

## MARKET

Heterogeneous. Customers and customer needs are not clearly identified. Customer motivations tend to be complex. The perceived value of the product is unclear. The trends in the market are not easily foreseen.

## COMPETITIVE SITUATION

Competition is diffuse, with a large number of competitors. Competitors' strategies are unclear. There are no typical characteristics of the firm in the industry.

## TECHNOLOGY

Technology is evolving. A variety of unknowns in process and product specifications and cost structure exist. Rates of change in products and production processes are both rapid and unpredictable.

## ECONOMICS OF MANUFACTURE

The key determinant of manufacturing cost is still unclear. Costs are not affected by size or location of plant. Raw materials are easily available.

## EXECUTIVE GROUP

Executives do not have any shared experiences—educational, cultural, or professional. They do not share a feeling of belonging to the organization.

|   | 1 | 2 | 3 | 4 | 5 | 6 | 7 |
|---|---|---|---|---|---|---|---|

Product

Process

## MARKET

Homogeneous. Customer segments are clearly identified. The customers' decision process and perception of value of the products are clear. Market trends are clear.

## COMPETITIVE SITUATION

Competition is easily identified. There are only few competitors, and their strategies can be identified and interpreted.

## TECHNOLOGY

Relatively stable technology and a high level of manufacturing sophistication. Products are relatively mature. Production technology improvements and cost minimization are seen as important.

## ECONOMICS OF MANUFACTURE

The key determinants of manufacturing cost are size of plant and capacity utilization. Locational advantages exist. Availability of raw materials poses a problem.

## EXECUTIVE GROUP

Executives share substantial experience together—educational, professional, and cultural. They share a sense of belonging to the organization.

*Figure 2.4.* Sample Questionnaire for Assessing the Required Extent of Local Responsiveness

O = Three years ago
X = At present
√ = Three years from now

Figure 2.5. Sample Questionnaire for Assessing the Required Extent of Global Integration

STRATEGIC

Capacity and manufacturing technology decisions are made with a view to provide multiplant linkages and multiplant sourcing potential.

MARKETING

Product and quality specifications are developed and coordinated to serve multiple geographically defined markets.

Pricing strategy, support to various market segments, assessment of the importance of various market segments to the corporation, market priorities for allocation of capacity and other such market-related decisions are made with the total worldwide corporate interest in focus.

The subsidiaries sell a substantial part of their output to the same multinational customers worldwide.

The customers have the same level of income, education, and motivations worldwide.

TECHNOLOGY

Development effort is carried out in multiple locations, each location specializing in a specific technical area and/or a product line. This output is shared by all subsidiaries.

MANUFACTURING

Substantial movements of semifinished and finished products exists between local subsidiaries. This movement is governed by formal agreements. Problems in one plant (e.g., quality of product or strike) can affect other plants and markets adversely.

CONTROL

Production planning, inventory and quality control, and cost control are managed centrally.

STRATEGIC

Capacity and process decisions are made on a project-by-project basis with a view to serving specific market areas.

MARKETING

Product and quality specifications are developed with a single, specific geographical market in view.

Pricing, support to various market segments, perceived importance of the segments to the corporation, allocation of capacity and other such market-related decisions are made with the needs of the local* market in view.

The various subsidiaries do not serve multinational customers.

The customers are very dissimilar worldwide.

TECHNOLOGY

Development effort is carried out in a single central location, and the results are passed on to all locations needing the technology.

MANUFACTURING

Local subsidiaries are basically independent of each other in terms of product flows.

CONTROL

Production planning, inventory and quality control, and cost control remain the responsibility of local subsidiaries. Corporate groups provide only broad guidelines or no guidelines.

Scales (1 2 3 4 5 6 7) are provided for each category. The TECHNOLOGY category has two scales labeled Product and Process.

33

Figure 2.6 shows the managerial perceptions of change in, for example, the polypropylene business for the period 1971 (three years ago), to 1974 (now) and 1977 (three years hence). The data were collected using a questionnaire similar to the one shown in Figures 2.4 and 2.5, in one large U.S.-based chemical firm. The overall managerial perceptions of change correspond well with the trends in the industry at that time. The benefits of using the questionnaire to identify managerial perceptions are several. For example:

1. If managers' perceptions, as identified by their responses to the questionnaire, do not match the industry trends, as identified by an independent analysis of the changes in technology, cost structures, and competitor behavior, then the managers' perceptions can be challenged.

2. The perceptions of change by different groups of managers can be compared. For example, in Figure 2.7, we show the perceptions of managers from three distinct groups—from head office representing the product division, area managers representing the perceptions of the national organization (and subsidiaries), and joint venture partners. It is interesting to note that while joint venture partners perceive a need for greater global integration, they also perceive a greater need for local responsiveness. A similar analysis of data from functional groups—technical, marketing, and general management, shows the same diversity of perceptions. While all three

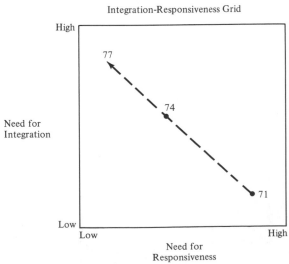

***Figure 2.6.*** Managerial Perceptions of Change—
Polypropelene Business, 1971–1977

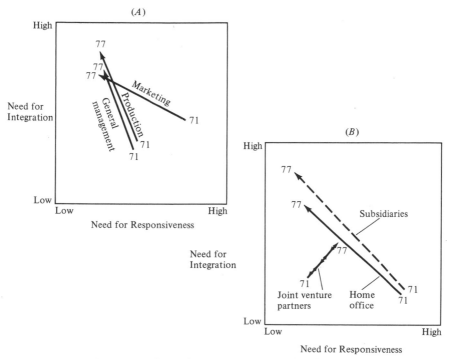

**Figure 2.7.** The Perception of Change of Functional Groups in the Poly-propelene Business

groups agree on where the business is headed, they disagree on where they are coming from and how much they have to change.

3. The charting of the differences in the perceptions of the various managerial groups suggests that the same "objective evidence" may be interpreted differently by various groups. They may perceive the changes required as significant (e.g. marketing) or relatively slight (general management), and even quarrel with the direction of change (joint venture partners). If the various groups perceive the *need for change,* the *extent of change,* and *the urgency for change* differently, internal tensions can develop. The questionnaire becomes an aid in identifying the differences in perceptions and making those explicit. That allows for a debate and facilitates narrowing of differences.

## IR Pressures May Affect Functions Within a Business Differently

We have assumed, so far, in identifying the pressures for global integration and local responsiveness that the unit of analysis is a discrete business. In some cases, however, functions within a business may respond differently to those pressures. For example, in the computer industry, integrated R&D is common. Manufacturing may be somewhat decentralized, and marketing fairly locally responsive, as shown in Figure 2.8. An integrated R&D function allows the firm to conserve scarce human resources, protect proprietary knowhow, and reduce the investment required in R&D. It also allows R&D to be centrally managed. On the other hand, the need for sensitivity to diverse national customers' requirements may suggest a locally responsive marketing function.

Functions such as R&D, manufacturing, marketing, and service may be used to identify pressures for global integration and local responsiveness, when each function represents a significant commitment of distinct types of resources and different underlying cost structures (significant economies of scale in R&D and the need for differentiated marketing tasks by country), and when internal mechanisms exist or can be developed to coordinate the functions that are managed differently.

## Global Business Versus Global Competition

We have so far examined the characteristics of a business using the IR grid and have identified factors that cause mobility of a business within that framework. However, the location of a business in the IR framework does not always identify the pattern of competition in a business. It is likely that if a business is high on global integration and low and local responsiveness, (e.g. semiconductors), it will be run, by most firms participating in that business, on a worldwide

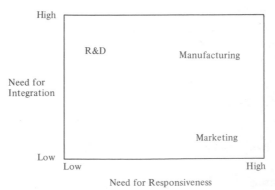

***Figure 2.8.***  IR Grid: Mapping Critical Functions

basis. On the other hand, a business high on local responsiveness and low on global integration (e.g. processed foods), is likely to be run with significant local autonomy. Businesses that are high on both dimensions (e.g. telecommunications, ethical drugs), may require a complex structure that accommodates the pressures of both integration and responsiveness. But those patterns do not identify the nature of competition that may exist in a given business. In the next chapter we shall examine the dynamics of global competiton.

# 3

# The Dynamics of Global Competition

In the previous chapter we developed a methodology for mapping the structural characteristics or the driving forces in a business. We also identified the way business characteristics change over time. While that analysis has allowed us to distinguish between a "global," a "locally responsive," and a "multifocal" business, it did not allow us to predict the nature of competition in those businesses.* For example, the detergents business would be seen as locally responsive in the IR grid. There are no overwhelming economies of scale in the manufacture of detergents. The technology is well known. Managing differences in distribution, promotion, and pricing across national markets are crucial. Based on that analysis, can we conclude that Unilever and Procter & Gamble are not involved in global competition? The computer industry will be regarded as a global business in the IR grid. Does that mean that all computer firms have to be global in their scope of operations or compete across the world? Computer firms like Nixdorf, ICL, Bull, and until recently Hitachi and Fujitsu competed primarily in their national markets, protected by privileged access to the public sector or to nationally defined customers. If we believe that the structural characteristics of a busi-

---

*Many of the ideas developed in this chapter are based on the work done by C. K. Prahalad and Gary Hamel. For example, see Gary Hamel and C. K. Prahalad. "Do You Really Have a Global Strategy?" Harvard Business Review, July–August 1985.*

ness—such as cost, technology, scale, customer profiles—*determine rather than influence* the pattern of a global competition, then the analysis developed in Chapter 2 is adequate. However, if we believe that competitors influence the patterns of competition as much as the underlying characteristics of a business and that often they change those characteristics through competitive innovation, then we need to pay special attention to the role of *key competitors' strategic intentions in determining the patterns of global competition.*

## COST STRUCTURE VERSUS CASH FLOW

Most managers believe that cost reduction (or gaining cost parity with Japanese and Korean competitors) is the essence of the competitive problem faced by Western MNCs. We would like to suggest that global competition is not about cost reduction *per se* but about managing *global cash flows.*[1] Consider, for example, the following scenario:

Let us assume that CPC, the consumer products MNC, has a dominant market share in the cooking oil business in Brazil. The product and the brand name are well established. Because of CPC's dominant share and the absence of large and viable competitors in that business in Brazil, CPC typically enjoyed very high levels of profitability. Let us further assume that Unilever, sensing the profit potential in Brazil for packaged and branded cooking oil, introduces a similar product. To gain market entry, Unilever prices its product about 5 to 8 percent lower and promotes it heavily with the trade. What should the manager of CPC Brazil do? Obviously there are no great economies of scale in manufacturing in the packaged cooking oil business, and CPC does not enjoy a competitive advantage based purely on size in Brazil. Switching costs to customers are almost negligible. By the criteria we developed in Chapter 2, packaged cooking oil is a "locally responsive" business.

We have posed this question to a large number of executives. In our experience, the response to the question is almost always "I will also lower prices and defend my market share" or "I will give better discounts to the trade and advertise more heavily" or "I am willing to sacrifice some profit margin in Brazil to defend my market share." When pushed to recognize the reality that any actions in Brazil—be it more advertising, more discounts, or price reductions—will all lead to deterioration of profits, managers typically would concede market share to the aggressor, in this case to Unilever. What are the lessons of this example?

1.  Even though packaged cooking oil is a locally responsive business, it cannot be defended locally (in Brazil) against a determined global competitor like Unilever without a significant profit penalty. Unilever, in reducing prices and increasing discounts to the trade in Brazil, exposed only a very small percentage of its worldwide cash flow in that business. On the other hand, CPC exposed a significant percentage of its worldwide cash flow. Any price reduction by CPC in Brazil to counter Unilever's actions would hurt CPC more than it is likely to hurt Unilever. The only viable strategy for CPC is to search for Unilever's cash sanctuaries—whether in Germany or in the United Kingdom—and take price action there. That is likely to put a "monkey wrench in Unilever's money machine" and reduce its ability to continue to fund market share battles in Brazil. Even though the characteristics of that business, as defined in Chapter 2, suggest that the business ought to be locally responsive, the ability of multimarket firms like Unilever and CPC to coordinate strategies and cash flows across markets creates a competitive arena that is global.

2.  The essence of global competition, as illustrated by the CPC–Unilever example, is the *management of international cash flows and strategic coordination,* even when global integration across subsidiaries in terms of product flows does not take place. If CPC is to become an effective competitor against Unilever, it has to have viable operations in markets like Germany and the United Kingdon—Unilever's profit sanctuaries. The ability to retaliate against Unilever is conditional on CPC's having operations in Unilever's profit sanctuaries as well as the ability to coordinate actions strategically between the two subsidiaries—say Brazil and Germany. It assumes that the CPC manager in Germany is willing or can be persuaded to take a short-term profit penalty in order to support the Brazilian operations. As every MNC manager knows, few organizations have the ability to coordinate subsidiaries' actions—as, for example, in Brazil and Germany. Moreover, the internal systems (planning, performance measurement, and compensation) in most MNCs act as impediments to such strategic behavior.

3.  DMNCs that are preoccupied with costs may find themselves strategically vulnerable. In the example above, even if CPC had lower costs than Unilever in Brazil, Unilever's actions would erode CPC's profit margin. Unilever could take a profit penalty in Brazil as long

as its profit sanctuaries remained uncontested in Germany and the United Kingdom. CPC's lower costs in Brazil allow it to sustain a competitive battle and to outlast Unilever only if Unilever also competes on a market-by-market basis and does not coordinate its strategies across markets.

## MANAGING CASH FLOWS

The game of global competition revolves around cash flows. Recognition of that fact allows managers to emphasize not just the cost side of the equation but also the price side. Figure 3.1 provides a framework for thinking about the dynamics of global competition.

### Managing the Cost Side

The goal of the strategist in managing the cost side is simply this: How do I get the lowest possible systemwide cost in this business? The factors to consider in determining the lowest possible net cost are the following:

#### Factor Costs

Factor costs refer to the location-specific advantages that accrue to a manufacturer. Included in factor costs are labor cost differentials between alternative manufacturing locations. Labor costs in South Korea, Taiwan, or Singapore are about one-fourth those in the

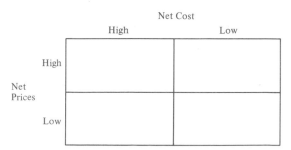

*Figure 3.1.* How the Sources of Competitive Advantages Can Be Visualized

United States. In a manufacturing process where the labor content is high, the net cost differential that can accrue to a manufacturer is obvious. A significant percentage of the reason for "outsourcing" from the United States and Europe is based on that rationale. In assessing the labor cost advantage, we are making the assumption that there are no great differences in productivity levels, that is, that the labor rate advantages are not neutralized by a productivity disadvantage.

Other location-specific advantages could include availability of cheap sources of raw materials or semifinished materials. The availability of natural gas in the Middle East and cheaper steel in Japan and Korea can lead to competitive cost advantages.

Availability and access to low-cost capital, as well as preferential tax treatment in specific locations, can prove to be advantages. The desire of many firms to exploit the tax advantages available in Ireland for overseas investors or the cost of capital in Japan, with its heavier reliance on debt than in the United States, are examples of this type of advantage.

*Exchange Rate Advantages*

The volatility of exchange rates during the last decade has brought an additional dimension to the problem of a competitor's cost advantage. Exchange rate fluctuations of 30 to 40 percent in a matter of six months are not unusual; this can either totally wipe out cost advantages or can suddenly make some manufacturing locations more attractive. For example, the strength of the dollar during the latter part of 1984 and in 1985 suddenly rendered manufacturing in Europe particularly attractive.

*Scale Advantages*

Cost advantages can accrue to manufacturers from the average age of plants and the level of their technological sophistication. Further, productivity advantages accruing from better utilization of equipment, materials, and labor can add an additional layer of cost advantage.

## Net Competitive Advantage

Competitors' net competitive advantage can be calculated by looking at the factors outlined above. A comparison between Caterpillar, the U.S.-based world leader in earth moving equipment, and Komatsu, a Japanese rival that has been systematically gaining market share over Caterpillar, is shown as an illustration in Table 3.1. While the table is a simplified presentation of a complex analysis, it points to the need for thinking about cost advantages in multiple dimensions rather than focusing only on the labor rate differentials.

### The Manufacturing System

The manufacturing system has to balance the three dimensions of the cost equation—labor costs, manufacturing scale and technology, and exchange rate fluctuations. In highly asset-intensive businesses like semiconductors, the cost of capital may become a very important part of the total equation as well. The total space within which a business can operate is shown in Figure 3.2.

The strategist's task is not to reduce the impact of any one of those dimensions to the exclusion of others but to strike a balance among the three factors, as well as to manage the system flexibly. That entails the following:

1. The business must have a portfolio of manufacturing locations that allows the firm to exploit both factor cost advantages and

**TABLE 3.1**　Komatsu's Cost Advantage over Caterpillar

| Factor | % of Cost | % Advantage | % Net Advantage |
|---|---|---|---|
| Raw material (steel) | 15 | 30 | 4.5 |
| Labor cost | 35 | 50 | 17.5 |
| Productivity advantage[a] | | | |
| Cost of capital[b] | | | 2.5 |
| Exchange rate advantage[b] | | (10.0%) | − 20.0 |
| Net advantage | | | 15–45 |

[a]Data not available.
[b]Estimated.
SOURCE: Komatsu Limited, Harvard Business School Case Clearing Services, 9–385–27, 1985.

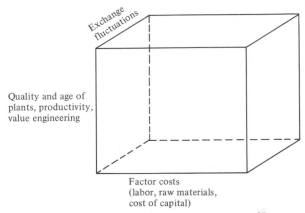

*Figure 3.2.*  The Dimensions of a Global Manufacturing System

the exchange rate differentials. Locating a plant in Mexico, for example, may accomplish both goals. However, it must be recognized that labor costs do not stay put and that the competitive advantages derived from low labor costs can disappear over time, as in the case of Singapore. Exchange rates also vary. For example, the British pound was at $1.05 in February 1985 and was up to $1.40 in June/ July 1985. That is a 30 percent change in a matter of four months. The business therefore should have not only a portfolio of manufacturing locations but also the flexibility to vary the loads assigned to its various manufacturing locations on short notice. That calls for a significant capability to integrate operations.

2. While the logic of a portfolio of manufacturing locations and flexible loading of those locations is appealing, there are several impediments to accomplishing that goal. The first impediment is the difficulty of integrating the activities of various national subsidiaries and varying the load assigned to them in the short term. Issues of performance evaluation, incentive compensation, national pride, and the stability of the work force interfere seriously with the ability to be flexible.

National policies in various countries also restrict flexibility in the short term. Although managers in the United States have traditionally enjoyed the ability to downsize the work force without too many difficulties, in Japan, in Europe, and in less developed countries, that is almost impossible in the short term. Closing plants may be even more difficult. Further, restrictions on the free movement of subassemblies and parts between various locations may be imposed by the fiscal authorities of countries concerned about transfer prices and/or the import–export balance.

In spite of the difficulties and restrictions on effectively balancing the various elements of cost in Figure 3.2, this methodology is appropriate for predicting medium- and long-term movements in the locus of manufacturing in various businesses. It is a methodology for *benchmarking* the competitive advantages that derive from all counts—low labor costs (compared to the United States and Western Europe), cheaper raw materials in several industries (like steel), lower cost of capital, and an undervalued currency. As a result, concentrating all their manufacturing in Japan till recently made eminent sense for Japanese MNCs. A strong yen, the fear of protectionism and the fear of losing markets will force them to locate plants elsewhere. On the other hand, U.S. manufacturers have had to contend with high labor costs, high rates of interest, an overvalued dollar, and high cost of materials like steel (because of an inefficient domestic manufacturing base in steel). The result has been a drive to locate plants overseas or to give up manufacturing and source the products from suppliers from South Korea, Taiwan, or Japan.

## Managing the Price Side

The concern of the strategist in managing the price side is simply this: How do I get the highest net price in this business? Because there are significant price differentials for the same product and "functionality" in different markets, by developing a portfolio of markets the strategist can maximize the bet prices for the system as a whole. The factors to consider are as follows.

### Structure of Markets

The market of each country is unique in terms of its competitive structure. The intensity of competition, which determines price levels in various markets, is dependent on the number and the type of competitors. Competing with purely national firms, which may be inefficient in a protected market like India, can lead to prices much higher than in an open and competitive market like the United States or Singapore. Further, competitive rivalry may also depend on the demand structure in a market. If the market is supply constrained, or if it is in the early stages of its life cycle, one can reasonably expect higher prices. The relative market share of competitors in the market of a given country may also give us clues as to competitors who are motivated to take price action and thus drive margins down. It is important to realize that prices are constrained by market structure, competitive rivalry, and competitors' strategic intentions in a given market and not by cost to the firm. Although that is obvious, firms continue to think of prices in cost-plus terms and miss opportunities to exploit the market asymmetries around the world.

In order to exploit the market asymmetries, the firm should have a market presence in a portfolio of markets. The need for a multinational market presence becomes obvious when we compare two firms with the same cost structure. Whirlpool, a large and efficient manufacturer of domestic appliances in the United States, may have cost parity with Sanyo, a multinational marketer of appliances. However, in order to exploit cost advantages fully against global competitors like Sanyo, Whirlpool must secure a viable market presence in multiple markets.

### The Value of Distribution and Brand Presence

Well-established brands with a quality image, like Sony in consumer electronics, command a premium. One could argue that the basic television set is an engineered commodity and the quality differential between established manufacturers like Sony and Philips and a newcomer like Samsung is trivial. However, Sony is able to obtain significantly higher prices than Philips, which has higher prices than Samsung. Established reputations allow for a price premium. Further, control over the distribution channels brought about by a product line also allows for a premium. This suggests that in addition to being present in multiple markets, a firm should attempt to develop in its key markets a brand and distribution presence.

### The Value of a Product Family

While the analysis so far has assumed a single business as the basic unit of analysis for competitive profiling, the value of a product family cannot be underestimated. For example, just as a firm can use its multinational market presence to cross-subsidize competitive battles (e.g. Unilever versus CPC in the example outlined before), a firm with a large product family can subsidize a given business within a market. For example, Sanyo or Matsushita, with a complete line of consumer electronics and appliances within the United States market today, can cross-subsidize any one of their businesses. In contrast, Whirlpool or Zenith, with their relatively narrow range of businesses, would find it hard to respond. More of that later. Further, Sanyo, with a family of businesses in the United States, has greater economies of scope and clout with the distribution channel. Sanyo can also introduce products with less incremental cost than Whirlpool or Zenith, which have less of a product scope.

### The Marketing System

Managing net prices is critical to managing a business's overall cash flow. That means firms should manage the *marketing system,* which comprises (1) a multimarket presence to exploit the price asymmetries brought about by competitive structure in various national markets, (2) a brand presence that allows for price premium, and (3) a product family in contrast to single businesses to leverage economies of scope, to control channels, and to provide opportunities for cross-subsidization, across businesses, within a given market. Those three aspects of the marketing system can be represented as a cube (shown in Figure 3.3). The strategist's role is to balance the three sources of price advantages available to the firm.

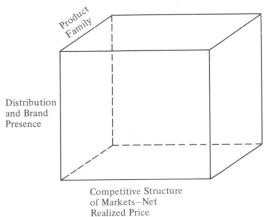

*Figure 3.3.* The Dimensions of a Global Market System

A firm's relative net advantages that accrue from managing the marketing system are more difficult to compute than the net cost advantages, even though equally real. Typically, a common product, say a 16-inch color TV set or 14-cubic-foot refrigerator, used as an index to analyze price differentials across markets and brands provides a crude but useful measure of the competitor's ability to manage prices.

The discussion of managing cash flows by managing the manufacturing and the marketing systems to minimize the net systemwide cost and maximize the net systemwide prices respectively suggests that a first order of business for the strategist is to arm himself with a *strategic infrastructure* that allows him to wage the war of global competition. The strategic infrastructure comprises:

1. A portfolio of manufacturing locations to leverage factor cost advantages and the ability to integrate them into a global network and to cope with exchange fluctuations
2. Constant attention to manufacturing technology and productivity improvements
3. A multimarket presence to leverage competitive asymmetries and exploit the resulting price differentials
4. A global brand and distribution presence
5. A product family that allows cross-subsidization opportunities, across products, in a given national market

Not all firms start with a strategic infrastructure. Caught in the global competitive battle, they have to find ways to remedy that deficiency. That explains the emergence of "strategic partnerships" among firms.


## BUILDING STRATEGIC INFRASTRUCTURE

The need for a strategic infrastructure—presence in multiple country markets as well as a manufacturing system that minimizes the total systemwide cost—to remain globally competitive is becoming obvious to many DMNCs. As a result, DMNCs that do not possess the strategic infrastructure are attempting to build one through a series of "strategic partnerships" with other firms that find themselves in a similar predicament. Figure 3.4 illustrates the pervasiveness of a wide range of collaborative arrangements in the information technology industry as of 1983. The propensity to form partnerships is

| | PERIPHERALS/ COMPONENTS | SMALL COMPUTERS | MEDIUM COMPUTERS | LARGE COMPUTERS | SOFTWARE | COMMUNICATIONS |
|---|---|---|---|---|---|---|
| AT&T | Telectron (1) | In house, Convergent Technologies (4), Olivetti (2, 8) | In house | No plans | In house, Intel (5), Zilog (5), Motorola (5), Digital Research (7), Others | In house, Philips (3, 8), Gold Star (3) |
| BULL | Trilogy Systems (2, 5), Magnetic Peripherals (2) | In house, Fortune Systems (2, 6, 8). | In house, Convergent Technologies (4), Ridge Computers (5, 8) | In house NEC (5, 8), Honeywell (5) | In house | In house |
| BURROUGHS | Memorex (1), Peripheral Components (2), Qume (4), Canon (4), Intel (9) | Convergent Technologies (4) | In house, Graphics Technology (1) | In house | In house, Midwest Systems Group (1), Graphics Technology (1), others | In house, Systems Research (1) |
| CONTROL DATA | Centronics (2), Magnetic Peripherals (2), Trilogy Systems (2, 5) | In house, Columbia Data Products (4) | In house | In house, Microelectronics & Computer Technology (5) | In house, Chrysler Corp (5), Northrop Electronics (7) | The Source (2), United Telecommunications (2) |
| DEC | In house, Trilogy Systems (2, 5) | In house | In house | In house, Microelectronics & Computer Technology (5) | Third-party agreements | Northern Telecom (5), Xerox (5), Voice Mail Int'l. (8) |
| HONEYWELL | Magnetic Peripherals (2), Synertek (1) | In house, Columbia Data Products (4) | In house, Bull (2, 6) | In house, Microelectronics & Computer Technology (5), NEC (5, 6, 8, 9) | Third-party agreements | Action Communication Systems (1), L.M. Ericsson (3, 5, 8), Keycom (3) |
| ICL | In house, Fujitsu (4) | In house, Logica (4), PERQ Systems (5, 9), RAIR (8, 9) | In house | In house, Fijitsu (5, 8) | In house, third-party agreements | In house, AT&T (6, 8), Mitel (8) |
| IBM | In house, Intel (2) | In house | In house | In house | Microsoft (4), Comshare (8), others (4, 7, 8) | Rolm (2), Merrill Lynch (3), SBS (2), Sears and CBS (3) |
| NCR | In house, Magnetic Peripherals (2) | In house, Convergent Technologies (4) | In house | In house, Microelectronics, & Computer Technology (5) | In house, third-party agreements | Comten (1), Ztel (2), Intel (8) |
| NIXDORF | In house, LSI Logic (4) | In house | Spartacus Computers (6) | In house, Auragen Systems (5) | In house, Spartacus Computers (6) | In house |
| OLIVETTI | In house, Hermes Precisa Int'l (1), Lee Data (2, 8), Ithaca (2, 8). | In house, Corona (2, 8), Kyocera (4) | In house, Stratus Computer (2, 8), AT&T (8) | IPL (2, 8), Hitachi (8) | In house, Digital Research (2, 8), Shared Financial Systems (2, 8). | In house, AT&T (8), Northern Telecom (8, 9), Bolt Beranek Newman (8) |
| SIEMENS | In house, IBM (4), Furukawa (3), Intel (4), Xerox (6, 8) | In house | In house | Fujitsu (8) | In house | In house, Corning Glass (3) |
| SPERRY | Magnetic Peripherals (2), Trilogy Systems (2, 5) | Mitsubishi (7) | In house | In house, Microelectronics & Computer Technology (5), Mitsubishi (7) | In house, third-party agreements | In house, Northern Telecom (7) |

(1) Acquisition (2) Equity position (3) Joint venture (4) OEM agreement (5) Technology development (6) Technology exchange or licensing (7) Joint product development (8) Marketing agreement (9) Manufacturing agreement   DATA: BW

***Figure 3.4.*** Strategic Partnerships in the Information Technology Industry

SOURCE: Reprinted from July 16, 1984 issue of *Business Week* by special permission, © 1984 by McGraw-Hill, Inc.

as prevalent in the biomedical and automotive industries as well. Many observers of the industrial scene in the developed world believe that the phenomenon is here to stay. Kenichi Ohmae, a proponent of this mode of creating global infrastructures, labeled the phenomenon "Triad Power"—a global configuration of American, European, and Japanese firms in strategic partnerships.[2]

## Motivations for Strategic Partnerships

As DMNCs increasingly recognize the need for a full product line, a broad base of technology, and a viable market presence in the critical markets, such collaborations are increasingly attractive. However, not all DMNCs entering such arrangements start with the same motivations. For example:

1. Some approach such relationships as a way of *buying time* before they create their own infrastructure. They start with the long-term goal of investing in the infrastructure on their own. Collaborations, as a result, are seen as temporary arrangements and as intermediate steps in a long-run competitive battle. Collaboration for such firms is an integral part of a competitive strategy.

2. Some DMNCs approach strategic partnerships from the perspective of reducing the investments required to build a global infrastructure. While it is easy to recognize the savings in investments that can be realized by gaining access to an established infrastructure—be it a distribution or service network, a technology, or a manufacturing location—through a collaboration, few recognize the limitations that form imposes on the strategic freedom of partners. While collaboration may reduce the initial outlay for building a global presence, it has the potential of increasing the strategic risk, if the motivations of the partners change over time. A significant number of such arrangements fail over time. Hence strategic partnerships approached as a temporary arrangement—"buying time"— have an outcome quite different from those approached as a way to reduce investment needed to create a global infrastructure.

3. Some approach collaborations as a way of leveraging short-term competitive advantages, such as a technological lead in a specific area that may have a very short window of opportunity.

## Stability of Strategic Partnerships

Irrespective of the underlying motivations of the parties to the partnership, a large number of such partnerships are being formed. Once they are formed, however, managing such collaboration agreements effectively is yet another matter. Firms often make the following implicit assumptions in entering into such agreements:[3]

1. The partners have similar or complementary motivations, and therefore the conflicts of interest in timing of new investments, introduction of new products, choice of manufacturing location, and scope of the manufacturing operations are unlikely. Nothing could be farther from reality. While it is relatively easy to agree on starting positions, as the business grows (or is beset with difficulties), partners' motivations and priorities change.

2. Even given a compelling technical or strategic rationale for the collaboration, the partners are likely to find difficulties in implementation. Partners often start with widely varying corporate cultures, and as a result the collaboration is often beset with managerial difficulties even from its inception. That is particularly true in European-American and American-Japanese collaborations. Continued commitment of top management to the success of the collaboration agreement and attention to differences in approach by the partners is critical for success.

In spite of all those problems, strategic partnerships are likely to continue to be pursued by firms in the short term.

Implicit in this perspective of the strategic infrastructure is the assumption that the firm possesses the logistical capability to tie all operations together, as well as the marketing intelligence data base to exploit the infrastructure. Further, it has the organizational savvy to structure the incentives for a wide variety of managers—subsidiary managers, central staff, and the business managers—to make it work. That is by no means an easy task, as we shall see in Chapters 8 through 11.

The strategic infrastructure provides the preconditions to be globally competitive. However, most firms either do not build the infrastructure systematically or do not use the infrastructure effectively once it is in place. In other words, the strategic intentions of firms may be a dimension as important to our understanding of the dynamics of global competition as the underlying infrastructure.

## STRATEGIC INTENT: THE MOTOR BEHIND GLOBAL COMPETITION

The discussion so far has concentrated on the nature of the armory that one needs to compete globally. It is important to recognize that the outcomes in global competition are determined not just by the size of the armory that the various players possess but also by how effectively and imaginatively they use their weapons.[4] The strategic intent of various competitors, or their long-term vision, may be as important as the size and quality of their armories. We should distinguish the strategic intent from the strategies: "Intent" is used here to describe long-term goals and aims, rather than detailed plans. For example, Komatsu, a Japanese manufacturer of earthmoving equipment, described its long-term vision, or strategic intent, as "Maru-C" or "encircle Caterpillar," the world's largest manufacturer of earthmoving equipment.[5] That was Komatsu's strategic intent way back in 1965, even though it was a small, weak player with no presence outside Japan. Its technology was inferior, and the product range and design were wanting. Komatsu could not have developed any detailed plans to take on Caterpillar during 1965–80, but the goal was clear. It was to be number one in the earthmoving business, and that meant beating Caterpillar. In other words, strategic intent is crucial for a firm to *aim for goals for which one cannot plan*. It is important to separate that orientation (strategic intent) from strategic planning or strategies. Strategic intent allows firms to build layers of competitive advantage painstakingly, to accomplish long-term goals. That is what Komatsu did over the period of 1965–82, when it was ready to take on Caterpillar. The same is true of a firm like Honda, which back in the 1950s was talking about being global when it was still a small repair shop with fifty employees. A firm's strategic intent allows it to think of resources and competitive advantages differently and to deploy them with greater imagination, as we shall see below.

## Building Layers of Competitive Advantages

In our research we can discern three types of firms—firms whose strategic intent is *global dominance*, even if, initially, they do not possess the strategic infrastructure to accomplish that goal; firms whose strategic intent is *defending domestic dominance*, even if they have operations in multiple markets; and those whose primary orientation is *local responsiveness*. The different strategic intents lead to very distinct approaches to competition and the use of competitive advantages, even if the strategic infrastructures appear not to be markedly dissimilar.

We shall use the color television (CTV) industry as an example for understanding the impact of the strategic intent on building and sustaining a global competitive advantage. We find that the Japanese CTV producers were concerned about building and defending a global dominance, while RCA, Zenith, and General Electric were more concerned about defending domestic dominance. Philips of the Netherlands and CSF Thompson of France were concerned about their goal of being locally responsive. Each group of players used a different complement of competitive approaches, leveraged their resources differently, and over a period of fifteen years, starting in 1970, reaped a different harvest in the international competitive arena. We shall use an analysis of the shifts in the competitive positions of the key players in the CTV industry during the period 1970–85 to illustrate the importance of strategic intent in understanding the dynamics of global competition.[6]

### *Loose Bricks: Building Layers of Competitive Advantage*

Japanese firms in the consumer electronics business started with the strategic intent of global dominance, even though their strategic infrastructure during the 1960s did not extend beyond a well-protected home market. During the 1960s they were major exporters of black-and-white TV sets. By 1967 they had become the largest producers of black-and-white TVs; by the 1970s they had closed the gap in color sets. Japanese producers used their cost advantage, derived primarily from their low labor costs, to gain volume in the United States. Once they had secured that initial volume, they moved quickly to invest heavily in process and product technology, from which they gained scale and quality advantages. By the early 1970s the Japanese advantage was not only low labor costs but also greater reliability and quality based on superior manufacturing technology.

Japanese manufacturers recognized the transience of low labor cost as well as technology-based advantages. Volatile exchange rates and increases in labor costs as well as newer manufacturing technologies were rendering the sources of competitive advantages they had quite vulnerable. Throughout the 1970s Japanese TV makers invested heavily in order to create a strong brand presence in global markets and a distribution presence, thus adding another layer of competitive advantage.

Making global distribution and brand presence pay for themselves meant a high level of channel utilization. The Japanese force-fed the distribution channels by speeding up product development cycles and expanding across contiguous product families. Thus by the early 1980s, the Japanese competitive advantage had evolved from low-cost sourcing, to a technological advantage resulting in lower costs and higher quality, then to a global distribution and brand presence across a spectrum of consumer electronic products. The strategic intent of global dominance provided a basis for building on tactical and short-term advantages, deploying resources in such a way as to build "layers of competitive advantage." The Japanese position today in consumer electronics is formidable.

## Defending Domestic Dominance

RCA was prototypical of firms with a defend-domestic-dominance orientation. RCA owned most CTV patents and should rightly be regarded as the "father of CTV." However, RCA did not invest in overseas markets and was quite happy to concede the private label and the small CTV market to the Japanese. It saw itself as not only defending the U.S. market—its domestic base—but also defending only segments of the market, primarily the market for higher-priced sets. As a result, RCA allowed a market position for the Japanese, was unaware of their long-term goals in the United States, and was blind-sided. The same was the case with other U.S.-based manufacturers, such as Zenith and General Electric, who were oriented to serving the domestic market and did not have a global orientation.

The Japanese threat was obvious by 1975–76, and American producers who were primarily concerned about domestic dominance were unable to respond. Convinced that the sources of Japanese competitive advantage lay in low labor costs, they transferred most of their manufacturing overseas. They also sought protection. Yet even with costs under control, these companies (RCA, GE, and Zenith) were still vulnerable because they had failed to understand the changing nature of the Japanese competitive advantage. Even as American producers closed the cost gap, the Japanese were cementing future profit foundations by investing in global brand positions. U.S. firms that tended to conceive of global competition in domestic terms and on a product-by-product basis could not justify investments in a global consumer franchise.

Having conceded non-U.S. markets, American TV manufacturers were powerless to dislodge the Japanese even from the United States. While Zenith and RCA dominated the color TV business in the United States, neither had a strong presence elsewhere. With no choice of competitive venue, U.S. companies were forced to fight every market share battle in their home profit sanctuary.

When American TV makers reduced prices at home, they subjected 100 percent of their sales volume to margin pressure. Matsushita could force such price action while exposing only a fraction of its own worldwide profitability.

We do not believe that American TV manufacturers will inevitably succumb to global competition. Trade policy or public opinion may limit foreign penetration. Faced with the threat of more onerous trade sanctions or charges of predatory tactics, global competitors may forgo a fight to the finish, especially when the business in question is mature and no longer occupies center stage in that company's product plans. Likewise, domestic manufacturers, despite dwindling margins, may support the threatened business if it has important interdependencies with other businesses (as in the case of Zenith's TV and data systems business). Senior management may consider the business important to the company's image (a possible motivation for GE's continued participation in the television business). The hope that foreign companies may never take over the U.S. market should hardly console Western companies. TVs were no more than one loose brick in the American consumer electronic market. The Japanese goal appears to be to knock down the entire wall. For example, with margins under pressure in the TV business, no American manufacturer had the stomach to develop its own video recorder. Today video tape recorders are the mainstay of profitability for many Japanese consumer electronics companies.

Companies defending domestic positions are often short-sighted about their competitor's strategic intentions. A company can understand its own vulnerability to global competition only by first understanding its rivals' intentions, and then carefully reasoning back to potential tactics. With no appreciation of strategic intent, defense-minded competitors are doomed to a perpetual game of catch-up.

## Local Responsiveness

Philips of the Netherlands is well-known virtually everywhere in the world. Like other long-standing MNCs, Philips has always benefited from the kind of international distribution system that U.S. companies often lack. Yet our evidence suggests that this advantage alone was not enough. Philips had its own set of problems in responding to the Japanese challenge.

Japanese color TV exports to Europe didn't begin until 1970. Under the terms of their licensing arrangements with European set makers, the Japanese could export only small-screen TVs. No such size limitation existed for Japanese firms willing to manufacture in Europe, but no more than half the output could be exported to the rest of Europe. Furthermore, because laws prohibited Japanese producers from supplying finished sets for private-label sale, they supplied picture tubes instead. So in 1979, although Europe ran a net trade deficit of only 200,000 CTVs, the deficit in color tubes was 2.7 million units. By concentrating on such volume-sensitive manufacturing, Japanese manufacturers skirted protectionist sentiment while exploiting the economies of scale gained from U.S. and Japanese experience.

Yet, just as they had not been content to remain private-label suppliers in the United States, Japanese companies were not content to remain component suppliers in Europe. They wanted to establish their own brand positions. Sony, Matsushita, and Mitsubishi set up local manufacturing operations in the United Kingdom. When the British began to fear a Japanese takeover of the local industry, Toshiba and Hitachi simply found U.K. partners. In moving the assembly line from the Far East to Europe, Japanese manufacturers incurred cost and quality penalties. Yet they regarded such penalties as acceptable costs for establishing strong European distribution and brand positions.

If we contrast Japanese entry strategies in the United States and Europe, it is clear that the tactics and timetables differed. Yet the long-term strategic intentions were the same, and the competitive advantage of Japanese producers evolved similarly in both markets. In both Europe and the United States, Japanese companies found an opening in the bottom half of the market—small-screen portables, along with other openings in the private label business in the United States and the picture tube business in Europe.

Philips tried to compete on cost but had more difficulty than RCA or Zenith. First the European TV industry was more fragmented than that of the United States. When the Japanese entered Europe, twice as many European as American TV makers were fighting for positions in national markets that were smaller than those in the United States.

Second, European governments frustrated the attempts of companies to use offshore sources and to rationalize production through plant closings, layoffs, and capacity realignments. European TV makers turned to political solutions to solve competitive difficulties. In theory, the resulting protectionism gave them breathing space as they sought to redress the cost imbalance with Japanese producers. Yet because they were still confined to marginal, plant-level improvements, their cost and quality gap continued to widen. Protectionism reduced the incentive to invest in cost competitiveness; at the same time, Japanese producers were merging with Europe's smaller manufacturers.

With nearly 3 million units of total European production in 1976, Philips was the only European manufacturer whose volume could fund the automation of manufacturing and the rationalization of product lines and components. Even though its volume was sufficient, Philips's manufacturing was spread across seven European countries. So it had to demonstrate (country by country, minister by minister, union by union) that the only alternative to protectionism was to support the development of Pan-European competitors. Philips also had to wrestle with independent subsidiaries not eager to surrender their autonomy in manufacturing and capital investment. By 1982 it was the world's largest color TV maker and had almost closed the cost gap with the Japanese producers. Even so, after ten years, rationalization plans are still incomplete.

Philips remains vulnerable to global competition because of the difficulties inherent in weaving disparate national subsidiaries into a coherent global competitive team. Low-cost manufacturing and international distribution give Philips two of the critical elements needed for global competition. Still needed is coordination of national business strategies.

Philips's national managers are jealous of their autonomy in marketing and strategy. With their horizon of competition often limited to a single market, national managers are poorly placed to assess their global vulnerability. They can neither fully understand nor adequately analyze the strategic intentions and market entry tactics of global competitors. Nor can they estimate the total resources available to foreign competitors for local market share battles.

Under such management pressure, companies like Philips risk

responding to global competition on a purely local basis. Its Japanese competitors can "cherry pick" attractive national markets with little fear that their multinational rival will focus total company resources on retaliation in key markets.

## The Three Cases Compared

We can come to the following conclusions based on the study of the evolution of the competitive structure of the CTV industry. The Japanese firms started with very few, if any, strategic infrastructure advantages. The U.S. firms, especially RCA, owned most of the technology; Philips owned the marketing and manufacturing infrastructure. The radically changed strategic positions of Matsushita (Japanese), RCA, and Philips during the 1980s can be explained by analyzing the investments made by the three firms in both building and leveraging the strategic infrastructure. RCA never built the infrastructure and is extremely vulnerable to actions taken by the Japanese in the U.S. market. It has few venues in which to fight the competitive battle. On the other hand, the story of Philips is a case of underleveraged infrastructure. Both RCA and Philips totally underestimated the Japanese competitive advantage, as their focus was on the strength of elements of the infrastructure, like product quality or cost, taken one at a time. The overall pattern of the development of Japanese competitive capabilities was not fully understood, because the stated strategic intent of Japanese competitors was not used as a basis to interpret their tactical moves. On the other hand, a well-developed and articulated strategic intent allowed the Japanese the ability to seize opportunities as they presented themselves and to build a coherent pattern of competitive advantages.

The need for a framework to interpret opportunities and to build on them, as in the case of Japanese competitors in the consumer electronics industry, suggests that the meaning of a competitive advantage depends on how a group of managers interpret it. The Japanese saw the low-priced private label market as the "thin edge of the wedge" in the United States. RCA did not see that as a threat. So given the same industry data, two groups of managers are likely to interpret the opportunities and threats differently, depending on the overall framework of "intent." The resource allocation patterns that develop as a consequence are likely to change the patterns of competition. One could argue that if all the key players operated with the same overall strategic intent of domestic dominance, then the industry structure would have been quite different. This argument assumes that we ought to go beyond a business's structural characteristics (Chapter 2) and the strategic infrastructure of competitors and focus on their intent as well. We could argue that global competition is more likely in "global businesses," as defined in Chapter 2, and among competitors who have a global strategic infrastructure. But we cannot rule out the impact of competitors who are motivated by global dominance and who are willing to seize opportunities along the way and build a presence.

## THE NEW ANALYTICS

In addition to the strategic infrastructure and the strategic intent, we want to focus attention on the capability of a DMNC to compete globally—its ability organizationally to coordinate strategic thrusts, as well as the analytical framework it uses to understand the emerging patterns of global competition. In the rest of the chapter we want to focus attention on the analytical framework for assessing the emerging patterns of competition. We shall examine, in depth, the organizational requirements in Chapters 8–11.

### The Concept of Market Share

The linkage between market share and profitability is well accepted by managers. The logic that underlies the linkage between market share and profitability can be stated simply as follows: Market share, relative to competitors, is a surrogate for accumulated volume, and accumulated volume is a surrogate for cost levels as the learning is internalized in the firm. As a result, firms with higher market shares are likely to be lower-cost producers. A low-cost position provides the potential for higher profitability. While that logic is valid in a variety of industries, as we have illustrated in this chapter, accumulated volume may not always be a good surrogate for lower costs or profitability. The manufacturing and marketing systems worldwide dictate profitability. Total overall cost in a market does not depend on accumulated volumes *per se* but also on exchange fluctuations, for example. We need to recognize the limitations of the linkage between "market share and profit potential" in a globally competitive environment.

## Market Share as Insurance

The capacity to cross-subsidize market share battles is an important element of global competitiveness. In order to do that, a DMNC must have a minimum market share in all the critical markets and also in the profit sanctuaries of key competitors. The market share of a U.S.-based DMNC in Japan, for example, may be such that the firm does not turn a profit in the Japanese market. However, its presence enables it to counter Japanese moves in the United States by taking price action in the competitors' profit sanctuary, Japan. In other words, a minimum market share, defined by the structure of a given national market, is required to defend profit sanctuaries elsewhere. DMNCs may, in this sense, be said to "exchange hostages."

## Market Share for Cost Competitiveness

Firms may want to determine what is the minimum global market share they need in a business to afford the minimum economic plant size, or a critical size of R&D effort, or a management structure. Increasingly, in several industries, a minimum market share may be required to support R&D investments, as in computers and semiconductors. Several firms are therefore separating the concept of a *manufacturing share* as distinct from market share. For example, more than 85 percent of all microwave ovens sold in the United States are manufactured by Japanese firms, even though the market share in terms of Japanese labels is not more than 40 percent. The same data for video recorders would be 100 percent manufacturing done by the Japanese but not more than 30–35 percent market share held by them in the U.S. market. Cost competitiveness is forcing firms to separate the concept of "manufacturing share" from "market share."

*Vulnerability of Large Domestic Share*

The arguments presented in this chapter should convince anyone that a single-market competitor or a multimarket firm operating on a purely "local-for-local" basis with no strategic coordination between markets is very vulnerable. RCA is vulnerable in the United States even though it has the largest share of the CTV market. So is Philips, if it does not coordinate strategies across country markets. In global competition, a large domestic share may be only a license to lose big.

## The Concept of Critical Markets

Central to the arguments presented in this chapter is the notion of critical markets. In other words, to defend itself against determined global competitors who can cross-subsidize market share battles, a firm should be a multimarket competitor. That does not mean the firm should be present in all markets. Critical markets may be determined by seeking, at a minimum:

1. Markets that are the profit sanctuaries of the key competitors in that business
2. Markets that provide volume and include the state of the art customers
3. Markets where the competitive intensity allows reasonable margins

## Resource Allocation

Resource allocation methodologies that are commonly used in most Western firms will need reexamination as well. The DMNC is often, for resource allocation purposes, seen as a collection of strategic business units (SBUs). In some firms they are called strategic planning units. Each such unit is seen as a discrete business with its own competitive mission. This implies that resources are allocated based on the missions for each unit. The SBU format and methodology for resource allocation do not allow a DMNC to allocate resources to core technologies, distribution, and brand development, all of which can cut across several SBUs, as well.

*Core Technologies*

Typically, the basis for defining SBUs in a DMNC tends to be product-markets served. Such a scheme for defining SBUs and allocating resources causes the organization to underestimate the importance of the core technologies that can cut across very diverse product markets. For example, Honda can be seen as a collection of diverse, often unrelated product market activities—cars, motorcycles, snowmobiles, outboard motors, power tillers, power generators, lawnmowers, and so on. Anyone reading that list of distinct product market operations can see that they all have in common a core technology—the technology of engines. It is important to speculate how Honda would allocate resources if it were organized as SBUs and how it might approach the resource allocation problem differently if it conceived of itself as consisting of a core technology called engines and a series of product markets exploiting that core. The Honda example is shown in Figure 3.5. Honda is exploiting not only the common technology across product markets but also brand recognition when its ads tease the consumer: "How do you put six Hondas in a two-car garage?" The advertisements go on to show the range of products—car, motorcycle, snowmobile, lawnmower, outboard motor, and a power generator.

Examples of core technologies abound: the compressors and small motors that go into General Electric's consumer businesses;

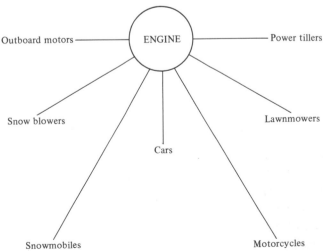

***Figure 3.5.***  Leveraging Core Competencies: Honda

the optical recording technology that spans such diverse businesses as compact audio disc and computer peripherals at Philips; the semiconductor technology at Matsushita and Philips; and many others. The issue to be faced is simply this: To get the appropriate global scale in R&D and manufacturing, is it important to go beyond the SBU framework and allocate resources to core technologies directly? An overreliance on the SBU framework is likely to lead to inadequate allocation and commitment to core technologies, as no single SBU is likely to seek "massive investments." Investments are likely to be scaled down to cope with an SBU's specific needs. Matsushita, for example, had to centralize the management of semiconductor technology (a significant departure from its famous and well-developed system of autonomous product division structure) for resource allocation, as no single business unit would make the commitment of resources that that technology demands.

## Scope of Operations

Emerging patterns of competition also suggest that we may have to reexamine the viability of strategies focused on discrete single businesses rather than on a family of businesses. Figure 3.6 is a representation of the consumer durable market in the United States. A series of "discrete" business clusters—small domestic appliances, major domestic appliances, and radios—are represented. A firm like

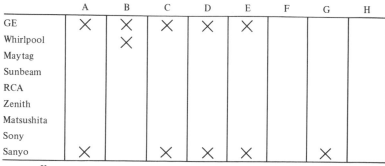

| | A | B | C | D | E | F | G | H |
|---|---|---|---|---|---|---|---|---|
| GE | X | X | X | X | X | | | |
| Whirlpool | | X | | | | | | |
| Maytag | | | | | | | | |
| Sunbeam | | | | | | | | |
| RCA | | | | | | | | |
| Zenith | | | | | | | | |
| Matsushita | | | | | | | | |
| Sony | | | | | | | | |
| Sanyo | X | | X | X | X | | X | |

Key:

A: Small domestic appliances   E: VCR
B: Large domestic appliances   F: Video games
C: Radio/hi-fi                 G: Personal computers/accessories
D: TV                          H: Home entertainment/security systems

***Figure 3.6.***   The Emerging Distribution Pattern in the United States

Whirlpool operates in one of the business clusters. On the other hand, a firm like Matsushita or Sanyo spans the whole spectrum. The range of products and businesses represented there has been built up patiently over a period of time, in the belief that there are distribution, logistic, and brand advantages to be gained by managing a product family rather than operating in single segments of the distribution chain. Most often, firms operating with a single business in such a situation, such as Maytag or Whirlpool, are unlikely to see Sanyo as a threat, if it is not promoting a set of products in their own "served" product markets. On the other hand, Sanyo could consolidate its position all around in the distribution channel and enter Maytag's or Whirlpool's arena by cross-subsidizing its battle from the cash flows from other businesses. For example, it can cross-subsidize market share battles in major domestic appliances from CTV and video recorder cash flow.

One could easily understand the difficulties that a firm like Maytag or Whirlpool, which participates in a single cluster of businesses, has in identifying Sanyo and Matsushita as potential competitors. General Electric, on the other hand, participated in most of the businesses during 1980, as shown in Figure 3.6. Why then does General Electric not retaliate against the Japanese? General Electric had embraced, during the 1970s, the concept of SBUs. Each business was a discrete SBU or was composed of several SBUs. Each SBU manager was measured on his or her performance, and cross-subsidization across SBUs would have meant that one SBU manager would take a profit penalty—a drop in performance—to help the other. Hence no attempt was made to cope with the competitive threats imposed by Sanyo or Matsushita. As each SBU became unprofitable, in spite of significant market shares in the domestic market, through the action of competitors, General Electric conceded market after market: It first sold off the small domestic appliance business, then decided to source the radio, television, and video recorder businesses from outside, mostly from Japanese and South Korean suppliers. The need for understanding the importance of a product family and the limitations of the SBU methodology need to be emphasized once more.

## Limitations of SBU Methodology

While the SBU methodology has gained a lot of currency, both the illustrations given above—the importance of core technologies and core distribution and brand investments—suggest that we need to reexamine the relevance and the adequacy of the methodology. For example, the time horizons for investments in core technologies (e.g. engines in Honda and optical recording of display technologies in Philips), and core distribution and brand investments are different from manufacturing and from product-market investments. An SBU methodology that forces one time frame on all those potentially different time frames for investment may be inappropriate. This raises a fundamental question for most DMNCs: Is the methodology for resource allocation—be it SBU or a similar one-dimensional view of the firm—adequate, or should the firm embrace a multidimensional view of the resource allocation process? It should be clear that we think that all complex DMNCs must have a complex and multidimensional view of the resource allocation process—both in terms of the *units of analysis* for resource allocation (e.g. product-markets, technologies, distribution, and brand investments) and in terms of *time frames* that senior managers use. Distribution and technology investments often have a longer time frame than manufacturing and product market investments.

### The Subsidiary Versus Business Group Dilemma

The resource allocation process is rendered complicated by the fact that the strategic missions of various subsidiaries may be dictated by central business groups depending on the nature of the market share battles being waged at a given point in time. The management of both the manufacturing and the marketing systems suggested by this chapter is that the autonomy of the subsidiaries may have to be moderated in the interest of overall global strategy. This means the allocation of resources and the nature of strategic control will depend on the "quality of sibsidiary–head office" relationships. In other words, resource allocation will depend on the way the subsidiaries and headquarter groups relate to each other.

## THE DYNAMICS OF GLOBAL COMPETITION

The dynamics of global competition suggest that we ought to move beyond the structural characteristics of a business and focus on competitors' underlying motivations. The imperatives of global competition are:

1. Building a strategic infrastructure of manufacturing and marketing system with the internal ability to coordinate the cash flow equation by managing the manufacturing system, and to coordinate the price side by managing the marketing system. It is also important to recognize the costs and benefits of a multicountry presence in manufacturing and marketing. Further, there are limits to the competitive advantages, primarily cost advantages, derived from technology or manufacturing.

2. We need to examine carefully the strategic intent of our competitors rather than just respond to their tactical moves. There is a significant competitive asymmetry between two competitors—one who believes in global dominance and the other who believes in defending domestic positions—even if the two are balanced in terms of resources and confront the same industry characteristics.

3. In order to become competitive and allocate resources in ways consistent with the demands of global competition, we need to reexamine many of the implicit concepts we use in management, including such basic concepts as the value of market share, as well as the methodology used for resource allocation. In other words, we must ask ourselves: *Do we need new rules of the game?*

# 4

# Responding to Host
# Government Policies

In the previous chapters we have assumed free markets, free flows of goods and funds, and free opportunities for investment, divestment, and strategic coordination across borders worldwide, ignoring the influence exercised by host governments. That is clearly an unrealistic simplifying assumption for the sake of clarity of exposition.

Host governments obviously implement all kinds of measures that limit the freedom of MNCs. Trade policies may tax and limit finished goods imports, require exports to offset MNC imports, impose local content requirements on goods made in the country by MNCs, or call for minimum export volume or for exports-to-production or exports-to-domestic sales ratios. Price control policies, applying to a wide range of products from pharmaceuticals to bathroom fixtures, have also occasionally wrought havoc with MNCs' global strategies. Public purchasing policies and procedures, technical standards, product certification policies, and a web of other seemingly innocuous regulations may constitute forbidding nontariff barriers to trade, preventing the globalization of whole industry segments. Policies toward industry structure and competition may limit investment opportunities or make it illegal to integrate certain foreign acquisitions into an integrated network. In some extreme cases, home or host governments' antitrust policies may force foreign subsidiaries of the same firm in different countries to compete actively against one another, as for instance in the case of Timken's European divisions in the roller bearing industry for decades. More generally, investment policies and constraints on divestitures may seriously hamper the strategic freedom of global competitors.

Similarly, exchange control regulations can frustrate attempts at cross-subsidization by locking cash in certain countries and making an active global market portfolio management impossible. A number of European companies, such as Rhône Poulenc and Volkswagen, have had quite profitable operations in Brazil but have found it extremely difficult to move funds out of Brazil to use elsewhere. Tax policies may also modify the relative attractiveness of various strategic options and increase the cost of integration or of active strategic coordination.

In sum, host governments often limit the scope for integration and coordination strategies, and they almost always modify the relative attractiveness of various strategic choices.

Occasionally, though, host governments can also influence some MNCs positively, by modifying the competitive conditions in their favor. Subsidies to encourage export-oriented investments make integration more attractive. Host governments may also shield certain MNCs from the full strength of global competition, for instance by giving them a privileged access to their domestic markets, sometimes in association with a national partner. Such a partnership may extend to sharing technology. While in most countries that may mean a one-way flow of technology from the MNCs, in some developed countries or in technologically sophisticated developing ones like India, it may involve true reciprocal benefits through MNC access to the work of public research institutes.

In sum, host governments should not be seen by MNC top managers exclusively as an impediment to global strategic freedom, to be avoided at all cost. Occasionally they may provide enough of a helping hand—through privileged market access, export credits, and subsidies—for smaller MNCs to face global competition to make it worthwhile for those smaller, often weaker, MNCs to relinquish wholeheartedly some strategic freedom to gain competitive strength through government support. Host governments can thus either hamper or help global strategies, depending on their policies and on the strategic options of the affected firms.

It is important, therefore, to make an analysis of host government goals, policies, and actions an integral part of the strategy formulation process in a global business. In particular, two related sets of issues are of critical importance in the context of the argument developed in this book:

1. Host governments affect industry structures overall, and therefore modify the options available to MNCs and their relative costs. It is therefore important to analyze why and how the competitive structure of a global industry is influenced by host government policies.

2. Host governments may specifically affect the individual position of a business, for a given firm, on the integration-responsiveness grid outlined in previous chapters. In particular, for businesses whose underlying structural dynamics (Chapter 2) and competitive dynamics (Chapter 3) drive toward integration, host government policies can blunt or even reverse those economic and competitive dynamics. In such cases those businesses may have to be run with a high level of national responsiveness, despite the economic forces toward integration. In other words, under what conditions should a business *for which economic and competitive conditions suggest integration* be managed either in a national responsiveness mode (area 2 in Figure 4.1) or managed with full recognition given to the need for complex tradeoffs between integration and responsiveness forces (area 3)?

Yet government policies almost defy generalized analysis! The diversity of national situations, economic and political, and of na-

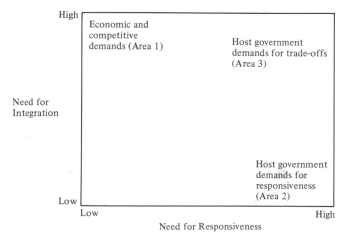

*Figure 4.1.* Discrepancies Between Economic, Competitive, and Host Government Demands in the IR Framework

tional policies is such as to frustrate attempts at generalization, particularly when governments try to use MNCs to help implement policies that have, *a priori,* very little to do with MNCs. How do we even compare Malaysia's concern for integrating its ethnic Malay population into a modern economy so far dominated by Chinese and Indian immigrants with Mexico's Institutional Revolution Party's concern for incorporating all political tendencies in Mexico (thus preventing the birth of a credible opposition), or with France's Gaullist concern for "grandeur" and military sovereignty and strategic independence?

Such immense diversity makes the choice of an appropriate level of analysis of host country policies by MNC managers difficult. In an analysis of government influence on MNC strategies, simply considering the manifest government policies—as they translate into investment codes, trade regulations, tax laws, and foreign exchange controls—while needed, would deprive the MNC managers of an opportunity to anticipate, and often even to influence, the shaping of policies. That is obviously not sufficient, yet there is no limit to political analysis. In some cases it is critical to carry it out in detail. In 1972–73, while negotiating the establishment of a major new plant, Ford's managers were able to anticipate with some confidence a smooth transition from Franco's dictatorship to a moderate democratic regime by carefully analyzing the social fabric of Spanish society and its likely political processes. On the other hand, Mitsui and GTE were caught off guard, with large-scale exposures in Iran, by the overthrow of the Shah. The purpose of this book is not to enter the realms of political analysis, for which there are detailed treatises available, or to compile data on investment codes, tax laws, and the like, for which also there are good sources available.[1]

Our comparative analysis of government policies toward global industries and global competitors suggests rather that an intermediate level synthesis is possible as a framework to analyze host government influence on global strategic choices. In brief, government policies are conditioned by (1) the nature of the industry they affect, both economic (how and why it is international) and strategic (why national control is or is not important given strategic and military considerations); (2) the stage of evolution of the industry in terms of worldwide demand (from nascent to dying); and (3) the relative competitiveness of the country and of its national firms in that industry. Specific geographic conditions (size, location of the country) also obviously play a role.

Based on those factors determining the scope of government policies, the potential for collaboration and conflict with MNCs, according to the strategies they pursue, may then be assessed in terms of convergence or divergence of interest, and the likely resulting industry structure can be analyzed. This chapter is, therefore, organized into three sections: (1) understanding the concerns and motives of host governments, (2) assessing the potential for collaboration and conflict with MNCs, and (3) drawing a series of managerial implications to cope with host government policies. The bulk of the analysis is presented in the second and longest section, while conclusions are presented in the third.

Our focus will be more on the policies of key countries in global competition, by their market size, the role of their companies, the location advantage they offer (e.g. cheap labor or energy), and their integration in the world economy. Specific issues and policies related to the least industrialized countries and to state-trading countries are not covered. The argument also applies mostly to industrial MNCs, not to extractive activities (which have been studied elsewhere extensively)[2] or directly to international service businesses such as financial institutions, transportation industries, and the like, although the approach presented here may have some relevance for service businesses.

## UNDERSTANDING HOST GOVERNMENTS

### Host Governments' Concerns

To clarify the issues, it is useful to separate host country concerns about the globalization of industries from those about the presence of MNCs. Even when globalization takes place through transactions by independent producers, traders, and distributors, in the absence of MNCs governments share a series of concerns. Conversely, the mere presence of MNCs in an industry, even operating in a nationally responsive mode, triggers another set of concerns. The two merge where global industries are populated by integrated MNCs, as in the electronics, automobile, and chemical industries.

### *Concerns About Global Industries*

First, we shall consider concerns about industries where international trade flourishes, even in the absence of MNCs. Concerns in those industries center on adjustment to international competition and conflicts between producers' and consumers' interests.

More intense international competition confronts governments directly with tangible economic interdependence. Freer international trade forces rapid adjustment of the national economy to competitive demands. Adjustment affects different groups within a nation differentially.[3] Whereas free trade favors consumers at the expense of national producers, protectionism does the opposite. Although nearly all governments now acknowledge the overall benefits of free trade and the resulting need for adjustment, they are concerned with its equity and efficiency. Equity issues dominate adjustment in declining industries: how should the costs of adjustment be shared among workers, investors, and consumers in declining industries? Issues of efficiency dominate adjustment to new, emerging opportunities: How should those opportunities be pursued efficiently? Will private corporations do it on their own?

### Concerns Regarding MNCs and Strategic Coordination of Subsidiaries

Multimarket competitors usually raise fewer host government concerns than integrated MNCs or mere free trade. When they invest primarily to serve the national market, local conditions by and large determine the characteristics and viability of their investments, and the response of national subsidiaries to policies may thus be expected to approximate that of nationally owned companies. Only the mix of skills available to the MNC and its portfolio of potential investments in other countries strongly differentiate the MNC subsidiary from its domestic competitors. Its behavior toward risk, in particular, may be different.[4]

But as soon as global competition, rather than market-by-market competition, takes place and is recognized by managers, it is likely to drive the choices of MNCs. Recognizing that reality, host governments fear that their national market may become a battleground where MNC market participation and objectives will be driven by the overall leverage they provide against other competitors. That, in turn, biases the competition between multinational and domestic firms. In particular, an MNC can engage in vigorous competition and depress prices in a particular country to block one of its global competitors, often with the result that smaller national competitors become the first casualties.

## Concerns Regarding MNC Integration Strategies

When international competition prevails—and once an individual national subsidiary is part of a global integrated network—international conditions weigh heavily on both the performance of the subsidiary and the operating and strategic choices of its managers.* In those circumstances government concerns are many.

Governments fear MNCs may quickly relocate their manufacturing operations in lower-cost countries in response to shifts in labor, energy, and raw material price competitiveness, as follows from our analysis in Chapter 3. MNCs' global scanning capabilities give them advanced notice and detailed information on the most profitable manufacturing locations, while their multinational nature will let them relocate easily without showing particular commitment to any country.

Whether such behavior on the part of integrated MNCs is actually widespread or not is irrelevant;† its mere possibility heightens government concerns.[5]

MNC integration also fuels fears of political dependency. Integrated MNCs in global industries give one state the means to influence the policies of another sovereign state. From the export of automobile components from Argentina to Cuba by a U.S.-owned subsidiary to the well-known Siberian gas pipeline embargo, examples abound where conflicts between states are acted out via global industries and MNCs.[6] The mere potential for such action creates dependency and is resented by host governments.

---

*In some cases the subsidiary "managers" are no longer its local management, since production and shipping schedules are managed centrally, marketing policies are coordinated centrally and so forth.*

*†The search for low-cost manufacturing locations is far from universal. In some industries, like pharmaceuticals, where production labor costs are insignificant (compared to R&D amortization and engineering and marketing costs) and where developing countries seldom provide the needed skills, manufacturing remains close to the principal markets. Further, in such industries the need for close interaction with key customers and some product tailoring may severely limit the advantage of distant, low-cost manufacturing locations. Even in the automobile industry, where integration of manufacturing is among the highest, companies claim to prefer manufacturing locations close to their major markets. (We may thus witness in the next few years a reversal of the move to "out-source" manufacturing in low-labor-cost regions. With automated manufacturing technologies, manufacturing may move back close to major markets in the developed world.)*

*The fact remains that even within a single region, such as the EEC, the MNCs are often rationalizing their manufacturing networks to increase scale of production as a response to competitive pressures, as observed in the chemical, machinery, instruments, and electrical engineering industries.*

When direct costs are small in relation to allocated costs, integration also offers an MNC the opportunity to bias financial results of subsidiaries to decrease the total MNC tax exposure. Transfer pricing and subsidiary remittances (royalties, fees, and so on) allow the transfer of income from high-tax to low-tax countries in ways that are difficult for government officials to detect.[7]

Host governments also show concern that the integrated MNCs will retain key competencies at the center and will farm out to their foreign subsidiaries only menial tasks that contribute little to the development of knowledge and skills in the host country. Even when competencies exist in host countries, for instance R&D centers, they are often confined to adapting global products to local markets, or else they report directly to global headquarters and seldom contribute to the overall technological development of the country or provide the host government with responsive technological capabilities for national projects.[8]

More generally, governments are also concerned with the disappearance of national decision centers in integrated MNCs and the emergence of a web of cross-border flows and relationships among subsidiaries. Some government officials feel that the response of integrated MNCs to national policies is particularly difficult to predict, or even understand, since those webs of cross-border relationships make MNC reactions quite different from those of national firms producing and selling the bulk of their goods in one country only.

Industry globalization and MNC integration may jeopardize the future of primarily national firms, as we discussed in Chapter 3. Access to foreign markets becomes a condition for competitiveness, and local national firms face a growing disadvantage. The investments needed to establish effective and controlled international distribution, to develop low-cost sourcing plants, and to run an efficient integrated network may exceed the resources of national firms. Those efforts may stretch a comparatively inexperienced management very thin. They may also increase tensions with the national unions, as we shall discuss in Chapter 5. Picking narrow segments, where resource commitments are smaller and managerial complexity less, may be self-defeating: As we discussed in Chapter 3, economies of scope and competitive cross-subsidization across segments may make it a futile effort.

In sum, the integration of MNCs, itself closely related to the emergence of global industries, adds to the concerns of host governments. Subsidiaries of integrated MNCs are more difficult to regulate, and their behavior is less predictable than subsidiaries of nonintegrated MNCs. That is more so when subsidiaries are operationally integrated with cross-border transshipments of products, but it also may be a concern when multimarket global competition takes place without actual logistical integration. It is not only integration that worries government officials but also the impact of global patterns of competition among MNCs.

Finally, integration not only increases the range of options available to the MNC, and thus limits the control that any government can exercise on the MNC, but also increases the MNC's bargaining power against host governments. Prior to a new investment, the MNC can put several alternative locations in competition to serve the same markets and can thus lead potential host countries to waive usual performance criteria and to outbid each other to grant incentives, thereby giving excessively good terms to the MNC. Once the investment is made, the integration of the new plant into a global network is a guarantee against expropriation: Once links to the rest of the system are severed, its value to the host government would be low.[9]

Beyond increasing an MNC's bargaining power, integration also shifts the mode of government intervention from regulation to negotiation. When an investment is made to serve a single national market, uniform conditions, independent from an MNC's operations in other countries, may apply; when an investment is made as an export platform, the interdependence between that investment and other activities is such that exactly the same host government conditions may be of very different appeal to different MNCs. Further, the number of potential investors or partners may be so reduced, in a global industry, as to make regulation unfeasible. Regulation in any case would negate the differences between firms, where such differences may make a given form of cooperation mutually beneficial with one firm but not with another.

## ASSESSING THE POTENTIAL FOR COOPERATION AND CONFLICT BETWEEN HOST GOVERNMENT POLICIES AND MNC STRATEGIES

The concerns summarized above raise difficult choices for host governments on how to make their national economies participate in global industries and on the role they are willing to let MNCs play. Our premise here is that host governments do take positions vis-à-vis MNCs in an increasingly pragmatic, rather than ideological, way.

Choices for governments in global industries cluster around three broad participation modes:

1. Governments can accept, and even encourage, the presence of integrated MNCs, in the hope that their economies will benefit from such presence. In that case, their approach is usually to bargain access to a large domestic market for an export-oriented investment with large positive balance-of-payment and employment effects. Ford's decision to invest in Spain in 1973 was the successful outcome of such a policy.[10] Such a policy is easier to implement when local labor costs are relatively low and the local market has strong growth potential, as was then expected in Spain. Ireland, with a small domestic market but free access to the EEC, has been able to attract many integrated MNCs but has often had to provide large subsidies to offset the costs of training, development, and an eccentric European location.[11]

2. Governments can also favor the autonomous development of internationally competitive national firms with the strategic intent to achieve dominance. That usually involves selective protection to allow import substitution along the usual infant-industry lines, followed by assistance to participate in international markets, and finally the relaxation of both protection and assistance once national firms achieve competitiveness. The well-known development of the automobile and consumer electronics industries in Japan provide textbook examples of this policy of active assistance to national firms in global industries.[12]

3. Governments may also sponsor international partnerships among national firms from various countries, or between pliable MNCs and national firms. Such partnerships involve joint R&D, coproduction, and reciprocal marketing. Well-known examples are provided by Airbus Industries, a partnership among national firms, and by C2I–Honeywell Bull, a partnership between a national firm (C2I) and a global one (Honeywell).[13]

## A Framework for Policy Choices

### Country and Firm Competitiveness

The choices among the three modes of global industry participation most often hinge on a few factors. First, the country's *level of competitiveness* in a global industry results from (1) the competitiveness of its production factors relative to those of other countries as they apply to the particular industry, and (2) the effectiveness with which firms operating in that country exploit those factors, relative to the effectiveness of firms operating in other countries. Relative *competitiveness of factors* is most critical in industries where global integration prevails, while *competitiveness of firms* may be crucial in industries where a mix of local and multinational firms compete.

With some oversimplification, it is possible to sketch the likely policies of a country according *to its mix of factor and firm competitiveness,* as shown in Figure 4.2. When both are high, domestic production by domestic firms and exports are likely to be favored by the government. That is the case in the Japanese auto industry, which combines the locational advantages of Japan and the process engineering capabilities of Japanese car makers into a uniquely productive manufacturing system. Where firms are competitive but national factors are not, outward foreign investment is likely to result, as in the U.S. consumer electronic industry. Where national factors are competitive but national firms are not, foreign inward investment is most likely to be called upon, as in Southeast Asia in the consumer electronic industry or in Ireland in the information technology industry. When neither the factors nor the firms are com-

Factors' Competitiveness

|  | Strong | Weak |
|---|---|---|
| **Strong** | Domestic production, large exports (e.g., Japanese auto industry) | Outward foreign investment (e.g., U.S. consumer electronics industry) |
| **Weak** | Inward foreign investment, export platform requirements (e.g., consumer electronics in Southeast Asia) | Imports, no national production (e.g., jet airliners in developing countries) |

Firm's Competitiveness

***Figure 4.2.*** National Policies and Competitiveness of National Production Factors and of National Firms

petitive, no national production is likely to take place, unless national defense considerations call for it and governments are willing to subsidize local firms.

## Host Governments' Priorities over Time

As we discussed briefly in Chapter 3, a nation's positions in an industry are dynamic, not static. As individual industries mature over time, the structure of national economies shifts as resources are transferred from industries where countries lose competitiveness to industries where they gain it. The magnitude and speed of that adjustment process vary with a country's exposure to international trade. Singapore, with the bulk of its GNP externally traded, has to adjust more quickly and more comprehensively than such relatively self-sustaining countries as the United States or Japan.

Government policies toward an industry are therefore likely to shift over time in predictable patterns. Government policies tend to concentrate on transition periods calling for an active adjustment process, particularly during emerging and declining phases of industry evolution. Strategically significant industries (e.g. military hardware, telecommunication equipment) receive more constant government attention. For emerging industries, the issues focus on how to secure an early competitive position for the national economy. In particular a critical issue is whether to try to entice MNCs into developing such new industries locally or, on the contrary, to foster the development of an indigenous national industry and support it beyond import substitution to achieve international competitiveness. For a mature industry, the adjustment costs of rationalization and decline provide tough issues: which jobs are shed, where, what the impacts are on the balance of payments, how significant the adjustment cost is, and how it is shared. Regarding MNCs in mature industries, the central issue for host governments is national consolidation versus international integration. In some cases (e.g. electricity producing equipment in France), governments may foster industry consolidation along national lines; in some others (e.g. ball bearings in Europe), regional or global integration may prevail. In strategically significant industries, the concern is usually to maintain a measure of government control over the suppliers—and thereby to restrict and orient MNC participation—while at the same time not incurring excessive diseconomies of scale by rediscovering and independently developing and producing systems and products that already exist elsewhere but remain classified, or the import of which would result in too much political and strategic dependence on the supplying country.

This section reviews typical government policies toward the three cases mentioned above—emerging, maturing, and strategic industries—and analyzes the likely interaction between corporate strategic choices of responsiveness and integration, and the policies followed by governments.


## Emerging Industries: Policy Choices and MNC Strategies

*Government Policies*

An early move into an emerging industry by acquiring and exploiting a technological advantage is a policy option coveted by government officials as a way to overcome the aging industrial base that characterizes much of the developed countries' economy. Such officials, assuming that faster and faster industry life cycles with global competition from the start call for the early identification, targeting, and integration of opportunities in emerging industries into a strategic vision, believe that a cooperative state–private sector set of institutional arrangements may perform those tasks more effectively than private firms acting alone. Economies of scope in data gathering and analyses, discussion of such analyses between business circles and government officials, and integration into a consistent framework may decrease both the cost and the uncertainty, for private firms, of committing resources to new emerging industries. To a large extent, that is the function of MITI's "ten-year visions" in Japan. Economic and technical uncertainties, high interest rates, and adverse fiscal conditions may discourage private long-term strategic investment in emerging industries, and therefore specific state action may be needed to support the development of such industries, from R&D subsidies and investment incentives to the provision of state-controlled "first-user" markets.

Before long, government officials face the issue of whom to support: national firms or MNCs. The choice hinges on an assessment of national firms' capabilities. In biotechnologies, the French support French pharmaceutical and chemical companies, while Ireland, with no such firms, has provided attractive terms for Schering-Plough to build a plant and a research center. The choice also hinges on an assessment of the availability of technology. Immediately after World War II, Japan bought European technology for its nascent car and electronics industries. But state-of-the-art technologies in truly emerging industries—where no supplier has yet established a clear technology lead or where such a producer is not willing to share it—may not be so easily available. Enticing either MNCs or national firms to enter a new industry locally usually involves significant protection, first to create a demand and then to allow the "infant" domestic industry to develop, although it may not be competitive by international standards. In some cases, the state may encourage the acquisition of foreign technology by independent national firms. Active competition for the domestic market (as in Japan) or early exposure to the demands of the international markets (as with the Brazilian commuter plane manufacturer Embraer) impose the search for competitiveness on the fledgling firms early.[14] On the other hand, the European practice of appointing a "national champion" among large (often state-owned) groups has had disappointing results: Rather than develop new skills to compete internationally, the "champions" too often continued to depend on the state for their development.[15] Once competitiveness is achieved, international expansion follows. Again, Japan is the clearest case in point.[16]

## MNC Responses

The autonomous development of internationally competitive national industries is an obvious danger to established MNCs and leaves comparatively little room for cooperation between international and national firms. To thwart such adverse developments, MNCs can take several approaches that decrease their likelihood of success and increase their likely cost to the point where governments will prefer the other option: courting MNCs to invest early in the new industry.

Yet such policies often divide international firms in an industry. Leading firms in a global industry may try to defeat policies of self-development by active competition (e.g. IBM against Japanese computer makers). Weaker competitors, on the contrary, may be all too happy to support such efforts. Fearing they would lose out in a unified global industry dominated by a handful of leading competitors, they welcome national efforts to fragment and segment markets. Host government efforts to develop national industries not only preempt large markets from the leaders but also make profitable partnerships possible with secondary firms where access to large markets can be traded off for technology transfers. The Bull computer group, for instance, is quite willing to transfer technology to Brazil to retain a presence in a market from which IBM would pull out under similar conditions. To retain a market presence in the large mainframe computer market segment, ICL, Siemens, and Amdahl are quite willing to offer access to their markets to Fujitsu's large computers, while Bull may provide the same to NEC.

Autonomous national development efforts can therefore be seen in quite different lights—as a mortal threat or a good opportunity— by "leader" and "follower" firms in the same industry.

Several observations can be made about the strategies open to leading firms. First, those firms may try to slow down the diffusion of technology. International patent protection can be trusted to achieve protection of technology in some industries where product characteristics are clear and patentable (e.g. pharmaceuticals). Where process know-how is important, preventing its diffusion may be critical, hence Michelin's extreme discretion about radial tire manufacturing technology or Texas Instruments' and the Semiconductor Industry Association's lobbying effort to stem the transfer of U.S. microelectronics process technology to Japan.[17]

Second, timing is crucial in the implementation of an autonomous development strategy. Priority goes to the buildup of a domestic market, whose rapid growth then catapults the national producers toward competitiveness. One of Japan's main advantages in that respect was the very rapid development of a domestic mass market for specific goods: TV sets, cars, stereo systems, and VCRs. Specific patterns of consumer behavior favoring widespread, quick adoption of new consumer products, and the control of distribution in the domestic market by national manufacturers both played a key role in that rapid development. Most other countries aspiring to play a leading role in global industries have smaller, less protected domestic markets. That would reduce their opportunity to achieve international competitiveness through fast domestic demand growth. Strong free trade policies may prevent the effective control, and sudden release, of domestic demand to the benefit of local firms only. While the outcome in Japan may have more to do with the structure and the loyalty of mass distribution than with formal trade barriers, official trade barriers play a more significant role in other countries.

Third, the integrated MNCs can try to lock national partners into early "unequal" cooperative agreements. Those agreements preempt the options of emerging national competitors while allowing the leading global suppliers to maintain an asymmetric relationship, if only because they control technology and market access. For instance, Boeing has entered into agreements with Aeritalia (the Italian state-owned aircraft manufacturer) and a group of Japanese companies for the "comanufacture" of the Boeing 767 wide-body twin jet, in direct competition with Airbus's main products. While the role of those "partners" is hardly more than that of risk-bearing subcontractors, it makes it more difficult for them to enter into agreements. Similarly, some of the many collaborative agreements in the information technology industry may be more valued by one of the partners because they effectively freeze options available to others.

Fourth, the payoffs for development strategies come only from success in the international markets, assuming that foreign markets can be penetrated, particularly countries whose mix of production factors no longer matches the requirements of the industry. Despite the publicity given to Japanese successes in motorcycles, cars, photographic equipment, and consumer electronics, foreign market penetration is seldom so simple as those well-known examples would have us believe. For one thing, global competitors fight back not only where they are best placed to win (e.g. IBM in the United States attacks companies leasing Japanese computers such as Itel and National Semiconductors) but also where they can inflict the greatest damage, that is, in the domestic markets of the new competitors (e.g. IBM fights Fujitsu in Japan as well). Besides, few distribution channels are as easy to penetrate as the U.S. mass merchandisers. With the exception of manufactured commodities such as low-end TV sets, VCRs, and other electrical and electronic consumer products, the intensity of the selling and service tasks act as strong import barriers. In a few industries, product features may allow those barriers to be overcome (e.g. by improving product reliability and modularizing design, as the Japanese did with photocopiers), but generally, distribution channels may not be easy to penetrate. Finally, national producers may resort to protectionism to defend themselves, from "orderly marketing agreements" to outright import bans, via cumbersome arrangements designed to slow down imports and to warn importers of further threats (such as the French decision to route all VCR imports to the central city of Poitiers for customs clearance, the site of a famous battle where the French defeated Moorish invaders in 732).

Weaker competitors clearly take another approach. The stronger and more dominant the industry leader(s), the more readily will the weaker competitors be tempted to join forces with emerging national partners against the leader. Conversely, governments favor equal partnerships with weaker firms rather than unequal ones with leading multinational suppliers. The "also-rans" band together to become viable competitors of major integrated MNCs. The Airbus grouping is a prototypical example of that approach; comparatively unsuccessful European companies banded together to share costs and risks and to combine their domestic markets (the French group had sold only about 250 "Caravelles," while British Aerospace was selling in small numbers a relatively broad range of jet aircraft, the BAC 111 being the only commercially successful one). Nationally responsive MNCs will also find it easier to cooperate flexibly with partners in various countries. Specific collaborative agreements can be implemented in one country or another without influencing the overall network.

The patterns of interaction between national governments' intervention policies in the development of new industries and corporate responses can be sketched as on the first row of Table 4.1. While nationally responsive MNCs often cooperate with governments that are willing to develop their own industries, large integrated MNCs try to increase the cost and difficulty for governments to develop emerging industries on their own. Small integrated MNCs may be tempted to enter into a partnership with an individual government while retaining the advantages of integration.

## Declining Industries: National Rationalization Versus International Integration

### The Policy Choices

Maintaining the competitiveness of maturing industries is another critical concern of governments, particularly where trade competition is intense. It usually involves rationalization of capacities, automation, work force reduction, and ultimately managing a gradual withdrawal from declining industries at an acceptable social and political cost.

Industry restructuring and modernization have become important concerns of most European governments. They are attempted through general policies (early retirement schemes, retraining and re-

**TABLE 4.1**   Bases for Cooperation or Conflict Between Government Policies and MNC Strategies

| Government Intervention Policies | Types of Corporate Responses | | |
| --- | --- | --- | --- |
| | *National Companies* | *Nationally Responsive MNCs* | *Integrated MNCs* |
| Development of new industries | • "National champion" <br> • Recipient of subsidies <br> • Control of domestic market (price/vol.) | Cooperation: <br> • Shared technology <br> • Export coordination | • Technology retention <br> • Lobby for equalization of terms <br> • Unequal cooperative agreements <br> - technology <br> - global market access <br> • Active competitive counterattack on emerging competitor's home base |
| Adjustment of declining industries | • National consolidation | • Shift to multinational integration <br> • Divestment if operations too small or too strategically significant to host country | • Integration as guarantee, but danger to relocate |
| National independence | • "National champions" <br> • Cooperative agreements | Fit | Increase the cost to government <br> • Good citizenship <br> • Exchange of value |

location grants, or special credit policies) or sectoral ones (state ownership, programmed capacity reductions, mergers and consolidation, and so forth). Those policies encourage both rationalization and orderly withdrawal. During the rationalizing and scaling down of national industries, governments are usually under severe pressure to intervene to give breathing space to hard-pressed national competitors. Protective measures have been taken by OECD countries toward textiles and clothing, footwear, steel, shipbuilding, automobiles, appliances, and others.

In industries where trade competition dominates, protection is easy to implement: Affected competitors are distant, and little retaliation is to be feared. On the other hand, threatened competitors may themselves turn global in their sourcing (e.g. designer shirts made in Asia) to try to capture the competitive advantages of production from developing countries. In a number of maturing industries, therefore, policies have been tailored to buy time through protectionism and to allow domestic suppliers either to manage an orderly withdrawal or to regain competitiveness by relocating part of their manufacturing offshore.

In some cases, industry repositioning and reorganization may allow competitiveness to be regained. Shifts from large firms to smaller entrepreneurial firms helped Italy maintain both its steel industry (via the development of mini-mills) and part of its textile and apparel industry (via networks of smaller and larger firms in the Prato region north of Florence, in particular).[18] Smaller, more agile firms, with low overheads, more flexible employment rules, and owner-managers, can thrive where large firms would not be competitive. Large firms can also sometimes regain competitiveness by aping smaller firms on their own and lowering costs. (General Motors' new Saturn subsidiary and IBM's personal computer "Independent Business Unit" provide two well-publicized attempts by large MNCs to cope with low-cost foreign competition.)

In short, where international trade competition is intense but foreign MNCs are not significant players, temporary protection can allow national firms to reduce their costs (by moving offshore, automating and/or reducing overheads) to reposition themselves toward less competitive, better protected market segments and, if nothing else succeeds, to organize an orderly withdrawal from the industry.

In maturing industries where MNCs are key players, the most logical MNC response is to integrate across borders. Complex manufacturing processes sensitive to economies of scale and experience often characterize those industries (e.g. automobiles, construction equipment, appliances, petrochemicals). Where MNC subsidiaries were originally sized to serve modest shares of discrete national markets, they may be hopelessly uncompetitive against worldwide competitors. In such situations, integration into an efficient logistic network of focused factories may be the only route to MNC survival. Yet, insofar as such rationalization leads to the closing of marginal plants and the concentration of production into fewer more efficient plants, it becomes a social and political issue.

For national governments the choice is often between international integration and national consolidation. Whether one or the other is preferred often depends on the existence of a potential national champion around which to regroup other companies, and on the assessment, on the part of the government, of the risks to national independence of losing control of the industry. A government may wish to consolidate the electrical engineering or the telecommunication equipment industry along national lines, but let the automobile or the ball bearing industry integrate into MNCs. The typical pattern of government policy choices can be sketched as in Figure 4.3.

## MNC Responses

For the corporations, responses to adjustment needs in declining industries are relatively straightforward. Nationally responsive MNCs

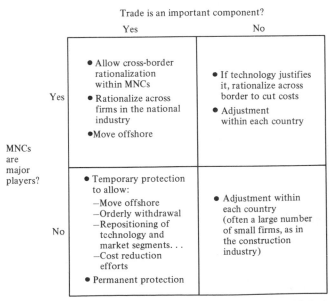

**Figure 4.3.** Policy Choices Toward Declining Global Industries

feel the pressure to integrate, particularly when they are smaller than their competitors, be they "local champions" or other major MNCs. In the 1970s, for example, Chrysler was among the first victims of the intensification of competition in the European auto industry. With relatively small operations scattered in various countries, it could compete effectively neither against the strong national producers (Volkswagen, Peugeot, Fiat, Renault) nor against its larger multinational rivals (Ford and General Motors).[19] Smaller nationally responsive MNCs therefore have a difficult choice: If they integrate they may still lose out to their larger global rivals; if they do not they may lose out to local competitors. For them the choice depends largely on an assessment of the willingness of host governments to extend protection toward them. The extent of national influence that goes with national responsiveness strategy has value to host governments, and they may be willing to accept economic inefficiencies as a price for control. In Europe, for instance, ITT has not integrated its telecommunication equipment manufacturing operations to the full extent that economic and technical considerations alone would have called for. ITT's management saw the less than optimal degree of integration as a way to maintain privileged access to public (Postal, Telephone & Telegraph) markets.[20]

To already integrated MNCs, integration is a guarantee against loss of competitiveness, and industry maturity only makes it more valuable. Only basic changes in value-added structure (e.g. from global hardware to country-specific software) or in manufacturing technology (that would eliminate economies of large scale) may threaten their advantage, beyond protectionist measures by governments. It is not surprising, therefore, to observe much empirical evidence showing that multinational integration strategies are most prevalent in maturing industries that are not seen as strategically critical by host governments.[21] In others, such as the electrical generating equipment industry, where integration would make economic sense, perceived strategic importance means that national domestic consolidations almost always prevail. The same is true in railway locomotives, with, however, some collaborative agreements among national suppliers to the various national railroads in Europe.[22]

The argument developed above is summarized as the second row of Table 4.1. Confronted with maturity and decline, national companies join forces to rationalize and consolidate their activities, often under the auspices of their governments. Smaller nationally responsive MNCs either undertake to integrate and rationalize their activity or let their subsidiaries join national consolidations and often partially or totally divest them. The choice between integration and consolidation often hinges on an assessment of national policies. Except in strategically significant industries, maturity comforts integrated MNCs in their choices.

### Strategic Industries: Host Government Control and MNC Options

Protecting national independence by controlling strategic industries runs directly against the globalization of industry and follows a logic of autarky. Global industries imply national specialization between industries or within each industry; thus they limit the independence of the individual country, for it now has to obtain from abroad a substantial part of the goods it needs but no longer produces. While that is nothing new (witness the efforts of European countries to gain independent access to spices, coffee, and tea in the sixteenth century), it raises difficult issues in critical industries. A broad-front self-engineered effort in a critical industry, whose technology evolves rapidly, may be a self-defeating effort beyond the means of a single country, as the French discovered painfully with computers and the British with combat aircraft.[23] Specialization would not satisfy dependency concerns, because excelling in one small global segment does not eliminate dependency in others. Calling in MNCs does not eliminate dependency either, since they are likely (1) to keep their most advanced research at home, (2) to specialize their activities by country, and (3) to try to avoid the diffusion of the technology within the host countries.

The need to (1) be global, (2) not specialize, and (3) retain control has driven government officials to encourage transnational cooperative agreements that offer more scope than autonomous national efforts and more control than MNCs. Well-known examples include various ventures in microelectronics, the C2I-Honeywell Bull agreements, the joint venture between General Electric and the French national jet engine maker SNECMA for jet engines, the Ariane satellite launcher, and the more recent partnerships among Rolls Royce, Pratt & Whitney, and several Japanese companies in the jet engine field.

Such partnerships are plagued with difficulties, however. First, the interests of the partners do differ with their starting positions. Their existing products may be at different stages in their life cycle, which makes the development of a joint timing difficult. European attempts to join forces in the engineering and production of digital switching, for instance, have been stifled by such differences: Some companies—Plessey in the United Kingdom, Siemens in Germany, and Italtel in Italy—have their own new systems to sell and amortize, while others, such as CIT-Alcatel in France, are looking for the early and fast development of a new system. Potential partners in such efforts may also perceive a better complementarity with non-European firms, which can provide market access and technology exchanges in other parts of the world; hence, the courting of AT&T by European firms or their willingness to collaborate with Japanese firms in the information technology industry.[24] Different priorities between national users, "juste retour" principles, and rivalry between partners for program leadership may also scuttle otherwise sound projects, as with the recent failure of the "Future European Combat Aircraft." Finally, most partnerships remain expensive to run; duplications are not quite totally avoided; management costs are high; and priorities may change over time, making ongoing cooperation difficult.

Partnerships may be attractive to MNCs, paticularly when national partners control and guarantee access to their home markets and share in research and development costs. Smaller MNCs may be more willing to join such partnerships than leading ones, for the same reasons that make them participate in national efforts to develop an independent industry.

Yet the possibility for independent MNCs to compete in truely strategic industries is quite limited. In the early 1970s, for example, Westinghouse's plan to establish a large nuclear energy engineering business in Europe were dashed by national concerns. Similarly, there are no MNCs in the military aircraft business.


## National Policies and Global MNC Strategies: A Synthesis

So far in this chapter we have presented the way host governments are likely to decide on policy alternatives toward their national industry's participation in a global industry, and we have discussed the strategic responses that MNCs in various positions may bring to government policies in different broad types of industry situations (newly developing, declining, strategically significant). In this subsection we recast the argument made so far into a broader discussion of industry structures as they evolve from interactions between government policies and business strategies.

### Cooperative Relations and the Exchange of Value

First, if governments and MNCs are to develop cooperative relationships, tacit or explicit, both must see an interest in entering and maintaining a relationship. That usually means a shared perception of mutual benefit in such a relationship, rooted in some exchange of value where both sides see themselves as better off than if the relationship did not exist. Table 4.1 clearly shows that the different MNC integration–responsiveness strategic priorities we discussed in Chapter 2 result in very different bases for exchanging value with host governments.

*Integration strategies* are expected to create, through the higher efficiency allowed by integration, an economic value of a monopoly nature. Such value is then shared between the MNC, which achieves the efficiency, and the host governments, which make such value possible by granting the integrated MNC continued license to operate in their territory. Except at the margin, the ability of host governments to influence the integrated MNC's operations is limited. Their bargaining position is relatively weak: Prior to an investment, the MNC can often put several locations in competition, limiting the performance requirements that the governments can impose. While the government's bargaining power may increase somewhat once the investment is made, the local investment is a mutual hostage: In operations within the MNC network, it brings taxes, employment, and exports to the country. Nationalizing it, or imposing such requirements that the MNC would opt out, would leave both sides worse off: The value of a stand-alone, specialized, world-scale plant cut off from its worldwide distribution channels, or even geared to produce highly specialized components only, is quite low. Conversely, to the MNC, the exit cost is not trivial. It becomes a missing link in the network and in some cases an awkward precedent. Host governments may nibble away at the MNC's advantage by imposing higher local content levels, higher taxes, localization of managerial ranks, and so on, but usually with little actual change. Conversely, MNCs may extract somewhat better terms over time, but usually the relationship is relatively stable. The strategic autonomy of the MNC is justified by its managers as a necessary condition of value creation.

Governments trade a measure of control for better economic performance.

The sharing of value can take multiple forms beyond the payment of taxes by the MNC and is usually a compromise along multiple dimensions that results from negotiations between the MNC and individual host governments. In some cases the compromise is implicit and tacit, particularly when there is a clear global leader of an industry. IBM, for example, is quite willing to incur "citizenship costs" in various countries in order to be allowed, tacitly, to continue to operate worldwide as its managements see fit. Thus, above the regulatory and legally required conditions, IBM takes costly actions to ensure that host country governments are satisfied with its presence. Those range from progressive labor policies—which have the added benefit of stifling unionization efforts in many of its subsidiaries—to grants for education or to conscious suboptimization of the globally integrated network to keep a fairly even trade balance in most countries. So, while IBM resists any attempt to impose the exercise of government control over its operations (witness the pullback from India or the aborted project to produce personal computers in Mexico), it can be quite generous, at the margin, with citizenship costs above and beyond what it owes host countries' economies. Where a few rivals are vying for a leadership position (as in the auto industry) or where competitive rivalry is made very intense by the nature of the industry (as in the semiconductor industry), integrated MNCs may be much less willing to incur citizenship costs; any such cost would penalize them vis-à-vis their competitors. It is only in exchange for some exclusivity contributing strongly to competitive advantage that they may accept exacting conditions from a host government, as Ford did in Spain in the 1970s.

*National responsiveness strategies* offer host governments quite a different tradeoff. Their logic is to provide the host country with most of the same advantages as those offered by a national producer and at the same time retain some of the advantages of multinationality. Autonomous national subsidiaries can be largely self-contained and responsive to national policies. Unlike integration strategies, nationally responsive firms trade off economic performance for social control; they may not be so economically efficient as firms pursuing integration strategies, but they give host governments a much larger measure of control over operations in their country and allow flexible cooperation. The typical exchange of value occurs here when government subsidies and market access are traded off against responsiveness of MNCs to national conditions and policies. Nationally responsive MNCs still bring to the country a range of know-how and skills not easily available locally. That makes them more attractive to national governments than independent national competitors.

*Multifocal strategies* are predicated on an intermediate exchange of value: The MNC gives some influence on overall strategic choices to national partners in exchange for support from the host governments. Rather than merely share value, the strategy of the MNC itself becomes an item for negotiation. To some extent the MNC, with the support of host governments, still attempts to achieve integration, but in a way negotiated to satisfy the requirements of host governments.

As noted earlier in this section, national governments will see one or another mode of exchanging value as most suitable, according to the nature of the industry, the national position (in terms of size, potential competitiveness in the industry, strength of domestic firms, and existing trade policies), and their own political priorities. Similarly, large leading MNCs in an industry may have different interests and different reactions to government policies, in comparison with their smaller, weaker competitors.

Again, weaker competitors in global industries may see great advantages in allying themselves with governments, provided governments help them to segment the industry in a fashion that allows them to overcome their competitive disadvantages vis-à-vis the industry leader(s). Essentially they are trading off their freedom to integrate and coordinate their international operations for protection by host governments. Governments may protect their markets (through import barriers) or their production factors (through subsidies for local R&D or labor).

In such circumstances, competitors following very different strategies may thrive, since the competitive disadvantage of the weaker companies may be offset by the political protection granted by governments. In the European computer industry, for example, it is possible for some of the weaker competitors, such as Bull or ICL, to survive against stronger competitors like IBM or DEC.[25] Governments influence the range of strategic options available to such competitors by (artificially) segmenting global markets on geographical lines and therefore making multifocal and local responsiveness strategies feasible and most attractive to weaker competitors in industries where economic conditions and competitive dynamics alone strongly favor integration strategies, but where such strategies would probably eliminate weaker, smaller competitors, be they national producers or smaller MNCs.

Host governments thus create conditions whereby key industries are served by a mix of competitors following different strategies. Globally integrated leaders, such as IBM in the computer industry, may provide host governments with benchmarks of economic and financial performance to challenge nationally responsive and multifocal competitors who seek government assistance. On the other hand, weaker MNCs following a multifocal strategy or allying themselves with national firms provide for national control over key industries—which integration strategies deny to national governments—and provide a viable alternative to integrated MNCs. Their existence, in turn, confers bargaining power on host governments in their negotiations with integrated MNCs. Conversely, integrated MNCs enforce competitive discipline upon otherwise inefficient suppliers. Maintaining a heterogeneous industry structure with integrated MNC suppliers, multifocal and nationally responsive firms, and national champions may thus serve the needs of host governments well.

When national control becomes the overriding priority, as for instance in military aircraft, only national producers or joint projects with such producers succeed. When their technological base is not sufficient, local producers acquire licenses from leading foreign suppliers and manufacture equipment nationally at great cost. Japan, for example, manufactures F-15 fighter planes under license from McDonnell Douglas rather than buy them at a fraction of the cost of producing them in Japan.

A phase of our research program identified the strategies followed by forty-eight firms in eleven businesses in Europe. Technical and economic characteristics, as outlined in Chapter 2, strongly favored integration strategies for all those businesses. Yet as government control over their market—measured by the share of sales in these businesses to the public sector customers—increased, the competitors with the smaller relative market shares increasingly followed multifocal and, as government shares of sales became predominant, local responsiveness strategies. Sample businesses were chosen so that government control over their markets would vary widely, while economic, technical, and competitive forces would consistently pull toward integration.

The results of the study are presented in summary form in Figure 4.4. On the horizontal axis, the various businesses are arrayed ac-

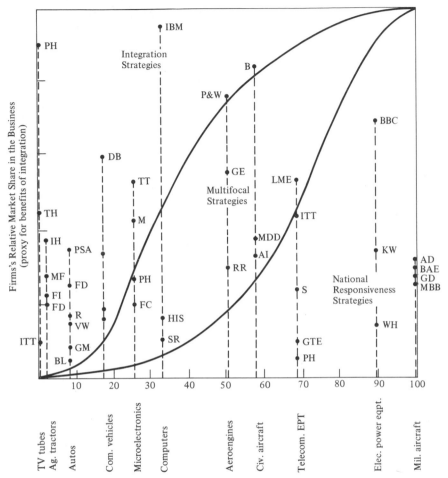

**Figure 4.4.** Comparative Patterns of Strategy and Competition in Selected European Industries, 1978–79

NOTE: Company names are represented by initials: P = Peugeot S.A.; FD = Ford of Europe; R = Renault; VW = Volkswagen; GM = General Motors; BL = British Leyland; DB = Daimler Benz; IV = IVECO; F = Ford; TI = Texas Instruments; TH = Thomson-CSF; AD = Avions Dassault; GD = General Dynamics; M = Motorola; PH = Philips; IBM = International Business Machines; HIS = Honeywell Information; LME = LM Ericsson; MF = Massey Ferguson; PW = Pratt & Whitney; GE = General Electric; BAE = British Aerospace; ITT = International Telegraph & Telephone; GTE = General Telephone & Electronics; BBC = Brown Boveri; KWU = Kraftwerk Union; WH = Westinghouse; FI = Fiat; B = Boeing; AI = Airbus Industries; IH = International Harvester; RR = Rolls Royce; MBB = Messerschmitt Bolkow Blohm; and MDD = McDonnell Douglas.

SOURCE: Yves L. Doz, *Strategic Management in Multinational Companies* (Elmsford, NY: Pergamon Press, 1986).

cording to the percentage of their total sales accounted for by public sector customers. The vertical axis measures the relative European market shares of various competitors. In the area to the left, above the two S curves, integration strategies predominate, that is, major competitors in businesses with low or moderate levels or sales to public customers. In those businesses, even smaller competitors integrate their operations and have to treat their businesses as global. In the area between the two S curves, *multifocal* strategies predominate. MNCs in that area follow multifocal strategies (e.g. Philips in microelectronics), form alliances between global and national suppliers (e.g. General Electric–SNECMA in jet engines), or develop international partnerships between national firms (e.g. Airbus Industries). To the bottom right of the S curves, MNCs with national responsiveness strategies and national competitors prevail.

In summary, policies constrain the strategic options open to integrated firms, to the point where they make it difficult for such firms to participate in certain markets, in particular those for defense-related strategic goods. They may also impose such performance requirements as to make participation unattractive to integrated MNCs. Government policies may also widen the options for weaker global competitors by offsetting some of the competitive disadvantages they would suffer in a competitive and homogeneous global industry.

## IMPLICATIONS FOR MANAGEMENT TO RESPOND TO HOST GOVERNMENT POLICIES

We can now draw from the analysis made in the central section of this chapter a series of implications, covering both the substantive impact of host governments on business positioning in the integration–responsiveness framework and the process through which to assess that likely impact.

### Government Policies and Business Positioning

The question raised at the beginning of this chapter can now be answered: When do governments so influence the economic and competitive conditions affecting a business that is necessary, or at least advisable, to reposition that business in the integration–responsiveness framework?

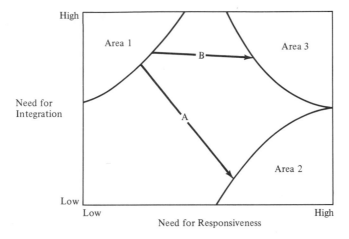

A. Move to Area 2 (national responsiveness)
  · Strategic industry with substantial government control over markets
  · Weaker global competitor seeking to acquire sheltered positions in
    protected markets
B. Move to Area 3 (multifocal strategy)
  · Weaker competitor in industry where governments are substantial buyers
    and value a measure of national control over suppliers

*Figure 4.5.* Consequences of Host Government Intervention on the Observed Position of Businesses in the IR
Framework

A move from integration to strategies of national responsiveness
is mostly advisable when the business is seen by host governments as
strategic enough to warrant extensive government control (Figure
4.5). Ideally governments might wish to turn to national suppliers,
but they may not be able, on their own, to keep abreast of technological developments or to gain access to export markets. In such
conditions they may prefer one or several multinational suppliers
rather than, or alongside, domestic ones, particularly when product
quality and reliability are strategically critical. In most countries,
therefore, the telecommunications equipment industry comprises
both national and multinational suppliers. As we discussed earlier,
countries do differ in their policies toward a given business on considerations of size, development strategy, trade policies, balance of
payments' stability, and so forth. Weaker global competitors may
thus seek to acquire sheltered profitable positions in protected markets and, where those markets are large enough, may be willing to
adopt national responsiveness strategies to serve them. The main difficulty with such an approach is that large developing countries with
protected markets often also have tight foreign exchange controls,

which make the movement of cash as difficult as the movement of goods. What is the value of a large market share in the Indian market in batteries or in radios if the cash flows from the operation have to be reinvested locally in areas increasingly unrelated to the corporation's worldwide business?

A move from integration to multifocal strategies, while usually driven by similar motives—concerns for control on the part of governments, fear of competitive weakness in a truly global industry on the part of the MNC—may be useful in a broader set of intermediate situations. In these, both the need to be responsive to local government concerns and the need to remain internationally competitive are important. The advantages and difficulties of a multifocal strategy have been discussed in the sections above, with one important exception, which will be discussed in detail in Chapter 8: A multifocal approach to world markets and to global competition is necessarily dialectical, and thus difficult and costly to manage. Yet, despite the loss of strategic freedom and the added managerial costs it entails, a multifocal strategy makes sense for smaller, weaker competitors in a number of industries in which governments themselves seek a tradeoff between control and competitiveness.

Again, different countries will make it more or less attractive for an MNC to adopt a multifocal strategy, based on their own desired tradeoffs. The relevant unit of analysis, therefore, is not a business as a whole. First, a business must be disaggregated geographically. In that business, some countries will be busily developing home-grown competitors, others welcoming integrated MNCs. Even in their attitude vis-à-vis the same MNC in a single business, they differ widely. Figure 4.5 portrays graphically the positions of various national governments vis-à-vis the same supplier of telephone switching equipment.

The Ecuadorian PTTs and the government, all too aware of the comparatively small scale of their country's market but enjoying relatively low labor costs, were quite happy to deal with the MNC on an "integrated" basis: They bought finished equipment efficiently produced on a large scale elsewhere, provided the company set up in Ecuador a large worldwide supply plant for a relatively low-technology, but labor-intensive, component. Offsets between imported finished products and exported components kept the impact on the balance of payments to a minimum. The Dutch, who already had in Philips a strong national supplier, were quite willing to deal with the MNC on an integrated basis and to purchase partly imported equipment. So were the Danes. As a gesture of goodwill, the company had located in Holland the central product development group for one of its product lines. It also had a significant plant in Denmark. Operations in Brazil, Mexico, Italy, and France, on the other hand, were fairly self-contained. Some had local shareholders, most were staffed by local nationals almost exclusively. In those four countries, national responsiveness clearly prevailed. The Brazilian operation, though, was still receiving components from other subsidiaries and exporting some of its production to neighboring countries. The critical point here is that a business with such internal variety cannot be run as a single, uniform entity. In an even more drastic way, Philips is running a global consumer transistor radio business, characterized by global cutthroat competition, and a separate self-contained radio business in India.

The balance that MNCs and governments find in their relationships is often compromised by changes in technology which modify both the MNCs' strategies and the governments' priorities. Shifts in technology not only affect the IR positioning directly, as discussed in Chapter 2, or through the competitive evolution they allow, but also indirectly through governments, because they also modify their policies. For instance, when telephone switching technology changed from electromechanical/analog to electronic/digital, national policy responses differed widely. The French, who were among the innovators in the new technology, promptly evicted the MNCs from the new technology and encouraged the sale of their local subsidiaries to the French electronics group Thomson-CSF. The Italians, whose state-owned producer Italtel was developing a digital electronic system, threatened to reduce the number of MNC suppliers from four to one and strongly encouraged MNCs to enter into a collaborative agreement with Italtel. Brazil was also tempted to develop its own system and used the shift to digital/electronic technologies as a way to "open" the industry to new competition and extract better terms from hopeful international suppliers. The Danes and the Mexicans, among others, acknowledged that digital/electronic switches were a software and microelectronics business, which did not offer good hopes for high local content and significant local employment, and were willing to deal with MNCs as integrated suppliers. Those various policy changes, along with many others in different countries, could have a significant impact on the structure of the telephone equipment industry.

Shifts in regulation can also have far-reaching impacts. Another segment of the same industry—station equipment—provides an illustration. So long as PTTs kept a monopoly on supplying station equipment, and so far as they were not too sensitive to costs, national responsiveness prevailed: They had equipment manufactured locally by MNCs or national firms and leased by the PTT. Once attachments were deregulated—letting independent station equipment suppliers sell their products to users directly—and/or once the PTTs became more sensitive to cost, in some cases as a result of privatization, integrated global suppliers of station equipment could succeed, at least at the low end of the market. While simple phones turned into a global market, supplied from Hong Kong or Korea, more complex and more customized equipment, such as PABXs, remained more local, particularly where service still is provided by PTTs.

The evolution of the station equipment business, as summarized here, also suggests the need to be segment-specific. To understand the likely impact of government policies, one needs to disaggregate an industry into homogeneous segments. To consider the telecommunication equipment industry in general is probably meaningless, while a more detailed view yields insight.

## An Approach to Assessing Host Government Policies

Above, we concluded that the relevant unit of analysis for understanding host government policies had to be relatively small: a business segment in a country. That suggests, first, that assessing host government policies is not a central staff job, at least not only. While teams of country risk analysts or social cost-benefit specialists are quite useful, they are not sufficient. Subsidiary managers themselves must play a key role in assessing host government policies, if only because they may have (almost) real-time access to critical information. We shall come back to the organizational arrangements and potential problems of having country managers successfully assume that kind of role; meanwhile, it is essential that local line managers see intelligence on government policies as a critical part of their job.

Once relevant information is obtained, action can be considered. From relatively minor investments to major strategic direction choices, a first guiding principle for action has to be *mutuality of interest.* This chapter has provided guidelines for analyzing when mutuality (or conflict) of interest exists between government policies and the integration-responsiveness priorities of MNCs.

Once mutuality of interest has been broadly established, more detailed analysis may proceed, specifically on the sharing of economic value or on the definition of roles in partnerships. Social cost-benefit analysis methods can be used to estimate the impact of specific projects (e.g. a new plant) on the host country, allowing MNC managers to develop a detailed understanding of the likely position of the host government.[26]

An analysis of specific risks can then be made in order to understand the nature of the exposure, and of the risks involved, within the overall integration–responsiveness strategic position. That may help guide detailed negotiations with the host government on specific incentives and performance requirements. While the specific techniques and methods needed to identify and assess specific risks and the methods to hedge against them, as well as the negotiation techniques to be used, are outside the scope of this book, they remain critically important. Even when mutuality of interest exists, the exact terms of agreement between MNCs and host countries can have a determining impact on the corporate return, on the MNC's ability to use operations in the country to bolster its worldwide competitive position, and on the evolution of the firm's global strategic posture over time.

# 5

# The Impact of Organized Labor

Just as our analysis in Chapters 2 and 3 ignored the influence of host governments on an MNC's strategic choices, it also made but passing reference to the impact of organized labor. There, we assumed a situation in which labor relations would not significantly hamper an MNC's strategic options or actions. While organized labor obviously does not enjoy the legal and fiscal powers of governments, however, in reality it may still play an important role in constraining the choices available to MNCs.*

First, although their importance relative to other costs is decreasing, labor costs still play a large part in determining cost competitiveness, as shown, for example, in our comparison of cost structures between Caterpillar and Komatsu. Wage levels, as influenced by unions and labor negotiation, thus play a key role. If not successfully controlled, labor cost disadvantages may considerably narrow the strategic options available to firms. Manning levels may be an even more serious problem for firms than wage levels, particularly in Continental Europe and in Japan, where employment cuts are particularly difficult. Again, that may have a deleterious effect on otherwise competitive firms. The plight of the French car maker Renault, with losses totaling more than $1 billion a year in 1984 and 1985, can be

*We are grateful to Professor Jacques Rojot, of INSEAD, whose willingness to share his insights regarding labor relations in MNCs contributed greatly to the writing of this chapter.

mainly explained by its inability to reduce employment when it was losing sales volume, falling behind its competitors in productivity, and incurring rapidly growing wage levels after the socialist government came to power in France, between 1981 and 1984.

While the impact of organized labor on MNCs is usually much less than that on national companies such as Renault, it can still be substantial. Plans to rationalize and integrate operations can be severely delayed, particularly in countries whose governments, under pressures from national unions, have pursued restrictive legislation. In several European countries, for instance, in order to carry out redundancy programs, MNCs need to show substantial losses of a permanent nature and to demonstrate that structural conditions make those losses unavoidable. Ford, for example, had to go through a long-drawn-out process before being able to close down a small, inefficient tractor plant in Amsterdam.

In many cases, MNCs have to buy social peace by committing not to integrate and rationalize their operations to the most efficient degree. General Motors, for example, was alleged in the early 1980s to have undertaken substantial investments in Germany—matching its new investments in Austria and Spain—at the demand of German metalworkers' unions as a way to foster good labor relations in Germany. One observer of the world auto industry suggested that car manufacturers were suboptimizing their manufacturing networks, partly to placate trade unions and partly to provide redundancy in sources to prevent localized social strife from paralyzing their network. Such suboptimization led to unit manufacturing costs 15 percent higher in Europe, on average, than an economically optimal network would have achieved. Union influence thus not only delays the rationalization and integration of MNCs' manufacturing networks and increases the cost of such adjustments (not so much in the visible severance payments and "golden handshake" provisions as through the economic losses incurred in the meantime), but also, at least in such industries as automobiles, permanently reduces the efficiency of the integrated MNC network.

Therefore, treating labor relations as incidental and relegating them to the specialists in the various countries is inappropriate. In the same way as government policies need to be integrated into strategic choices, so do labor relations. The evidence, however, is much more elusive. While MNC–host government negotiations are most often visible and explicit, the interactions between MNC management and unions are often private and even tacit. Only in deadlocked conflicts, such as long strikes, contested plant closing decisions, and the like, do interactions become visible. Therefore, although the tangible evidence of union power vis-à-vis MNCs is limited, it may also be beside the point: Union power may be more important when it quietly persuades management to do or not to do something than in the instances of open conflict, where it usually ultimately loses, albeit at great cost to the MNC. Managers will seldom admit openly to have yielded to union demands—for obvious reasons—and will thus minimize their importance, at least publicly, so the evidence on the extent and results of quiet, private, often tacit union pressure is elusive.

The organization of this chapter is somewhat parallel to that of Chapter 4. We shall start by reviewing the concerns of labor movements regarding MNCs, dealing with them in greater detail where they differ from those of host governments, and in a more perfunctory way where they parallel those of host governments. We shall then analyze the actions taken by organized labor toward MNCs and explain why they have met with only modest success, paticularly at the supranational level. Finally, we shall draw managerial implications from those analyses.


## UNDERSTANDING UNIONS' CONCERNS

Many of the unions' concerns about MNCs closely resemble those of host governments. Problems of free trade and adjustment to global competition concern unions as they do governments, with the unions taking—naturally—the side of producers' interests. Job losses to international competition in maturing industries has become the main preoccupation of unions, both because it is of most direct conern to their members and because it weakens their power by shrinking their membership base and reducing their fundraising ability.

MNC presence in an industry often is of relatively little concern *per se,* partly because MNCs often offer better terms and conditions than national firms, as will be discussed later. But MNC integration heightens the concerns of unions, who see in it both the threat from industry globalization and the MNC bargaining power derived from integration. In this section, we shall thus first review concerns about MNC integration.

## Concerns About MNC Integration

The first and foremost concern of unions parallels that of host governments: that the MNC will respond quickly and ruthlessly to changes in competitiveness of labor between countries and will therefore close down plants whenever their location is no longer competitive. Their assumption is, like that of governments, that the MNC's scanning capabilities, its experience in operating in multiple locations, and its experience in starting up new plants in diverse foreign countries will make its relocation of manufacturing faster, easier, and less costly than that of national companies. Further, the MNC places labor forces of various countries in explicit competition by being able to use layoff or close-down threats as a bargaining tool against national unions in wage negotiations. Multinational car manufacturers, for instance, very clearly threatened British unions with a plan to move manufacturing to Continental Europe unless British workers abandoned work rules that limited productivity, showed restraint in negotiating for wage increases, and curbed unrest.

The frustration of bargaining with MNCs, whose options are wider than those of national firms, is compounded with the distance between national unions and the "true" decision-makers. In a national firm or a nationally responsive MNC, union leaders can usually reach top management and deal directly with managers who have the power to decide. In an integrated MNC, managers in a subsidiary usually do not have the power to decide alone, except in the most mundane matters of labor relations. Even when local management has, in fact, considerable latitude to decide, it may still hide behind the existence of regional or global headquarters to justify a tough stance. Such a multilevel bargaining and decision-making structure allows MNCs to enjoy and exploit a wider range of negotiation options and to frustrate unions' efforts to pin them down in negotiations.

Further, the actual stakes and interests of integrated MNCs often look inscrutable from the standpoint of unions. Decisions are based on global optimization criteria, unknown to unions, and on data of which they see only a fraction. That explains the importance given by unions to "disclosure" as a necessary step toward strengthening the hand of unions in negotiatons with MNCs.

Another concern that unions share with host governments is the fear of the international division of labor, whereby MNCs keep the highly skilled tasks in their home country and farm out only menial tasks. While unions, representing mostly blue-collar workers, may be less sensitive to the issue than governments, it is still often a sore point in negotiations between unions and MNCs. One implication of such policy by MNCs is particularly disturbing for unions: the growing specialization and segmentation of labor between countries, within the same MNC, which make consistent transnational bargaining increasingly difficult and unlikely. International division of labor may also be an issue within the subsidiaries themselves: Senior technical, supervisory, and managerial jobs are filled by home country expatriates, who deprive local national employees of career development opportunities. While MNCs vary a great deal in their use of expatriates, heavy reliance on expatriates, for instance by Japanese companies, can become an issue for white-collar unions.

Unions are also concerned that MNCs will not fit well into national labor relation frameworks and, at the extreme, will not be fair players. For example, MNCs, having data on comparable plants in their own network where labor relations are organized differently, may try to depart from national practices and impose whatever labor relations framework seems most conducive to high productivity. Union officials also fear MNC managers will try to impose employment practices, contractual arrangements, and labor relations and negotiation frameworks imported from their home country. Too wide a departure from national standard practices would weaken union power and compel unions to deal with a wider set of circumstances. While union leaders admit that such tendencies on the part of MNC managers often result from lack of knowledge of the national environment and lack of familiarity with usual practices, they often suspect the MNC managers of deliberately trying to put them off balance by negotiating directly with the workers—often a departure from national norms. Here too, the Japanese, who try to export their style of labor relations overseas, meet with, at best, lukewarm reaction on the part of the unions.

Beyond the specifics of labor relations, MNCs are also suspected of trying to avoid unions altogether by tying the workers into a mix of benefits and commitments that makes them less receptive to unionization. Union leaders find this a problem particularly where white-collar workers predominate in number: They admit privately that nonunionization may satisfy individual employees, but argue that it weakens their collective power. It also weakens the unions by making them smaller and less representative. Such companies as IBM and Hewlett-Packard, and more generally U.S.-based MNCs that do not accept unions as a fact of life, are primary targets of criticism.

While that list of frequent concerns would suggest considerable union antipathy toward MNCs, the relation is tempered by a number of advantages, supported by concrete evidence, that union leaders owe to MNCs.

## A Union Perspective of the Advantages of MNCs

First, MNCs avoid being cast in the role of the villain because tensions betwen them and national unions have often been less than the unions' tensions with domestic companies. Since World War II, MNCs have been active predominantly in sectors where employment has grown faster than in sectors dominated by national firms. A number of the early global industries in which employment crises have been most severe in developed countries are not populated by MNCs: coal mining, steel, shipbuilding, textiles and garments, agriculture, and so on. Meanwhile employment grew in the automobiles, electronics, machinery, pharmaceuticals, and prepared food industries and in other sectors where MNCs play a leading role. The first sectors where MNCs have had to rationalize actively in the face of global competition have not been big employers—for instance, petrochemicals. Only recently, with the fall in employment in such industries as automobiles, electronics, and machinery, have MNCs confronted mass layoffs in Western Europe and the United States, where unions are best established and most militant. But even in those industries, MNCs have usually fared better than their national competitors in maintaining employment. While one could argue that MNC competition is causing employment losses among national competitors, that oblique but powerful argument has seldom been pursued actively by unions, if only because it would divide union members into those who work for MNCs and those who work for their national competitors. Unlike national firms, therefore, MNCs have seldom offered an obvious target for criticism by the unions.

Second, within a given sector, MNCs often give better terms, better working conditions, and higher wages than national firms. While in some cases that is an explicit citizenship cost gladly accepted by the MNC, it has the advantage of placating the most direct union pressures. In fact, in the eyes of some governments, MNCs may yield too easily to union demands and jeopardize national policies to limit inflation by reducing wage increases. In 1979, Ford of Britain showed willingness to make significant concessions to its unions, prompting the British Government to intervene by threatening Ford with cancellation of public sector fleet orders, should Ford yield to union demands.

Third, although data are scarce, there is little evidence to support the concern that MNCs close down plants any faster or more ruthlessly than national firms when faced with loss of competitiveness. In fact, as we argued in Chapters 3 and 4, by integrating their operations MNCs may be able to stem losses in competitiveness where local national firms would falter.

Fourth, except maybe for the paucity of research and development personnel, it is difficult to substantiate the argument that the MNCs employ lower-skilled personnel, in the same sector, than national firms. And the R&D deficiency argument cuts both ways: A country with relatively scarce researchers and engineers may gain more employment leverage from their being employed by national firms (which will presumably start by exporting), than from their being employed by MNCs, which may well exploit the results of the R&D work industrially in other countries.

As to the wider argument about skill levels, the reverse of the usual argument may in fact be true: MNCs skim the labor market, particularly in developing countries. They may well attract the best, and most docile, locally available labor, and be willing to pay a premium over local wages to maintain such access to the best labor. MNCs also put extensive emphasis on manpower training, an effort not always paralleled by local firms. That leaves MNCs open to the argument we made regarding R&D: Are they siphoning off the best and most productive talent to the detriment of local firms? While that can clearly be a preoccupation of host governments—particularly in the developing countries—it seems not to have become a preoccupation for unions.

Finally, studies of the impact of MNC investment in host countries, for both the home and host countries, are somewhat inconclusive, but they certainly do not suggest that host countries lose, or even that home countries incur substantial job losses because of "outsourcing" by national firms. While home countries do incur substantial blue-collar job losses, they result from loss of national factor competitiveness, not from out-sourcing by domestic firms nor from integration by MNCs *per se*. In fact, the available evidence suggests that out-sourcing and globalization of national firms allows them to maintain, and to develop further, white-collar employment in the home country, which would be lost—as would blue-collar employment—in the absence of out-sourcing and internationalization by national firms.

Given the tempering factors briefly reviewed above, unions have arrived at a position where the issue is no longer to nationalize or ban MNCs (except for some extreme left fringe groups). MNCs are neither good nor bad, in the eyes of union leaders, but should be better controlled—that is, there should be more safeguards to prevent them from being ruthless with their workers in their strategic choices.

The concern with control and, therefore, with increasing the unions' relative power vis-à-vis the MNCs has led union officials, over time, to a three-pronged approach toward MNCs.

The first path of approach entailed direct multinational bargaining. The original concept was to extend across borders the systems of union–company relations that existed within single countries. As we shall discover below, that approach met with little success. The second was more oblique: to acquire influence over MNCs by enlisting political support and obtaining the support of governments and international bodies. Such an indirect approach was slower but met with comparatively more success than direct transnational bargaining. The third path of approach was for unions to increase their national strength in traditional ways and to bargain with MNCs from their strengthened national base. So far, that has been the most effective approach. The three approaches are analyzed, and their future potential assessed, in the following section.

## UNION ACTIONS TOWARD MNCs

### Direct Multinational Bargaining

While the extension of domestic practices toward national firms to the international arena and to MNCs appears the most logical approach, it is also the most difficult for the unions to implement successfully.

Transnational bargaining started with the organization of International Trade Secretariats (ITS) as international federations to which national trade unions in a specific industry became affiliated.[1] While such ITSes existed in Europe for a long time, they received new impetus in the 1950s and 1960s with the entrance of such powerful American unions as the United Auto Workers. The ITSes originally saw the development of MNCs as an opportunity for new activities and for the enhancement of their influence, relative to the national unions. To match the geographical spread of specific MNCs, the ITSes created "world councils" for major MNCs, which regrouped representatives from the various national unions active in each MNC. The idea was to establish a "world council" for each MNC, with the objective of international coordination among the national unions, which would create an opportunity for collective multinational bargaining between the MNC and its "world council."

The various ITSes set up a number of world councils, for instance the International Metal Workers' Federation for Philips, General Electric, ITT, Siemens, and councils in the chemical industry, with Saint Gobain, AKZO, and Dunlop-Pirelli, among others. In the late 1960s, the "world councils" of several MNCs held meetings with the management of the companies, initially of a consultative nature, with the objective of achieving wage parity within the European activities of each MNC. Following the early success of those meetings—despite their consultative nature—some union leaders, led in particular by Charles Levinson, believed they could move toward direct transnational bargaining. They took intermediate steps, such as information exchange between national unions, encouragement of workers' participation efforts, and suport for national bargaining situations. After a few years, though, except for the coordination and exchange of information about MNCs, progress toward multinational bargaining had by and large stalled. The only true instance of multinational bargaining took place in U.S. companies between their domestic and Canadian operations only. The relative failure of transnational bargaining illustrates the limits to international labor actions, so a brief review of the reasons for its failure should be interesting.

The difficulties met by unions in multinational bargaining stem from three main sets of factors: (1) limits derived from the structures and origins of trade union movements and labor relations frameworks in various countries; (2) economic and political limits; and (3) the structure of employment within MNCs themselves.

*Structural Limits to Multinational Bargaining*

Various structural conditions make transnational bargaining particularly difficult.[2] First of all, bargaining structures and frameworks remain national and differ sharply from one country to another, and the pressures to make them converge are weak. Workers' wage comparisons are most visible within the same country, not across countries, where lack of information, exchange rate fluctuations, differing tax structures, and differing fringe benefit schemes cloud comparisons. In any case, workers are more sensitive to what their neighbors in a different industry earn than to purchasing power comparisons with distant unmet foreign workers in the same industry, or even in the same MNC.

In continental Europe national unions control very broad industry unions (for instance, the Federation of Metal Workers in Germany covers a wide range of industries). The breadth of such representation makes it difficult for those unions to deal effectively with narrow workers' categories and with single MNCs without creating tensions within their membership. They are geared toward broad deals on a national basis.

Union structures differ by country. Trade unionism developed independently in different countries in the nineteenth century, embodying in its structure the diversity of economic and political conditions in Europe, as well as the ideological orientations of early trade unionists. In France and Italy, unions split across ideological and political lines, with communist unions playing an important role. Some of the left-wing unions represented workers in large companies but did not become members of the ITS. Democratic concepts of unionism in Northern Europe and the United States differ profoundly from the "class struggle" views still held by the communist unions in Southern Europe. As a result, agreement on concrete practical actions toward MNCs is often difficult. Consensus between unions on transnational bargaining is difficult.

The negotiation contexts themselves also differ. First, they are more or less centralized, with emphasis being placed at various levels. Negotiations take place primarily on a regional basis in Germany, on a national basis in Sweden, on an industry basis in France, on a plant basis in the United Kingdom, and so forth. Second, the role of public authorities varies, with the government being intimately involved in labor negotiations in France, for instance, and not at all in the United States. Again, such diversity of negotiation contexts makes it difficult to develop an effective transnational bargaining context toward an individual MNC. The difficulty is further compounded where the same MNC may be exposed to multiple industry unions in a given country.

Finally, the legal framework of labor relations also differs deeply from country to country. On such basic aspects as the right to strike, Germany is much more conservative than France, while it is more progressive on the workers' representation and on co-determination. Again, those differences constrain the world councils' ability to develop a practical unitary position toward an MNC; what is legally acceptable in one country is not in another.

## Economic and Political Limits to Transnational Bargaining

Not only do workers seldom compare their situation from country to country with a view to equalizing it, but they also compete from country to country. Their main interest is to protect employment in their own country and their own subsidiary. Economic conditions may make agreement difficult: Various countries go through different economic cycles, or the products of this or that plant in an integrated MNC are more or less affected by recession or expansion. The economic and financial situations of various plants in the MNC are thus seldom uniform. When they are not uniform, the potential for transnational bargaining is weakened: Workers' interests differ too much from one country (and one plant) to another. Only when the overall corporate system is in crisis, and when pressures lead to systemwide integration, is the potential for coordinated international action relatively strong. To a large extent that was the situation in AKZO in the early 1970s, one of the few cases of active involvement of a "world council" in discussing rationalization and integration with management. Most often, though, internal differences within the MNC between various countries make joint action difficult.

Joint transnational bargaining would require on the part of the unions a long-term coordinated view of collective workers' interests across countries, and the ability to make short-term tradeoffs between locations on the basis of long-term collective interests. Like many other political institutions depending on short-term members' support and competing for workers' votes, unions are not easily able to make such tradeoffs against specific short-term subgroup interests in favor of long-term collective interest.

Local national unions, like national governments, also show little enthusiasm toward multinational bargaining: Having to abide by its results would weaken their power and decrease their autonomy. One of the main stumbling blocks for transnational bargaining has been, indeed, the local unions' unwillingness to transfer some power to ITSes. ITSes have thus worked relatively well in the gathering and sharing of information—a function that national unions could easily agree to—but not in implementing transnational actions, a function that would encroach on the power of national unions. National governments, no matter what their political orientation, have seldom supported transnational efforts on the part of unions, which they have usually seen as a threat to their sovereignty and, in some cases, to their key role in managing labor relations. International unions have found their staunchest supporters among transnational intergovernmental bodies, such as the EEC and the OECD, whose officials often suffer the same frustrations at the hands of national governments.

### MNC Limits to Transnational Bargaining

MNC managers have also made it difficult for transnational bargaining to succeed. First, the meetings with "world councils" have been only consultative and informal; management has carefully avoided being dragged into actual negotiation in this arena. Essentially, most MNCs have been willing to talk, but not to negotiate. Second, MNCs have avoided the creation of other channels and have made sure that their own structure of management of labor relations emphasizes national differences and national responsiveness, in tacit support of national unions against supranational ones.[3] MNCs have also avoided providing opportunities for group meetings between MNCs and trade unions, for fear that this would lead to an international and interindustry alignment of conditions toward those most favorable to workers.[4] Finally, and maybe most important, the strategic choices and the policies of MNCs themselves have had divisive consequences that make transnational collective bargaining difficult.

While on the surface MNC integration would correspond to transnational bargaining (and MNC national responsiveness to national bargaining), integration has side effects on labor management that are not conducive to transnational bargaining. First, strategies of integration usually reduce labor content. Larger, new, specialized plants replace older, smaller, multipurpose plants. That shift is an opportunity to modernize the process technology and also to use more automated processes, which the smaller scale of nationally responsive plants would not justify. Indeed, one of the chief sources of high unemployment in Europe, as against the United States, over the last decade has been much faster growth rates in capital-intensity and labor productivity in Europe than in the United States, leading to a stable employment level in Europe versus rapid job creation in the United States.[5] Second, strategies of integration often lead to labor stratification, with skilled blue-collar jobs disappearing and employment growing for unskilled labor and for white-collar technicians and engineers.[6] The shift toward labor stratification is more clear in industries where electronic technologies substitute for electromechanical ones, such as in telecommunication switchgear and in office equipment. Third, the growing global competitive pressures that go with integration lead MNCs to review their various activities and, often, to deintegrate and subcontract activities or stages in the production or distribution process that yield them the least competitive advantage. Unlike the situation of the 1950s and 1960s, when labor was scarce, the current employment situation and the specific role of integrated MNCs lead to more direct competition between the work forces of different countries and create more differentiation between the home and host country work forces, as well as between MNC and non-MNC employees in host countries (through labor stratification). None of those changes is conducive to a reinforcement of multinational bargaining power. If anything, MNC integration reinforces the bargaining power at the local level of existing skilled workers who play a key role in the integrated network and who might be difficult to replace quickly, locally or in a lower-labor-cost country, should the MNC move its manufacturing to another location in response to labor strife.

All the factors listed above—the organization of union structures and labor relation frameworks in various countries, the diversity of economic and political conditions in various nations, and the strategies and tactics of MNCs in dealing with labor—contributed to the failure of direct transnational bargaining. By the late 1970s, it became clear to trade unionists that such bargaining was unlikely to succeed. They thus emphasized another approach, which had been pursued for a few years but less actively promoted initially: international disclosure and regulation, which they hoped would lead to multilateral regulation through transnational organizations.

## Multilateral Regulation Through International Organizations

Multilateral regulation corresponds to an expectation on the part of unions that supportive legislation could be passed in a coordinated fashion, in several developed countries, to place constraints upon the MNC along a number of dimensions. In particular, such regulation would force MNCs' internal transactions to be more "transparent" to outside parties, including national and international unions, and also limit the situations in which MNCs could avoid extensive bargaining with unions at the national or international level. Among the many proposals for multilateral regulations, two stand out: the OECD conduct guidelines* and the "Vredeling Proposal."

### The OECD Guidelines

The OECD Council of Ministers decided in 1975 to establish a "Committee on International Investment and Multinational Enterprise" (CIME). Among other roles, the committee set out to define uniform standards of behavior applicable to MNCs. Those guidelines covered a wide set of domains, and CIME sought the assistance of two existing advisory bodies to the OECD: the Trade Unions Advisory Committee (TUAC), representing major national unions, and the Business and Industry Advisory Committee (BIAC), representing employers. Of particular concern to the BIAC members was the reaffirmation of "equal treatment" by OECD member countries between domestic firms and MNCs, one issue the importance of which was shown in Chapter 4. Of the various aspects covered by the guidelines, two concerned labor relations: the employment and labor relation guidelines, and the disclosure of information. While the guidelines were not intended to be a substitute for national laws and regulations, they provided a "code of conduct" for MNCs that had been agreed upon by the OECD member governments. The CIME, however, decided to make the guidelines not mandatory but only voluntary, in view of the legal and institutional complexity of making

*Other institutions, such as the International Labor Organization and the United Nations, have also drafted codes of conduct, but their influence has remained slight, partly because members of the United Nations could not agree on whether to include state-owned enterprises among MNCs (the Eastern bloc countries wanting to exclude them) and because the ILO declarations do not really contribute a detailed code of conduct. We have thus decided to concentrate our attention on the OECD guidelines.

international regulation of investment and multinational management actions practical.[7]

Although the guidelines provided no enforcement mechanisms, being only advisory, CIME did provide the possibility for member states or the TUAC to raise specific cases for consideration by CIME as a way to contribute to the better definition of what practices fall within or outside the standards of conduct approved by the guidelines. Over the last ten years several cases have been brought to the CIME's attention. They have involved such issues as the parent company's responsibility for liability resulting from a subsidiary's bankruptcy (e.g. the Badger subsidiary of Raytheon in Belgium), the transfer of workers from one country to another to replace striking workers (Hertz in Denmark), the appropriate level of discussion between unions and MNCs on future plans (Viggo/British Oxygen), plant closure (Ford Amsterdam), quality of work life (Warner Lambert), and participation of local MNC employees at international trade union meetings (Philips Belgium).[8] In several of those cases, CIME's attention led to a renewal of negotiations between the MNC and the unions. In the Badger case it led to a reversal of corporate position (Raytheon finally accepting corporate liability for the severance payments to workers in the Belgian affiliate it closed down).

The variety of topics brought to the attention of CIME, and the small number of cases, make any attempt at generalization difficult. A few points, however, are relatively clear. Although the unions seem to have failed in their effort to make the guidelines mandatory and to transform CIME into the equivalent of a court of justice, the guidelines have some impact and tend to be followed by most MNCs.[9] Indeed, in formulating and implementing MNC strategies and policies for a business, it makes sense not to ignore the guidelines. First, as pointed out above, the guidelines comprise provisions favorable to MNCs in the section not dealing with employment, such as the principle of nondiscrimination on the part of governments between domestic and multinational firms. Second, being singled out by unions for violation of the guidelines puts the company in an unfavorable light from the standpoint of host governments and public opinion in host countries. It brings the company into the spotlight and may damage its image in some constituency. Consequently, most companies prefer to avoid it. Third, frequent violation of the guidelines by MNCs would fuel union demands for a mandatory system, which would make codes of conduct mandatory and create some judicial enforcement mechanisms.

## European Economic Community Proposals

Beside the attempt to regulate behavior at the supranational level (represented by the hopes the unions placed in codes of conduct), unions have also tried to obtain international organization support toward multinational collective bargaining. That requires providing enough "transparency" to the MNC to overcome the disadvantage of lack of union information on overall multinational strategies. It also requires a capability to pull the MNC into negotiations on issues of relocation and integration, plant closure, and so forth.

While some of the earlier EEC-proposed "directives"—such as the ninth directive on protection of minority shareholders in MNC subsidiaries in the EEC—required the provision of extensive economic and operational data by the MNC on strategic coordination and operational integration of its EEC activities with that in the rest of the world, the main pressure toward disclosure came from the "Proposal on Procedures for Informing and Consulting the Employees of Undertakings with Complex Structures, in Particular Transnational Firms," commonly known as the "Vredeling Proposal" from the name of its originator.

The thrust of the Vredeling Proposal is to force the company to provide detailed information on future global strategies to individual subsidiaries and to have the management of the subsidiaries inform the workers and "consult" with them on those plans. Original drafts of the proposal also provided for workers' access to the decision-making centers at corporate headquarters, should agreement not be reached at the subsidiary level.

Implementation of such a proposal would obviously have devastating results for MNC strategies. First, it would probably result in the leakage of confidential information about future plans, manufacturing costs, and so forth, to competitors. Second, the MNC would have to provide data on all changes in the integrated network to subsidiaries, even when they are not directly affected. Third, the distinction between "consulting" with workers and negotiating with them is very thin and difficult to enforce. The MNC management could thus see any significant strategic move hamstrung in a maze of *a priori* negotiations with unions.

Those potential results led to an outcry by MNC managers and to the realization on the part of member states of the EEC of the impracticality of the proposal. Through multiple negotiation sessions and many drafts since its original 1980 drafting, the proposal's contents have been much watered down, and it has also become clear that such legislation is unlikely to be adopted by the Council of Ministers of the EEC.

## *Limits to Multilateral Regulation*

Limits to multilateral regulation are manyfold, which may explain why both the OECD Code of Conduct and the Vredeling Proposal have had little impact. First, neither the OECD nor the EEC proposal has as its goal the support of unions. They make tradeoffs between the interests of various parties to economic activity. As such they have to accommodate the demands of managers and investors no less than those of labor. Second, the economic and political context in which those issues are approached has evolved. The importance of maintaining or restoring the international competitiveness of OECD or EEC countries is much better understood in the mid-1980s than in the mid-1970s, when the codes of conduct and the reasoning leading to the Vredeling Proposal originated. The political balance in most European countries and in the United States has swung from state interventionism to a much more liberal approach, where freedom of economic activity is encouraged. High unemployment has shifted union concerns toward more immediate issues than controlling MNCs, such as adjustment in mature industries (steel, coal, shipbuilding, and so on) and the impact of new information and manufacturing technology on industrial and service employment.

As we suggested earlier, though, this means not that MNCs should disregard the OECD code of conduct, in particular, but that more drastic measures evolving toward tighter multigovernmental regulation of MNC policies in support of union control are unlikely.

## The Strengthening of National Constraints Toward MNCs

The conditions summarized above as limits to multilateral regulation, in particular the large unemployment, have also caused the locus of initiative of union action toward multinationals to move away from the ITSes back to the national unions and to national negotiation arenas. The inherent conflict between national unions of various countries, which compete for the same jobs, and the relative weakening of industry-specific unions in each country to the advantage of larger multisector trade union centers have combined to make it increasingly difficult for the ITSes to have an impact. Their credibility has also been recently weakened by the recognition of their failure to trigger a shift to multinational collective bargaining with MNCs. Trade union solidarity across borders has become difficult to achieve, except on the broader macroeconomic issues where ITSes have little to contribute.[10] Further, failing to see international organizations such as the EEC or the OECD exercise sufficient influence in their favor, national unions have fallen back to the position of attempting to obtain the support of their own governments in regulating MNC activity.

The approach of national unions has been somewhat incoherent, however, with measures that on the one hand tended to improve the solidarity of national unions in their dealings with MNCs and, on the other, particularly since 1979, expressed a stronger support for protectionist measures, which pit the interests of home country workers against those of host country workers. Those two somewhat contradictory sets of trends are summarized below.

### Home Country Solidarity with Host Country Workers

Coordination of national actions has been the easiest route for unions, mainly because it calls for no new bargaining or regulatory structure and can be achieved informally on an *ad hoc* basis, and partly because unions are able to leverage their influence with national governments to obtain legislation and rules toward MNCs.

Those actions have followed different approaches. First, unions have sometimes encouraged governments to pass legislation or impose regulations that extend domestic home country standards to home country's MNCs' activities in other countries. Most of those actions have focused on the extension of working conditions and workers' benefits of the home country to countries where they are not mandatory. In Sweden, for instance, legislation has been passed barring from preferential state credit Swedish companies that do not comply in foreign countries with Swedish employment conditions. Similar actions have taken place in other countries on issues of occupational hazards, safety, health, and even wages. While those home country union initiatives are cast in a socialistic tone ("workers of the world, unite!") they are also self-serving: By increasing the cost of producing abroad for the home country MNCs, they make it less likely that MNCs will relocate manufacturing facilities overseas. Back in the 1960s, international wage equilization was already a theme of the United Auto Workers in the United States, which was concerned about the major car manufacturers' overseas investments.

Second, unions have sometimes encouraged legislation that would give them a say on the governance of home country MNCs. German co-determination is the best known example: International union officials were appointed to the board of major firms as representatives of the workers. Although the union representatives' power was limited in various ways—they participated in debates but had no voting power—co-determination was seen as a way both to influence management and to gain access to strategic information about the MNC. Co-determination originally had the MNCs, both German companies and large subsidiaries of foreign MNCs in Germany, scared. After a few years of practice, however, the general consensus is that workers' representatives have by and large been co-opted into the ranks of top management and that on most issues their priorities and views are not radically at odds with those of top managers or of investors. In other countries, such as Britain, France, and Italy, where union leaders might have had extreme views, co-determination has not taken hold, and unions have avoided it carefully anyway.

Third, unions have sometimes engaged in solidarity actions across borders, for instance when workers at the Continental European plants of U.S. car makers have refused to produce parts similar to those made by striking plants in Britain. While examples of such actions abound, they have seldom amounted to much in actual economic consequences on the MNC.

Fourth, in some countries, such as Germany, unions have insisted on bringing representatives of foreign subsidiaries' unions onto work councils and other labor relations bodies to ensure that the point of view of labor in the host countries is heard. Management of MNCs has often resisted such efforts, in which they saw a prelude to international collective bargaining.

Overall, the impact of home country unions has been minor. As we discussed earlier, patterns of specialization and integration within the MNC tend to divide workers between home and host countries. The home government, usually more concerned with the competitiveness of their national firms than with the promotion of foreign workers' interests, has seldom supported unions in those actions, with the exception of the Swedish socialist government. Most other governments, while they may pay lip service to social equity, are not seriously interested and in some cases are openly hostile.

With the deepening of the crisis, home country unions have often turned to direct protectionism, from the UAW's support of the Burke–Hartke Act in the United States to Renault's workers' demonstrations against the import into France of Renault cars made in Spain. In a static view of defending their membership, unions have generally preferred protectionism to free trade. When supported by national governments, that is an obvious threat to integrated MNCs, particularly to those which out-source part of their production. While U.S. companies in the consumer durable goods industries are most directly threatened, many European companies would also be threatened. Protectionist pressures have been blunted so far, though, by the reluctance of governments to shift to protectionism and by the evidence that short-term employment protection costs dearly.

### National Action in Host Countries

MNCs in host countries have often been a privileged target of union activism. For ideological reasons, communist unions have singled out MNCs as a culprit for many woes. MNCs also are easy targets, in particular when they are integrated: While disruptions in one location can paralyze the whole network, and strikes are thus costly, MNCs also have an image of worldwide wealth and power, which does not endear them to public opinion when they cut employment in this or that country. Local companies, with desperate financial conditions but better political relations, do not usually offer such an easy target. MNCs thus have often borne the brunt of social strife on issues not directly related to their multinationality. The lack of familiarity of MNC managers with local legal and political conditions has sometimes needlessly worsened social conflicts by polarizing situations that local firms would have resolved through compromise. The MNC lack of familiarity with the local situations, and their management's lack of nuance in negotiations, also sometimes make them tempting targets. That disadvantage in local understanding may also explain why, on the whole, MNCs have tended to offer better terms and conditions than local firms, often as a way to buy labor peace.

The unions' ability effectively to single out MNCs as targets has been somewhat limited, though, by most governments' acceptance of nondiscrimination principles whereby MNCs are treated similarly as local firms.

Overall, then, the differential impact of national unions' actions on MNCs—compared with the impact on local firms—has seldom been significant, and attempts to rely on national governments to tighten their control of MNCs, be they home country or host country governments, have had little success. Quite to the contrary, certain governments, such as that of Singapore, have stifled development of strong national unions so as not to scare MNCs away. The inescapable fact that countries compete against one another in global industries drastically limits any government's capability to yield to union demands, no matter how sympathetic that government is to union positions, without compromising national competitiveness.

## CONCLUSION

While one might conclude that by and large unions have failed to influence MNCs, that would be an erroneous conclusion. Unions may have succeeded more in what they quietly deterred MNCs from doing than in what they attempted to force MNCs to do. Therefore, to conclude, from the lack of apparent success of labor unions to gain a say in the strategies and management of MNCs, that unions can safely be ignored in making strategic decisions in MNCs, and then handled at the margin, would be very dangerous. The overriding conclusion is therefore simply that possible union actions and their potentially serious consequences should be taken into consideration when making integration, rationalization, and divestment decisions. While day-to-day labor relations are best handled at the local subsidiary level, where the experience resides, overall labor relations strategies are best considered centrally in the MNC network.

# 6

---

# Evaluating Interdependencies
# Across Businesses

In our discussion, so far, of top management's task in a DMNC we have assumed that the basic unit for analysis and management is a discrete, stand alone business. That is a valid assumption only if the various businesses in the DMNC's portfolio are not interdependent or if we can ignore, for purposes of strategic management, the interdependencies among them. In this chapter we shall identify the *source* of interdependencies among businesses in a DMNC and examine ways to determine *the criticality* of various interdependencies.[1]

## SOURCES OF INTERDEPENDENCIES

The various sources of interdependencies in the portfolio of a DMNC can be illustrated by examining the high-fidelity audio business at Philips.[2]

### Vertical Integration and Technology

Product and component flows across businesses (vertical integration) as well as technology linkages, such as sharing a common core technology across several businesses, can create interdependencies.

Let us take the hi-fi business as an example. Figure 6.1 illustrates the nature of component and technology linkages in the hi-fi business. Hi-fi, as a worldwide business, was part of the Audio Group, which included phonograph, radio, and tape businesses. Hi-fi products were created partly by various combinations of subassemblies from the phonograph, radio, and tape businesses. Further, the hi-fi business within Philips depended on the Components Group (Elcoma) for components. Elcoma also sold those components to third parties as a discrete business in its own right. Hi-fi was also dependent on another division, called ELA, which developed and manufactured specialized audio components. The simplified chart of product and technology flows among the various groups illustrates the nature of linkages. The managers of hi-fi could not start their day with the simplifying assumption that they were managing a discrete, stand-alone business.

## Logistics

The logistics imposed by the product development and manufacturing system can create a series of interdependencies.

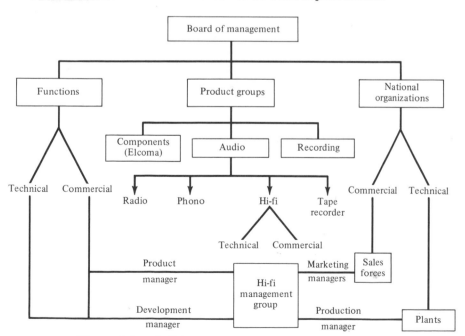

***Figure 6.1.*** A Schematic of Linkages: Hi-Fi Business

The market for hi-fi was worldwide. The manufacturing system supporting the hi-fi business was spread over several international production centers (IPCs) in France, Holland, Belgium, and Singapore. Those plants produced, in addition to the components needed for the hi-fi business, components and subassemblies for other businesses. That manufacturing configuration resulted as much from the firm's history of incremental commitments to the plant as the business expanded as from careful analysis of the total development and manufacturing costs associated with the system. As most manufacturing plants associated with the hi-fi business served other businesses as well, hi-fi management could not request drastic changes (either increases or decreases) in output from any location. In a sense, the manufacturing plants were selling capacity, and the hi-fi business group had to negotiate the capacity that would be assigned to it. Any changes in the negotiated allocation of capacity was contingent on the demands imposed by the other businesses the plants served. The agility with which the hi-fi business could respond to market demands was restricted by the very nature of the underlying manufacturing and development system.

### Host Governments

Host government demands can impose interdependencies across businesses that would otherwise be discrete and stand-alone.

The host governments—France, Holland, Belgium, and Singapore—where the IPCs of the hi-fi business were located, were also hosts to a large number of other businesses of Philips. For example, Philips had a significant presence in the defense and telecommunications businesses in France. The French government was concerned about Philips's maintaining component manufacturing capability in France. Any move on the part of either hi-fi management or Elcoma (Philips's component business) to reduce supplies of components from France, it was felt, could negatively affect the ability of Philips to maintain its presence in the defense and telecommunications businesses. As a result, the choice of manufacturing location in the hi-fi business (a strategic choice given the pressures for cost reduction in that business) was constrained by its possible impact on unrelated businesses like defense and telecommunications. The linkage between the two sets of businesses—hi-fi and defense systems—was the result of managerial perceptions of the possible reactions of the

French government. The impact of a reduction in component capacity in France, brought about by the need to be cost competitive in the hi-fi business, on the ability of Philips to continue to sell defense systems in France was not easy to determine. The linkage was nebulous and hard to define. It was, however, a real issue for managers.

Philips was the largest employer in Holland. Reducing capacity, or "out-sourcing," by Philips had serious implications for Holland's employment situation. As a result, the Dutch government did not look kindly on attempts to out-source. Philips's top management had to be sensitive to the political implications of reducing capacity in Holland, and no business could make that choice unilaterally without considering the implications of such a move on Philips's total operations.

The Belgian government was equally concerned about employment sustained in that country by businesses like hi-fi. Its approach to protecting employment was to link the purchase of Philips computer equipment by the Belgian public sector with Philips's continued manufacturing presence.

Singapore's government was less concerned about employment *per se.* It was more concerned with becoming a center for high-technology manufacturing, thereby upgrading the skill levels in the country. Singapore's concern translated into its demand for locating product development centers there. The development could relate to any business requiring high technology, not just hi-fi.

## Distribution and Marketing

Competitive advantages derived from distribution and marketing considerations, as well as the costs of marketing, might force interdependencies across businesses that might otherwise be discrete and stand-alone.

In the case of the hi-fi business at Philips, managers had to make choices regarding the marketing of hi-fi products in various country markets. In all the important markets of Philips, the national organizations had built up an impressive distribution and service organization around the audio-video products, as well as major and small domestic appliances. Hi-fi managers could use the existing marketing infrastructure, including channels, salesmen, and promotion provided by the video business or the appliance business, or could start a dedicated marketing infrastructure for hi-fi. In some countries hi-fi products were sold partly through specialized dealers—a further complication in the choice of a marketing approach. The cost of a dedicated infrastructure in various countries was prohibitive. On the other hand, it was extremely difficult to interest the video marketing group in providing support for the relatively small hi-fi business when its chief concern was to maintain market share in the video business. The appliance business had a reputation for standard products rather than for high-technology, state-of-the-art products, an image that the hi-fi business group was trying to promote in the minds of the consumer. The need to leverage distribution investments indicated an alliance with the established video group. This would make hi-fi's marketing strategies dependent on the strategies of the video group, an interdependence, the merits of which were not obvious.

### Corporate Image

The need to maintain and leverage a corporate image can and often does impose interdependencies across businesses.

Philips was concerned about the image hi-fi would create and its impact on the other consumer businesses in its portfolio. The hi-fi business represented state-of-the-art technology, and corporate management felt that the benefits of that image had to be exploited by other businesses as well. That meant hi-fi managers would have to work closely with other businesses and pursue opportunities for leveraging the Philips brand in a variety of consumer businesses, yet another source of interdependency.

## WHICH INTERDEPENDENCIES ARE CRITICAL?

The example of the hi-fi business at Philips illustrates the multiple sources of interdependencies. Depending on which interdependency is seen as critical, the position of the hi-fi business in the IR grid would change, as illustrated in Figure 6.2. If the hi-fi group felt that leveraging technology and the benefits of an in-house supply of components was critical to hi-fi's business success then the interdependency between the component business (Elcoma) and the hi-fi business would be critical. That would force the hi-fi business to take

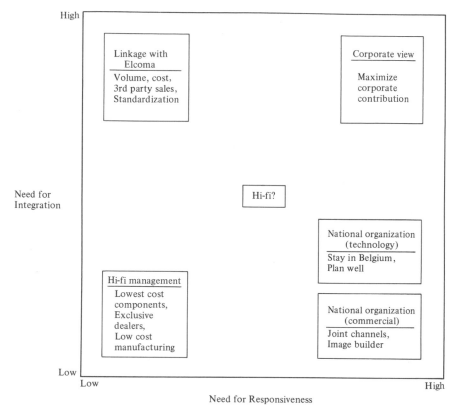

*Figure 6.2.* Multiple Interdependancies: Impact on Hi-Fi Business

on the characteristics of the component business in the IR framework. Dominant strategic concerns would relate to cost reduction, technology transfer, economies of scale, and standardization of products and product modules. On the other hand, if the central strategic concern is market development, and if sensitivity to differences in customer tastes and preferences is seen as the critical element of success, then the hi-fi business would take on the characteristics of a nationally responsive business, as shown in Figure 6.2.

The desire of host governments to link "unrelated" businesses together for public reasons, or the desire of corporate management to leverage a business along multiple dimensions (in the case of hi-fi along the technology dimension and the distribution dimension), can easily push the hi-fi business into a mode where the need for both global integration and local responsiveness are high at the same time. It is not uncommon in such circumstances for managers running the business to hope for an extreme stand-alone mode, where they are allowed to source components from anywhere, have a dedicated sales force, and primarily sell to OEM customers like Sears. The four possible configurations of the hi-fi business, depending on which is seen as the critical interdependency, as depicted in Figure 6.2, raise an important strategic question: How do we make a choice?

The difficulty in making explicit choices regarding the appropriate interdependency to leverage in a case like the hi-fi business arises from the fact that the "costs and benefits" of managing or not managing an interdependency are difficult to estimate. Some of the cost-benefits are more readily identified than others. For example, the value of shared manufacturing resources can be computed by estimating the additional investment that would be required to get into that business as a stand-alone operation. On the other hand, the cost-benefits of a shared distribution and marketing infrastructure are much more difficult to assess. Some aspects of that choice, such as the additional salesmen required or the warehousing costs, lend themselves to analysis, but other aspects do not. Typically, judgments regarding the impact on distributors and the sales force of adding a new business to an existing line of businesses are difficult to quantify. Judgments regarding the possible reactions of a host government on the various salient businesses a DMNC may be involved in, in that country, as a response to its actions in a nonsalient business are even harder to come by. The organizational costs of coordination of the interependencies are the most difficult to assess, even though very real, as we shall see later. In other words, costs and benefits are both tangible and judgmental. Some aspects of the equation can be quantified, others cannot be.

## EVALUATING INTERDEPENDENCIES

While it is very difficult to understand all the sources of interdependencies and identify the costs and benefits associated with them, strategic management requires that managers make some choices rather than try to manage all interdependencies as if all were crucial to success. While no one simple formula will provide the answer, we can identify a set of questions that can help in developing a comprehensive cost-benefit picture.

## Costs Associated with Managing Interdependencies

The costs associated with managing interdependencies tend to be primarily organizational and therefore difficult to quantify. Consequently, most firms ignore those costs. However, the costs are real. Some recurring symptoms of those costs follow.

### Loss of Top Management Focus on a Business

The most basic cost associated with attempts to manage interdependencies is the loss of focus on the performance of a specific business. The quality of a discrete business—its investment requirement, quality of returns, growth potential, market share, product leadership, quality of management—can be measured. An interdependent set of businesses creates difficulties in measuring the quality of any one business. For example, the performance of a component business is likely to be influenced by the quality of other businesses. Investment requirements, for example, in the case of hi-fi business, may have to take into account the investment requirements of the component business as well. The minimum size required to be cost-efficient may be quite different in the component business as compared with the hi-fi business, in which case the firm may have to carry additional capacity in the component business or find suitable third party buyers.

A discrete business provides top management with the option of continued investment or divestment. It allows an opportunity to measure managerial performance, uncluttered by a maze of accounting complications caused by joint costs and transfer prices. The management group can identify its performance with the success of a discrete business much more easily than with that of various interdependent organizational subunits.

### Loss of Flexibility

Increasingly, a large number of businesses require flexibility and quick response time to market needs. That is obvious not only in the consumer electronics industry, which is characterized by very short product life cycles, constant addition to and changes in features, and cost reduction, but also in such diverse industries as medical electronics, engineered materials, instrumentation, and information technology. Businesses that operate as discrete, stand-alone entities can respond quickly. If they are part of an interdependent set of businesses, then the response time to accommodate market needs—be it in product development or in increasing capacity—is constrained by the managers' ability in that business to convince others of both the need for and the urgency of the change. Strategic priorities of businesses that are part of the interdependent set may differ enough to make agreements on priorities difficult to negotiate.

## Reduced Innovation

Innovation and entrepreneurship tend to flourish when organizational arrangements allow for "freedom to act." In discrete, stand-alone businesses, where managers have control over most of the critical resources they need, such action is possible. DMNCs concerned with innovation, like Hewlett-Packard, 3M, and Harris, have prided themselves on operating small, discrete businesses within the large umbrella of the corporation. Even IBM, whose mainline business was managed with probably one of the most interdependent management systems, created separate independent business units (IBUs) to provide the opportunity for new businesses, like the PC business, to emerge and grow. When innovative ideas have to be negotiated with several other businesses, and when resource commitments have to pass the test of several groups of managers not close to the market place addressed by the innovation, entrepreneurship is often the victim.

## Loss of Visibility of Business Performance

The performance of a stand-alone business is relatively easy to compute, as we can identify both the assets deployed in support of the business and the returns of that business. As a result, managerial motivation and performance evaluation are relatively easy. In an interdependent set of businesses, shared resources, joint costs, and transfer prices cause even the accounting for results to be "muddy." Further, as managers do not have the freedom to make business decisions like volume, location, levels of investment, and prices pertinent to that business without concern for the impact on other interdependent parts, they cannot be held totally responsible for results. Both goal setting and performance measurement become confused. Confused perceptions of responsibility, based on responses of a set of managers, illustrated in Figure 6.3, result. It is obvious that no one feels particularly accountable for overall business performance results, like profitability or market share, even though they all feel responsible for selecting the scope of the business, like picking market niches in which to compete.

## Costs of Coordination

Coordination of interdependent businesses has other organizational costs. First, coordination means more management time, often more managerial layers, and more time spent in committee meetings. Often managerial attention is focused on "oiling the wheels of the organization" rather than on competition. In one DMNC we studied, managers often spent 50 to 70 percent of their time with managers

| Key Managerial Tasks | National Organization | Organizational Units | | | Other Product Divisions |
| --- | --- | --- | --- | --- | --- |
| | | Product Division | | | |
| | | Technical | Commercial | IPC | |
| Profit responsibility | X? | | X? | | |
| Market share | ? | ? | ? | ? | |
| P-M niche | X | X | X | X | X |
| Price | X | ? | X | | |
| Product specs | | X | | X | |
| New products | | X | X | | |
| Product line | | | X | | |
| Market testing | | ? | ? | | |
| Volume | X | | | | |
| Market/segment | X | | X | | |
| Distribution channels | X | | | | |
| Sales force allocation | X | | X | | |
| Deliveries | | X | X | | |
| Advertising | ? | | X | | |
| Emphasis on service | | | X | X | |

*Figure 6.3.* A Case Study of Managerial Perceptions of Responsibility

from other businesses on which they were dependent. The process of negotiation on priorities, resource allocation, transfer prices, and such issues consumes a significant amount of managerial attention and time. An internal focus is one of the costs of coordination.

Yet another cost of an interdependent system is the cost of carrying the inventory. The number and the complexity of interrelationships across businesses increases the difficulty of responding to changes in the market place. Changes in the demand for end products must be reflected in demand for subassemblies and components made in plants around the world. That results in a phenomenon best described as the "internal business cycle." Essentially, small shifts in the end product markets result in very large fluctuations in component demand as a result of a series of adjustments each stage makes to the forecast of the previous group as well as time lags in detecting the shifts in demand at various levels in the chain. The phenomenon, first described by Forrester during the early 1960s, is now well known.[3] A consequence of it is that inventories accumulate at different stages of the pipeline, even if only small shifts were required at the end product level. The inventory penalty can be considerable, often 25 to 50 percent more for an interdependent system than for stand-alone businesses.

## Benefits Associated with Managing Interdependent Businesses

One might get the impression that there are only costs associated with managing an interdependent system. There are also distinct benefits.

### Cost Reduction and Control over Value Added

The most obvious benefit of managing interdependencies is that sharing resources reduces cost. The incremental investment required to enter a business may be considerably reduced by sharing the resource base.

A less obvious advantage is that a degree of vertical integration provides managers control over the value added chain. Such control can provide an opportunity for active price management. By capturing the margins that would normally accrue to middlemen or suppliers, the managers of an interdependent system can enlarge the margin they have at their disposal to fight competitive battles. We are assuming that the internal suppliers are as efficient as external suppliers, so that the margins are available to the firm for use in a competitive situation.

A degree of self-sufficiency also provides significant bargaining advantages with suppliers; it allows managers to understand the cost structures better and provides a credible threat to suppliers.

## Technological Integrity

A technologically oriented DMNC is willing to pay the costs of coordination in return for the technological integrity that it can bring. For example, IBM managed its mainline businesses as one interdependent system, with all its attendant costs of corporate staff, because providing a compatible line of equipment was critical to IBM's strategy. IBM not only provided a whole line of equipment, it also ensured that the products were all compatible, which gave IBM customers a sense of security.

Technological integrity can also include the ability to keep critical know-how in-house. Often, proprietary know-how is contained in special purpose components. Further, keeping a critical mass of talent in related technical disciplines can lead to ease in product development. Firms like AT&T, IBM, NEC, and Philips have maintained core skills in-house for that purpose.

## Sustaining a Global Infrastructure

As outlined in Chapter 3, global competition requires a strategic infrastructure—global brands, distribution coverage, manufacturing presence, sales, and service support. Most often the costs of building and maintaining such an infrastructure are beyond the capabilities of a single business. DMNCs like Matsushita, Philips, Hitachi, and Sony have developed a family of products that can utilize the same strategic infrastructure effectively. On the other hand, RCA and General Electric do not have a global infrastructure in their appliance and consumer electronics businesses. At best they can boast of global sourcing. No single business unit, be it audio or video, in General Electric, for example, can support the massive investments required to build a global marketing network.

### Nature of Competition

Increasingly, the nature of global competitors is changing. In several businesses, such as consumer electronics, computers and telecommunications, medical electronics, machine tools, and financial services, the largest competitors are broadening their product lines. A broad product line allows a competitor to cross-subsidize products and businesses, develop a bargaining advantage with distributors and dealers, and pay for "core technologies" common to several businesses. The costs of paying for "core technologies," leveraging distribution advantages, and the opportunities for cross-subsidization are forcing firms wedded to the concept of decentralization, like 3M, Hewlett-Packard, and Matsushita, to reexamine their ideology of decentralized management.

### Bargaining Leverage with Host Governments

DMNCs with a wide range of products, spanning a variety of levels of technology, can develop multiple bargaining theaters in their relationships with host governments. That essentially takes two forms. One, a DMNC could offer to manufacture a low- or medium-technology product in a developing country in exchange for getting privileged access to public sector markets and/or large contracts. A case in point would be the offer by Brown Boveri to manufacture small motors in developing countries as an inducement to obtain contracts for power systems and heavy equipment.

DMNCs can also use a broad product range as a bargaining tool with developed countries. For example, in return for guarantees to maintain a certain level of employment, a DMNC could get the government of France or Belgium to provide privileged access to public sector markets, balancing a high-cost production center for radios with a respectable market share in computers or telecommunications equipment. That type of bargaining also takes on another form, known as "offset agreements." For example, General Electric, in return for an order estimated to be worth more than $1.2 billion for jet engines for the Canadian Air Force, agreed to an offset of more than $800 million dollars. The offset involved not only developing Canadian vendors for Canadian General Electric's requirement but also developing world product programs for General Electric, from Canada. The world programs involved such diverse businesses as electrical components, broadcast equipment, and filaments.

In all three forms of negotiation, corporate managers tend to use a broad portfolio to create a bargaining advantage. In the process, they create a linkage between the strategies of otherwise unrelated, distinct businesses.

## MANAGING INTERDEPENDENCIES: FINDING THE BALANCE

From the foregoing section it is obvious that evaluating the criticality of a set of interdependencies across businesses, like the hi-fi business at Philips, may not be a simple exercise in examining the value-added chain in tangible economic terms. That kind of analysis, derived from the analysis of vertical integration, is often suggested as the methodology appropriate to the analysis of interdependencies, a complex web of relationships, caused by a variety of considerations—competitive, organizational, and political. We believe that assessing the value of a set of interdependencies deserves analysis of costs as well as not so easily quantifiable judgments. We suggest developing a balance sheet comprising the factors shown in Table 6.1.

**TABLE 6.1**  A Balance Sheet for Evaluating Interdependencies

| *Potential Assets* | *Potential Liabilities* |
| --- | --- |
| Cost reduction and control over value added | Loss of top management focus on a business |
| Technological integrity | Loss of flexibility |
| Sustaining a global infrastructure | Loss of innovation |
| Matching key competitors and competition | Costs of coordination |
| Bargaining leverage with host governments | Loss of visibility to performance of a business |

Table 6.1 illustrates the essential dilemma. The potential assets are primarily substantive items that are amenable to detailed economic analysis. Data can be gathered to justify a position on almost all the items listed on the assets side. In debates about how many interdependencies should one try to manage within a DMNC, the asset side of the balance sheet gets more attention. The potential liabilities tend to be primarily organizational, and the effects are hard to identify in the short run. It is also difficult to produce hard data to justify most elements other than the incremental inventory needs in an interdependent system over a stand-alone system. The liabilities, therefore, are more subject to a corporate ideology, such as decentralized operations, as in 3M, Hewlett-Packard, and Matsushita, or a totally integrated management, as in IBM.

## The Search for a Balance

Increasingly, DMNCs are forsaking an "either/or" position and recognizing that costs and benefits must be considered explicitly, even if not all aspects lend themselves to quantification. The tradeoff is between "strategic advantages" and "organizational costs." This kind of soul-searching is leading to a series of significant reorganizations in a large number of firms.

• IBM has moved from a totally integrated DMNC, managing all interdependencies across its businesses (other than Federal Systems group), to one that manages most (not all) interdependencies across its mainline businesses; manages some as independent business units (IBUs) not subject to the same disciplines of staff review as the main line businesses; manages some as quasi-interdependent, which means only some aspects of the businesses are seen as linked; and engages in some joint ventures and collaboration agreements. The transformation of IBM over the last seven years is rendered schematically in Figure 6.4.[4]

• Hewlett-Packard, dedicated to decentralized management and individual entrepreneurship, has recently recognized the need to coordinate its efforts in its computer effort. Decentralization, as a philosophy, is giving way to centralization and coordination.[5] The transformation at Hewlett-Packard is shown schematically in Figure 6.5.

The implications of this search for balance—balance between the strategic advantages of coordinated effort and its organizational

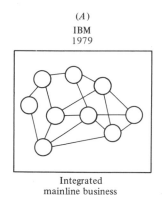

*(A)*
IBM
1979

Integrated
mainline business

*(B)*
IBM 1984

Mainline    Some    IBU    JV
            links

***Figure 6.4.***   Transformation at IBM: A Schematic

costs—are forcing large DMNCs to reconsider their approach to re-source allocation. Instead of allocating resources to discrete busi-nesses, DMNCs are examining ways in which the resource allocation process can be changed to consider those costs and benefits explic-itly. In several DMNCs it may be advantageous to move away from a "discrete business" *as the only unit of analysis* for resource allo-cation decisions and examine the opportunities and costs from dif-ferent perspectives. For example, *core technologies* that serve several businesses, and *distribution and brand investments* that transcend any one business may be distinct units for resource allocation and corporate attention as well. Resources may be allocated to core tech-

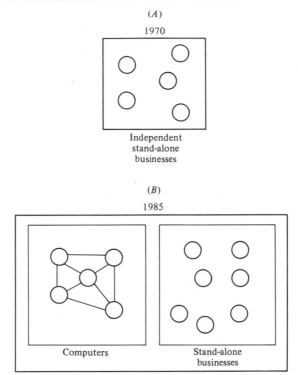

*(A)*

1970

Independent
stand-alone
businesses

*(B)*

1985

Computers

Stand-alone
businesses

*Figure 6.5.*   Transformation at Hewlett-Packard: A Schematic

nologies and distribution in addition to specific product-markets. For example, Philips may allocate resources to optical media (a core technology) as well as compact audio discs (a product-market using optical recording technology). Such an approach to resource allocation forces firms to deal explicitly with the costs and benefits of interdependencies.[6]

# 7

# Building the Corporate
# Portfolio of Businesses

In the first five chapters we argued that the basic unit of analysis for developing a global strategy is a discrete business. In Chapter 6 we considered interdependencies across businesses and suggested that a DMNC should manage only critical interdependencies. While the strategic worth of managing interdependencies across businesses is intellectually easy to comprehend and defend, we have to recognize the associated administrative and managerial costs. There is a need to balance such costs against their perceived strategic worth. In this chapter we shall focus attention on the problems of top managers who have to manage a portfolio of businesses, each with a distinct integration–responsiveness requirement. We move in this chapter from the identification of the strategic management requirements of a single discrete business, or the building blocks of a DMNC, to the problems of managing an entire portfolio of businesses.

## IDENTIFYING STRATEGIC VARIETY

We can summarize the basic approach to determining the appropriate strategic posture for a business in the DMNC's portfolio by following the schematic shown in Figure 7.1. The steps involved are:

  1. A basic economic analysis of a given business at a given point

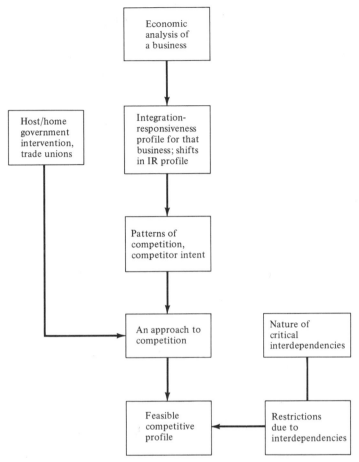

*Figure 7.1.*   A Framework for Strategic Analysis

in time determines the balance of "integration and responsiveness" forces, using the framework developed in Chapter 2. That allows us to classify businesses as "global," "local," or "multifocal." Essentially, the procedure enables us to understand the "existing rules of the game" in that business.

2. While the procedure so far provides us with a snapshot, it does not indicate the possible movement of that business over time within the IR grid, due to changes in the underlying economics, technology, and customer preferences, or resegmentation of the business

by determined competitors. In order to maintain and improve the competitiveness of a business, managers must understand the changes that are possible as well as those that are under way.

3. The IR grid gives us an opportunity to identify the economic structure of a business, but not necessarily the patterns of competition that are likely to develop in it. As indicated in Chapter 3, we need to understand the motivation of key competitors and how they may modify the "competitive game." A locally responsive business in the IR grid may still be subject to global competition.

4. Both host governments and to a lesser extent trade unions can modify the patterns of global competition either by modifying the underlying economics or by restricting the choices open to competitors. In some cases, host governments may sustain competitors who could not survive without their assistance.

5. Finally, in Chapter 6 we considered a basis for identifying the critical interdependencies that need to be managed. An interdependent set of businesses extracts a price. The degree of freedom with which the strategist may maneuver is restricted. He is burdened with considerations that affect the whole set of interdependent businesses rather than a single business. The interdependency also increases administrative difficulties. On the other hand, it might provide opportunities to develop complex strategies that are often unavailable to competitors who do not enjoy the same scope of businesses. The tradeoffs are as much analytic as they are judgmental.

It is important to remember, in the whole exercise, that developing an appropriate strategic posture is more than a simple one-time analysis. Positioning a business for global competition calls for a good analysis of the underlying economic structure, an understanding of political forces, creativity, and managerial judgment. In the choice of a competitive strategy, managers must avoid "determinism" and simple "recipes."

In a DMNC, the complex process for developing a business's strategic posture, as outlined above, leads top managers to the recognition that they have to find methods by which they can cope with the *strategic variety* represented by the various businesses, both intellectually and administratively. Simplistic methodologies that advocate "generic strategies" or a uniform administrative system, irrespective of the nature and competitive characteristics of the businesses in the DMNC's portfolio, while intellectually appealing and administratively easy, tend to mask the opportunities and risks.

Top managers in DMNCs must recognize and explicitly cope with strategic variety.

## Sources of Strategic Variety

It is important to recognize that the sheer number of distinct businesses does not necessarily lead to strategic variety. It is the differences themselves, in the businesses' natures, as identified in the IR grid, that lead to strategic variety. For example, at Corning Glass Works (Figure 2.1, Chapter 2), it was the dispersion of businesses in the IR grid, all the way from semiconductors (global), to Corningware (local), to television (multifocal), that created strategic variety. One could easily conceive of a DMNC with distinct businesses that are all global or all local. For example, Beatrice Foods, a giant U.S.-based dairy, packaged foods, and consumer products DMNC, had more than a hundred business units around the world. But all of them were considered primarily "locally responsive" businesses and were managed as such. Even though Beatrice Foods comprised more than one hundred distinct businesses, top managers in that DMNC had much less strategic variety to cope with than Corning Glass Works had with six businesses. At Corning, each business was distinct and had a different IR profile. The first source of strategic variety is the extent of dispersion of businesses in the IR grid.

Even if all businesses in a DMNC are in one strategic category, strategic variety can be caused by the intentions of key competitors. For example, Unilever and Procter & Gamble, also in packaged consumer products businesses around the world, think of themselves as caught in a global battle even though most of their businesses would fall into a "locally responsive" category in the IR grid. That means top managers at Unilever and Procter & Gamble must provide for greater strategic and administrative variety than Beatrice Foods, which ran "locally responsive" businesses, on a local basis. A firm's competitive orientation or its strategic intent adds a further layer of complexity to top mangement's task.

Strategic variety is further compounded by active host government intervention. As we saw in Chapter 6, even when businesses are quite distinct, host governments have a way of creating interdependencies across businesses. They can further complicate competitive battles by providing preferential treatment to some competitors.

Further, if a business is involved with joint ventures or consortia-type arrangements, the variety with which top managers must cope is increased.

## Administrative Variety

The strategic variety in a DMNC portfolio cannot be managed without attendant administrative variety. Often managers recognize the DMNC portfolio's strategic variety but attempt to manage it with a uniform administrative system, with a formal structure of systems and procedures. As the administrative components—planning, budgeting, compensation, and career planning systems—orient the attitudes and behavior of managers, a uniform system, applied across all businesses, tends to mask the strategic variety inherent in the portfolio. In Corning Glass Works, for example, top managers had to realize not only that they had to contend with a wide strategic variety but also that it called for an equally wide variety of administrative arrangements.[1]

### Sources of Administrative Variety

Administrative variety is created by the variety of businesses in the IR grid. The simplified portfolio of businesses that Philips's top management had to contend with as of 1978 is shown in Figure 7.2. It is obvious that no single administrative system, however comprehensive, can cope with such variety. The administrative processes had to be fine-tuned to reflect the needs of the businesses within that portfolio. Even managing the strategic *status quo* required significant administrative differences among businesses.

While Figure 7.2 shows the complexity of the Philips portfolio at a given point in time, over time, as we saw in Chapter 2, the locus of various businesses within the IR grid changes. Not only should senior management recognize and cope with the differences in the administrative needs among businesses at a given point in time, but they should also be capable of accommodating the change in the strategic needs of businesses, almost on a real-time basis. An ability to adjust the administrative process quickly and proactively is a competitive necessity.

The presence of consortia arrangements and joint ventures fur-

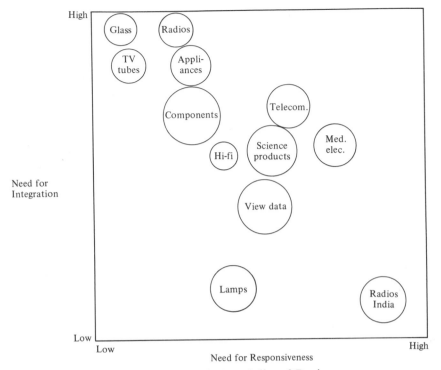

***Figure 7.2.*** Philips's Portfolio of Businesses

ther complicates the problem, as they reduce the degree of freedom top managers have, to manage the administrative process.

## Types of Countries

The problems of strategic variety and its attendant administrative variety are endemic to any diversified firm, whether multinational or not. Multinationality brings yet another problem: a need to understand the differences between countries and the demands such differences impose on the administrative processes.

Different countries have different institutional arrangements. For example, France, Japan, and South Korea have active policies aimed at managing and modifying industry structures. The United States, in most industries, allows industry structures to evolve. Countries like China and India have stringent rules regarding transfer of technology. Malaysia likes joint ventures with "Bhumiputras" or sons of the soil (native Malays) as a precondition for DMNC entry into that country. These examples indicate the strain imposed on a DMNC's top management group's administrative versatility.

Further, within the same country, different businesses in the DMNC's portfolio may require different approaches. For example, in the defense and telecommunications business, Philips may want to present a "local face" in France and enjoy the benefits that accrue from that approach. On the other hand, in the consumer electronics business, Philips may be required to be competitive, to behave "globally," disregarding France's specific interests. That type of conflict, between the needs of different businesses within the same country, leads to further complexities.

## COPING WITH COMPLEXITY

The work of a DMNC's top management can best be described as coping with complexity and balancing the often conflicting demands for providing focus to specific businesses by differentiating the organizational and administrative context, and at the same time maintaining some semblance of uniformity and order. The dimensions along which complexities arise are illustrated in Figure 7.3:

1. The strategic variety imposed by the number of distinct businesses with different IR profiles
2. The rate of change in the competitive dynamics in the businesses in the DMNC's portfolio (The faster the pace of change, the greater is the need to anticipate and change the administrative infrastructure that supports those businesses.)
3. The differences in the DMNC's geographical markets in the various businesses in its portfolio

Given the three dimensions of complexity, top managers of DMNCs have attempted to reduce the complexity with a wide variety of strategies. Some of the more common approaches are listed here.

### Reduce Strategic Variety

One common approach is to reduce the variety of businesses in the portfolio (remember that strategic variety refers to the differences in the strategic characteristics of businesses as captured in the IR grid,

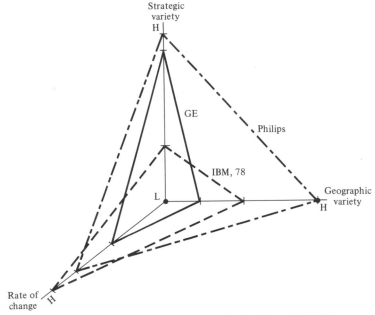

***Figure 7.3.***    Sources of Complexity in a DMNC

not to the number of businesses). Until about 1978–79, IBM followed this approach. IBM recognized that it had to cope with a fast-changing and dynamic set of businesses, as well as cope with the global spread of operations. In order to do so efficiently, the company developed an extremely complex organization. IBM, with its technology, could have added other businesses to its portfolio, such as telecommunications. Telecommunications outside the United States was an exclusively public sector business at that time, and the addition of the telecommunications business would have forced IBM to work closely with local postal, telegraph, and telephone authorities (PTT) and put on a "local face," a prerequisite for doing business in that industry (as illustrated in Chapter 4). The need to work in "partnership" with local PTTs often implies losing one's autonomy in product specification, product development, choice of manufacturing locations, and transfer of technology—the very elements of strategy that IBM protected and managed centrally in its other businesses. That would introduce "strategic variety," a whole new set of business characteristics that IBM's administrative system, designed to cope with the demands of its main line of business—computers—could not handle. The choice for the top management of firms faced with the dilemma outlined above is simple: Do we pursue the new opportunity (telecommunications in IBM), which is technically feasible and possible for us, and pay the price of increased strategic variety and, consequently, increased administrative variety, or do we forgo the opportunity and protect the integrity of the administrative system geared to the mainline business? IBM gave up the opportunity for some time. The issue for top management is, once again, balancing the strategic worth of an opportunity with its administrative and managerial costs.

IBM also walked out of opportunities in India during the late 1970s. The Indian government required IBM to enter into a joint venture, manufacture locally, and bring in products that IBM felt were inappropriate, given the size and the development of the market in India at that time. Irrespective of the merits of the arguments on either side, if IBM had conceded to the requests of the government of India IBM's strategic variety would have increased, as shown in Figure 7.4. Conceding autonomy over elements of strategy would have required significant changes in the way IBM's administrative system functioned at that time. Given the size of the market oppor-

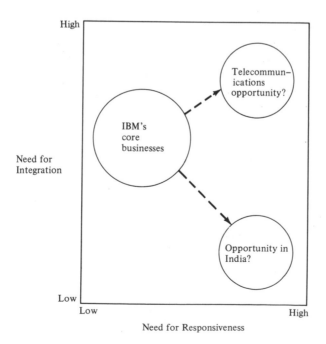

*Figure 7.4.* IBM's Portfolio, 1978

tunity that India represented at the time for IBM's businesses, one could argue that the decision to give up that market opportunity in favor of protecting the integrity of the administrative infrastructure was a sound one.

The choices that IBM made to reduce the complexity of the top management task during the 1970s are illustrated in Figure 7.3. IBM reduced the strategic variety by opting out of some businesses, like telecommunications, as well as opting out of some countries, like India. It managed a portfolio of businesses that had similar strategic characteristics (low strategic variety) and operated around the globe, but only in countries that allowed it strategic freedom (low geographical variety).

Are those choices realistic for DMNCs other than IBM? One could argue that even for IBM those are not realistic choices in 1985. It is not easy to sacrifice potential markets as lucrative as telecommunications, even if they require a whole new way of doing business. Further, in most businesses, once a DMNC opts out of a potentially large market like India, it is very hard to get back in. In other words, it is becoming increasingly difficult to give up business opportunities to maintain and protect the integrity of the current administrative system. As outlined in Chapter 6, IBM has made significant changes in its top management structure during 1979–85 to cope with emerging opportunities.


## Contain Administrative Variety

Yet another approach to reducing the complexity of the managerial task is to contain the complexity of managing a large number of distinctly different businesses by grouping them into sectors or groups. The concept is that each sector or group will have within it businesses that are strategically similar. While there may be no commonality across sectors, in terms of the strategic and administrative characteristics, within a sector one could expect numerous commonalities. This approach indicates that the top mangement explicitly recognizes that the requirements of the various businesses in the portfolio are so distinct that to gain competitive focus they need to group them. The executive management in such a system (for a group of businesses) rests with the sector executives.

General Electric's organization of sectors can be interpreted in this light. General Electric grouped its businesses as follows:

1. *Consumer Products and Services Sector,* which included a lighting business, major and small domestic appliances, television, GE broadcasting, and GE cablevision (Even though some of these businesses had a minor position overseas, they were primarily domestic or "local" for GE and were managed as such.)

2. *Technical Systems and Materials Sector,* which included the aircraft engine group, aerospace, medical systems business, information and communication business, and engineered materials (These represented high-technology businesses with significant overseas opportunties, and in all of them GE had a significant position overseas. They all required great sensitivity to local needs and most are politically salient.)

3. *Industrial Products and Components Sector,* which included electronics components and systems, motors, the contractor equipment business, and industrial products and components (All these businesses had their technology base in the United States and exported worldwide.)

4. *Power Systems Sector,* which included nuclear energy, the turbine business, power delivery group, and energy systems division. (All these businesses, when they sold outside the United States, had to contend with complex financial arrangements and political pressures.)

5. Utah International, acquired under Jones's stewardship and involved in mining operations, was kept distinct

6. Finally, the International Sector, which included all trading companies and the management of all affiliates

GE also reduced its managerial complexity by reducing its involvement in the international arena. While one of the top exporters of the country, GE is best described as an international company and not as a multinational. GE's assets and markets were concentrated, in most of its businesses, in the United States. When it did business overseas, it exported primarily technology-intensive products. GE's approach to coping with complexity is depicted in Figure 7.3. In Chapter 3 we discussed the competitive implications of not being a multimarket participant.

GE's portfolio in the IR framework may look more or less as shown in Figure 7.5. While all the individual business units may not fit the broad categorization scheme shown, the figure represents the overall concept of the GE organization.

GE's approach is quite popular and is employed at 3M, ITT, and other such large, diversified DMNCs. The underlying assumption is

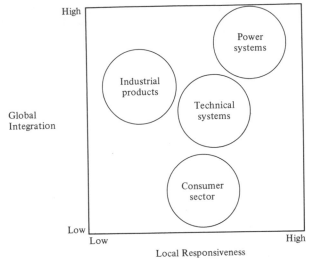

*Figure 7.5.*   GE's Portfolio of Businesses

that top managers can make one-time choices regarding the appropriate group to which a business should be assigned. That is not, in a technology-intensive business, an easy task. For example, ITT's digital PABX business was aligned with ITT's public switching business. The alignment was justified on the basis that the technology was the same and that the critical success factor was the ability to manage the technology. However, it was soon obvious that while the technology was the same, the markets were quite distinct. While customers in the public switching business were the PTTs (government-owned in most countries), customers for digital PABX (a business better managed as part of the office products business) were in both the private and the public sectors. ITT transferred the PABX business from public switching to the office products group during 1978. The example suggests that while grouping similar businesses together to reduce complexity is valid, top managers ought to evaluate constantly whether businesses should be reassigned from one group to another for competitive effectiveness. Frequent changes can be dysfunctional and disruptive.

### Categorizing Countries

DMNCs that operate in many countries can reduce the complexity by categorizing countries for selective management attention. For example, let us consider three geographically contiguous countries:

Singapore, Malaysia, and Indonesia. Are they all equally important, and do they deserve the same type and quality of management attention? The answer is obvious.

1. For most Western firms, Singapore is a strategic country. For example, at one time GE and Philips each employed more than 10,000 people in Singapore, and it was the export platform for a large number of their businesses. Radio, small domestic appliances, and television sets were made in Singapore for the global markets of GE and Philips. Singapore's government gave DMNCs freedom to operate; with its low labor costs and an efficient infrastructure, Singapore became an integral part of the global network of manufacturing locations of several DMNCs like GE and Philips. Singapore is a crucial link in the global network, so for management purposes it is a *strategic* country.

2. Malaysia, Singapore's neighbor, does not allow the same freedom for DMNCs to operate. There are several restrictions imposed on DMNCs, including the following requirements: (a) DMNCs are allowed to operate only if they form a joint venture with the "sons of the soil" (Bhumiputras), and (b) employment policies of DMNCs, like all other firms in Malaysia, must give preference to native Malays over citizens of Chinese and Indian origin. One could expand the list of restrictions. While Malaysia enjoys a low labor cost advantage, it is less attractive to the DMNC. The restrictions on the decision-making process within the DMNC as well as the perceived shifts in policies make Malaysia less attractive as an integral part of a DMNC's global network for a set of businesses. While it is not attractive as a supply base for global markets, it is still an attractive location—both as a market and as a manufacturing source—at least for the region. We may call such countries *tactical* from the DMNCs' point of view.

3. Malaysia's neighbor, Indonesia, is a very large consumer market but is less attractive as an integral part of a DMNC's network as the difficulties in doing business there and the restrictions it imposes on DMNCs are quite onerous. The operations of a DMNC in Indonesia as a result, may just be on a "local for local" basis. We may call such countries *opportunistic*.

We are arguing that a globally competitive DMNC should participate in all countries—leveraging the factor cost advantages as well as participating in the development of the local markets. However, it is unrealistic to believe that all countries are equally attractive or that the operations in all countries are equally critical to a DMNC's continued competitiveness. Top managers may want to categorize countries using objective criteria for management purposes. Strategic countries deserve the most attention, and opportunistic countries the least. That approach raises doubts regarding the appropriateness of the concept of regional management. Since Singapore, Malaysia, and Indonesia are geographically contiguous, should they be grouped under the same region? Our answer is, probably not. The strategic roles assigned to the countries, not the accident of their position on the globe, must determine the extent of management attention.

Again, it is dangerous to take a one-time view of the importance of various countries to the DMNC. The importance of countries changes as policies of governments change and as markets develop. For example, China and India, which are emerging as huge, attractive markets, may still be considered opportunistic countries. No top management could ignore the opportunities as large as these, even if risky. Top managers must constantly evaluate their assessments of countries. At the same time, they need not manage as if all countries were equally deserving of senior mangement attention.

## The Administrative Solution

None of the approaches for coping with complexity described so far is without a price. However, whether we opt out of businesses or countries (as IBM did during the 1970s), opt out of geographical spread (as did GE), or categorize countries for selective management, the following conclusions are inescapable. Each of those approaches, although reducing complexity, also reduces the ability to exploit business opportunties. Further, top managers must constantly evaluate the continuing validity of their approach to reducing complexity. Some DMNCs, such as Philips, unwilling to give up any opportunity, have developed yet another approach. They have created a very complex administrative system that is intended to allow them to manage the complexity brought about by the variety in the nature of businesses, rates of change in them, and the variety of countries in which they operate. Philips is also willing to operate with a wide variety of joint venture and consortia arrangements. In contrast to IBM and GE, the range that Philips is willing to manage is shown in Figure 7.2. The price that Philips pays for such diversity is a lack of focus for a given business.

## CONCLUSION

A portfolio of businesses in the DMNC setting can lead to intellectual and administrative complexities. Top managers have tried a wide
variety of approaches to cope with that complexity. Often, the solutions are transient in that the circumstances change, necessitating
a change in the approach, and they extract a cost, a missed opportunity. As the competitive battle intensifies, few DMNCs are willing
to give up opportunities for the sake of organizational and administrative ease. Strategic management in such a setting is emerging as
the real challenge for top management. We shall turn to that challenge in the next chapter.

# PART II

# MANAGEMENT RESPONSIBILITIES AND TECHNIQUES

# 8

---

# Control, Change, and Flexibility

In Part I we focused attention on the emerging nature of global competition and the economic and political imperatives with which a top manager in a DMNC must come to grips. In Part II, starting with this chapter, we shall discuss both the managerial tasks that derive from the emerging nature of global competition and the mechanisms that top managers can use to create and sustain the organizational capabilities required to be competitive. The managerial implications of the analysis of global competition presented in Part I are:

1. We need a methodology for mapping the characteristics of a business that allows us to distinguish a global from a local and a multifocal business. In order to compete effectively in a global or a multifocal business, we need organizations that can manage global integration of activities. At the same time, a local or a multifocal business requires the ability to be "locally responsive." Global integration is accomplished through a tight linkage of the subsidiaries with the headquarter staff. On the other hand, a locally responsive strategy needs relative autonomy at the subsidiary level. In a multifocal business, the relative balance of subsidiary autonomy and centralized control over subsidiaries emerges as an important issue.

2. The underlying characteristics of a business—its position in the IR framework—change over time. As a result, top managers must

be sensitive not only to the relationships between headquarters and subsidiaries at any one point in time but to changes in that relationship caused by changes in the underlying structure of a business and its competitive demands. Managing "change" in the nature of relationships between headquarters and subsidiaries is as important as assessing and establishing the extent of "control" that headquarters must impose on the subsidiary.

3. Global competition can take place even in "local" businesses. That means top managers must have the ability to coordinate strategies and to assign differentiated strategic missions to different subsidiaries and product groups, as competitive conditions demand. This calls for "flexibility" in the headquarters–subsidiary relationship.

4. The role of host governments further complicates the nature of the headquarters–subsidiary relationship. As we outlined in Chapter 4, many businesses are subject to host government influence. Managing such businesses demands an ability constantly to balance the needs for global coordination with the need for local responsiveness. The issue of control and flexibility in the relationships between headquarters and subsidiaries is of primary concern in such a situation.

5. The increasing need to manage interdependencies across businesses selectively also creates its own organizational demands. Top managers must constantly evaluate not only the strategic worth of managing interdependencies but also its organizational cost. The process of making these tradeoffs requires that the organization have the inherent capacity to adjust and readjust to the emerging competitive demands—a heightened need for "flexibility."

6. Top managers cannot easily reduce the organizational demands of managing a DMNC by opting out of businesses or out of countries (reducing strategic variety). A large portfolio of businesses is required to leverage corporate resources—be it technology, distribution, or brand presence. A viable market presence in critical markets is required to cope with the demands of competition—to have the ability to counterpunch and neutralize competitor's moves. Such considerations suggest that top managers who are unwilling to give up opportunities to leverage corporate resources or to compromise the competitive position of a business must end up with a complex organization. In other words, *creating and maintaining a sustainable competitive advantage in a DMNC requires the ability to manage a complex organization.*

## STRATEGIC CONTROL, CHANGE, AND FLEXIBILITY

The central capabilities that managers have to develop at the business level in a DMNC organization are these:

1. Efficiency in executing agreed-upon strategies through a process of control of subsidiary actions
2. Ability to change the nature of the headquarters–subsidiary relationships to reflect changes in strategic direction
3. Flexibility sufficient to exploit opportunities as they emerge, and to react to unanticipated problems within the context of an overall vision

In Figure 8.1 we outline, using the IR framework, the types of business characteristics that would focus top managers' attention

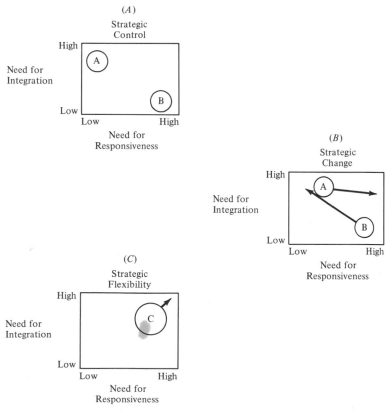

***Figure 8.1.***    The Three Tasks of Senior Management

toward the three distinct tasks of control, change, and flexibility. A global business or a business subject to global competition would focus managers' attention on "control of subsidiaries' activities" in order to develop a global response. Changes in the underlying characteristics of a business would require a refocusing of the strategic orientation of both the headquarters and subsidiary managers, resulting in a change in the relationships between the two. Often in salient businesses, a local and a global approach must be *simultaneously* managed, and that calls for a flexible approach.[1] Needless to say, the three capabilities outlined above affect the nature of the relationships between headquarters and subsidiaries. Often the organizational demands of control and execution of a given strategy are in conflict with the organizational processes that facilitate strategic change. In the rest of the chapter we shall define the nature of the managerial tasks of control, change, and flexibility, one at a time, as well as identify the impediments to developing those capabilities. We shall develop a framework for understanding and managing the organizational processes involved. In the next chapter we shall discuss the organizational mechanisms that top managers can use to build those capabilities.

## CONTROL: THE ESSENCE OF IMPLEMENTATION

A critical task of top management in a DMNC is the exercise of control. Control is the essence of implementation. We recognize two aspects of control:

1. Control is established by headquarters over subsidiaries in order to manage global integration of an interdependent network of operations. Typical examples of such control would relate to plant loadings, logistics around the world, technology transfer, and transfer pricing. Control in a business requiring global integration primarily relates to control over operations.

2. Strategic control is more subtle. It involves the assignment of different strategic missions to subsidiaries, depending on the nature of competitive interaction at a given point in time. As we saw in Chapter 3, the ability of a DMNC to respond to a move by a competitor in its primary profit sanctuary by taking actions in the competitor's profit sanctuary is the essence of global competition. That kind of coordination requires a shared view of strategy between headquarters and subsidiaries, a shared interpretation of the nature

of competitive threats, and an ability to coordinate strategic missions assigned to various subsidiary managers.

Both aspects of control—global integration and strategic coordination—are at the heart of the relationships between headquarters and subsidiaries. They form the essence of the debate regarding centralization and decentralization. In effect, the ability of headquarters to influence the actions of subsidiaries is a function of the nature of dependencies built into the multinational network.

## Basis for Control

The dependency of subsidiaries on headquarters for resources—technology, export markets, or management and financial resources—facilitates control.

The dependency of a subsidiary can take one of several forms:

1. The pattern of resource deployment in a business may be such that no one subsidiary has the skills or the facilities to duplicate the total capability of the parent in that business. Figure 8.2 shows the pattern of cross-shipments of IBM products around the world during the late 1970s. It is obvious that all subsidiaries are interlocked in a complex web of relationships, and no subsidiary could survive without the total. Further, the pattern of product and component flows is orchestrated by the central staff. That gives them significant influence over any one subsidiary. The nature of control over subsidiaries in such a situation is significant, irrespective of the size of the subsidiary, its technological maturity, or the sophistication of its management. The dependency of the subsidiary rests on the fact that it represents only a partial and not the total capability of the parent. IBM represents an extreme case of careful planning on the part of the company, over a long period of time, in deploying resources and skills around the world in such a way that no one subsidiary or region can be independent of the rest of the IBM.

2. A variant of the overall IBM pattern of resource deployment is the development of subsidiaries that serve primarily as sourcing platforms. Austria for Philips and Singapore for General Electric and Philips are good examples. An overwhelming portion of the subsidiary's resources is devoted to serving other markets in the DMNC's network. As a result, headquarters can have significant influence on decisions regarding capacity, technology used, product mix, and such operational decisions as plant loading.

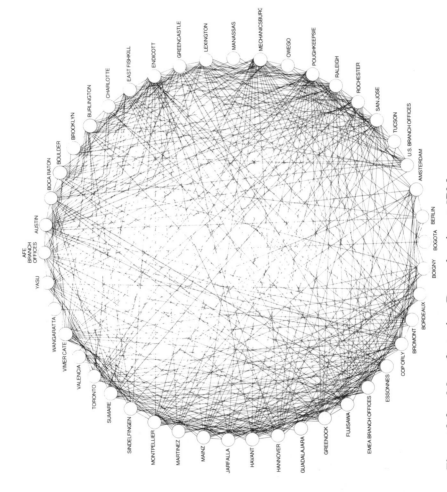

*Figure 8.2.* Manufacturing Dependencies at IBM

SOURCE: Original company document

3. If the subsidiaries are dependent on the parent for technology and/or management resources, the parent can use that dependency to influence the actions of subsidiaries. A significant proportion of U.S. DMNCs in technology-intensive businesses use the dependency of subsidiaries on technology as a basis for control. That dependence could be based on access to a central design data base, as was the case for Dresser. All subsidiaries in Dresser's compressor business prior to 1980 were linked to headquarters. When the Reagan Administration imposed an embargo on shipments of compressors to the Soviet Union, the French government insisted that Dresser (France) honor the contract and supply the compressors to the Soviets. Dresser's headquarters in the United States was forced to sever its ties with Dresser (France). Dresser top management ordered the computer links between Pittsburgh and France cut off, thus temporarily immobilizing the French subsidiary. The Dresser incident is an illustration of the influence that headquarters can impose on the subsidiary, if the subsidiary is dependent on the parent for technology or management support.[2]

4. The three illustrations above may lead the reader to the inappropriate conclusion that the only mechanism available to headquarters in exercising control over subsidiaries is to ensure a pattern of resource deployment that keeps subsidiaries dependent on each other, with headquarters providing the crucial coordinating link.[3] While maintaining a level of dependency at the subsidiary level facilitates operational control (global integration), strategic control is as much, if not more, dependent on having the key subsidiaries share *a common vision* with headquarters. The ability of headquarters to assign differentiated strategic missions to various subsidiaries, as a function of an overall global strategy, depends on the ability of headquarters to involve the key subsidiaries in evolving that strategy and communicating it effectively. Further, top managers must recognize that subsidiaries' performance must be measured according to their assigned strategic mission in the overall global network rather than as stand-alone, autonomous businesses. Let us, for example, consider CPC and Unilever locked in a battle for the packaged cooking oil market around the world (described in Chapter 3). The role assigned to the German subsidiary of CPC, let us assume, is to attack the profit sanctuary of Unilever in Germany, so that CPC's Brazilian cash flow can be protected. The strategic mission assigned to the German subsidiary of CPC is clear—reduce the profitability of Unilever in its most important market, even if it means taking a profit

penalty in Germany in order to protect the cash flow of CPC Brazil. Such strategic coordination requires that all subsidiaries perceive the threat of Unilever as urgent and important and are willing to make sacrifices in their operations to protect the integrity of the whole. It also requires top managers to ensure that the contributions of the CPC managers in Germany are measured differently. Measurement of the contribution of CPC managers in Germany must go beyond the profit contributions made by Germany as an autonomous unit and must incorporate the strategic contributions made by them to protect the overall cash flows of CPC.

## Impediments to Control

While dependency of subsidiaries on headquarters enhances the ability of headquarters to manage global integration and strategic coordination, a variety of factors act as impediments to such control. Some of the key impediments to strategic control are:

1. Historical evolution of the headquarters–subsidiary relationships. While the case of IBM cited above is an example of headquarters' continuing to maintain control over subsidiaries and never having lost it, in most cases the outcome is different. Most subsidiaries have evolved as fairly independent organizations. Opel, the German subsidiary of General Motors, is an example. For more than fifty years Opel had developed the technical and managerial resources required for it to operate autonomously. It developed its own product line. Until 1978–79, the strategic coordination and operational integration between General Motors in the United States and Opel in Germany were nonexistent. Opel had the skills and the size to manage its own affairs. Strategic coordination in such a situation, where the subsidiaries have grown up as autonomous entities, is very hard to develop. Resource dependency, which allows IBM to control subsidiaries, did not exist in the case of General Motors when it started contemplating coordination of strategies. A lack of resource dependency had to be compensated for by a shared recognition on the part of the subsidiary and headquarters of a common threat posed by Japanese competitors and by Ford in Europe. Further, the subsidiary and headquarters had to recognize that unless they could establish a reciprocal dependence between U.S. operations and Opel, GM's competitors could "cherry pick" them. A fundamental change in the nature of the headquarters–subsidiary relationship was called

for. Often the extent of change in the historical pattern of relationships causes the biggest impediment to strategic coordination.

2. Headquarters managers may lack an understanding of the skills and limitations involved in operating in environments dissimilar to that of the parent. For example, an operating environment that is highly regulated (e.g. India), subject to very high levels of inflation (e.g. Brazil), or a low-technology environment (e.g. Indonesia) can cause confusion if headquarters managers do not explicitly take into account those peculiarities.

3. The presence of joint venture partners can create an impediment to strategic coordination. Often the motivations of the joint venture partners are not congruent with those of the parent, which can lead to significant difficulties.

4. In businesses where host governments would like to influence strategy at the local, subsidiary level, global coordination and control can become complex. Implementing choices of production location, technology, transfer prices, product range, and pricing dictated by global competition can become problematic in such a situation.

5. Strategic coordination often tests the "loyalty" of local managers. While it could be argued that if the DMNC did not coordinate its strategies worldwide, its competitors could take advantage, in the short term it presents country managers with difficult dilemmas: Should they agree to out-sourcing, to changes in product mix, or to a reduction in profits in their own operations to help out another subsidiary for the overall benefit of the DMNC? Those questions present real moral and ethical dilemmas. The interests of the country must somehow be balanced against the interests of the DMNC.

## Control over Global Operations

Control over global operations represents a complex tradeoff for top management. While the analytical framework developed in the previous chapters can provide a clear picture of what needs to be done, the managerial and organizational realities of control (global integration and strategic coordination) make the task quite ambiguous. Control may be exercised only on a few subsidiaries critical to the business. For example, one could argue that only those subsidiaries that are sourcing platforms, or are located in profit sanctuaries of potential competitors, and large volume markets need be controlled. All other subsidiaries may be subject to less rigorous control. It is useful to think about the feasibility of exercising operational control and strategic coordination in a business within a DMNC by carefully articulating the factors that enhance the ability of headquarters as well as those factors that impede its capability to exercise control over subsidiaries, as shown in Table 8.1. The ability of a business group in a DMNC to implement a global strategy cannot be taken for granted. The difficulty is not in the analysis of the need for such a strategy: The main impediment is in creating the organizational capability—or the preconditions discussed above.

## Managing Strategic Redirection

So far, in discussing strategic coordination and global integration, we identified the managerial task involved in implementing a specific strategy. We were concerned with *efficiency of implementation.* However, as we discussed in Chapter 2, the characteristics of a business can change as a result of changes in technology, competitive dynamics, changes in the competitive focus of customers, and actions by host governments. Top managers, in anticipation of those changes, and sometimes in response, have to change the strategy of the business. Strategic redirection of a business requires a change in the underlying relationships between headquarters and subsidiaries, which may have been cemented over a long period. In other words,

**TABLE 8.1**   Control over Subsidiary Operations in a DMNC

| *Factors Enhancing Headquarters' Capability to Control Subsidiaries* | *Factors Impeding Headquarters' Capability to Control Subsidiaries* |
| --- | --- |
| Dependency of the subsidiary on resources of headquarters: technology, management, export markets, finances | Historical evolution of headquarters—subsidiary relationship; extent of autonomy of subsidiary |
| Shared strategic vision and competitive strategy | Host government regulations |
| Systems that recognize contributions to global strategy | Presence of joint venture partners |
| Loyalty to the DMNC | Loyalty to country, host government policies |

efficiency of execution or desire for control over subsidiaries suggests the development of well-defined and well-understood roles for subsidiaries and headquarters, and a clear balance of power in resource allocation decisions. Redirection requires changing established relationships. The ability of a DMNC to redirect strategy in a given business is often impeded by the very efficiency with which the prior strategy was executed. Changing existing relationships can be extremely difficult.

Let us look at an example of strategic redirection to see the sort of changes needed in the underlying relationships between headquarters and subsidiaries. As we outlined in Chapter 2, the chemical industry was undergoing significant change during early 1970s. Prior to 1970, most ethylene oxide plants in Europe had capacities around 50 million to 60 million pounds. Technological changes and the investments made by a few firms, such as ICI, increased the most economic plant size from 50 million pounds per plant to between 120 million and 150 million pounds. MNCs competing in that business had to build large plants and gain the economies of scale or be shut out of the market by more cost-effective competitors. The change in the characteristics of the business is shown in the IR framework in Figure 8.3. What are the managerial and organizational implications of such a change?

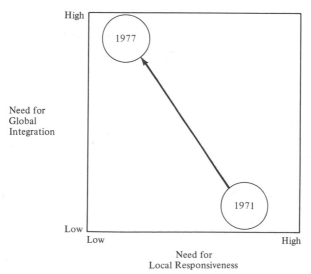

**Figure 8.3.** Changing Competitive Dynamics of the Ethylene Oxide Business

In the DMNC we studied, the overseas subsidiaries, especially those in Europe, enjoyed a certain level of autonomy in operations consistent with the strategy of the business during early 1970s. Each subsidiary was self-sufficient. Each subsidiary operated with a dedicated plant and its own marketing and sales force. Most subsidiaries, however, had a continuing dependence on headquarters for R&D and technology, even though their dependence varied. While headquarters still approved all capital budgets, especially budgets for plant and equipment, the decisions were primarily made by the subsidiaries. While subsidiaries were dependent on headquarters for aspects of their operations, the *relative balance of power* in decision-making rested with the subsidiaries. With the change in the nature of the business—due to technological changes and the investments made by competitors—that relationship had to change. For example, no single subsidiary could absorb the output of a new plant with 150 million pounds of capacity. The output had to be shared among two to five subsidiaries, which till then were quite autonomous. The need for central coordination of outputs, logistics, transfer prices, market forecasts, and raw material purchases meant that subsidiaries could not be autonomous and that they had to coordinate their decisions with other subsidiaries. Headquarters had to take on that role. More importantly, the capital costs of bringing a large plant on stream represented a different level of risk to the corporation, further reinforcing a stronger role for the headquarters staff. The change in the nature of the business, and as a consequence the change in strategy, forced a necessary change in the relationship between the headquarters (business group) and the subsidiary managers. Subsidiary managers had to give up their autonomy in a variety of decisions, and their roles had to change. The business manager and his staff at headquarters had to learn new ways of managing their relationships with subsidiaries.

Strategic redirection of the type described above would not take place unless the underlying organizational relationships between subsidiaries and headquarters were altered. The balance of power had to tilt from the subsidiaries to the business group.


## MANAGING FOR FLEXIBILITY

While strategic redirection often involves the process of reorienting the relationships between headquarters and subsidiaries, flexibility requires the ability to *shift between orientations,* almost on a decision-by-decision basis.

The dilemma for DMNCs in a wide variety of businesses is clear. The desire to build and leverage global market positions and technology forces DMNCs to consolidate manufacturing and technical resources to obtain overall cost savings. A consistent direction and goals to guide the actions of subsidiaries is seen as a must. On the other hand, that ideal is constantly challenged by the persistent demands imposed on the business by host countries. The goals of a host country may be at variance with the goals of the DMNC, as we have seen in Chaper 4. Further, host country demands may never stand still. The public switching business is an obvious example. The technology-intensity of this business forces DMNCs like LM Ericsson, Siemens, ITT, Northern Telecom, and AT&T to be globally integrated. On the other hand, in most of the world, PTT departments controlled by governments are the main customers for public switching equipment. Telecommunications is also a defense-sensitive business. As a result, in almost every country, governments seek to and do influence the choice of specifications, location of manufacturing, and pricing of such equipment. In order to sell switching equipment, subsidiaries must be seen to have a "local face" and must be sensitive to the demands—both current and anticipated—of host governments. The perspective of subsidiary managers who constantly interface with host government officials is an important input to strategy making. On the other hand, the need to maintain a local face can lead to duplication of resources—duplicating manufacturing locations or building plants with a scale that is suboptimal, sourcing components from local vendors—and increases in costs. That often is the price for accessing markets such as telecommunications.

The inherent conflict between economic and political imperatives often turns the management process into an advocacy process, with the subsidiaries presenting and providing a country perspective and the business managers and the headquarter staff providing and defending a global perspective. The need for flexible, country-specific approaches must be balanced with maintaining a cost-competitive base of global operations. A constant dialog between managers, a process of internal negotiations, and flexibility become key. In a sense, managing businesses that occupy the "High-High" position in the IR framework needs a different organizational capability from that of a global business. Organizations must allow both the country and the global perspectives to emerge and be visible. Decisions may favor one or the other perspective, and the slant toward either may depend on the nature of the problem. A very big order from China and India for public switching may force the DMNC to accommodate the interests of the host governments; on the other hand, a similar request from Kenya or Sri Lanka may be rejected. The strategic decision process must be flexible, suggesting that relationships between headquarters and subsidiaries must also be kept flexible.

## The Managerial Dilemma

Organizing for strategic control would itself be a large-scale managerial undertaking in a DMNC. If we add to that the need for anticipating and responding to strategic changes and skills for flexibly responding to opportunities, the complexity of the managerial task is compounded. The three tasks demand very different and often conflicting sets of managerial skills as shown in Table 8.2. It is obvious from the table that top managers cannot overemphasize any one of those tasks. If a business in a DMNC was well geared to

**TABLE 8.2**   The Variety of Managerial Tasks

| Managerial Criteria | Control | Change | Flexibility |
|---|---|---|---|
| Purpose | To implement a given strategy | To modify a given strategy, develop a new strategy | To be opportunistic within the framework of an overall strategy |
| Task | Identify and implement a set of HQ–sub roles | Change the existing set of HQ–sub roles to meet the demands of new strategy | Create adequate room for continuous readjustment of HQ–sub roles based on the merits of the case |
| Measure of accomplishment | Efficiency of implementation | Ease of change | Extent of flexibility |

"control"—to implement a given strategy—then it may find itself hard pressed to anticipate and change strategic direction. Excellence in execution requires very clear delineation of roles between headquarters and subsidiaries and a clear balance of power between the two groups. However, strategic change requires undoing the existing relationships and establishing a new set of relationships—or establishing a new balance of power. Flexibility may require an inbuilt ambiguity of power relationships that allows for different groups—product managers, country managers, and functional managers—to take leadership in sponsoring different issues that affect the total business.

## *Limits to Formal Structure*

Traditionally, managers confronted with the need to develop organizations capable of maintaining a delicate balance among strategic control, the ability to redirect strategy, and a capability for flexible response fall back upon formal structural solutions. Formal organization structures like the product or area organization forms represented in Figure 8.4 are used. In our experience, such traditional structures fall far short of the needs of managing a global business, save for a few very specific cases.

A product or an area organization imparts great clarity to the tasks that need to be performed as well as the roles and responsibilities of the headquarters and subsidiaries in getting them done. For example, a worldwide product structure focuses attention of managers on maintaining product and technological superiority and overall cost management. While it enables the management group to focus on worldwide operations, such a structure often induces a level of insensitivity among headquarters managers to local and national differences and host government demands. Managers tend to minimize or ignore the need for product adaptation and customized marketing approaches.

A traditional product organization, in its "pure form," is intended to leverage global integration opportunities at the cost of local responsiveness. It is an appropriate organizational form if managers can make a one-time choice on which factors to leverage (and which to ignore) for gaining and sustaining competitive advantage. This pure form is an efficient form of organization if the business is not too complex and permits those one-time choices to be made.

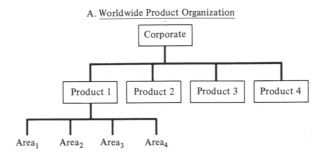

A. Worldwide Product Organization

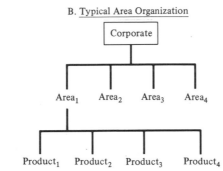

B. Typical Area Organization

***Figure 8.4.***    Formal Organization Structures

Further, we assume that if there are tradeoffs to be made between global integration and local responsiveness needs, they are few and far between. Given those simplifying assumptions, a unidimensional structure (one that leverages a single dimension in the IR grid) like the product organization is appropriate. The choice of such an organizational form also assumes that senior managers are willing to sacrifice strategic flexibility in favor of strategic control and efficiency of implementation of simple strategies. Such a choice also renders strategic redirection very traumatic, as significant structural changes will be needed before a new set of headquarters–subsidiary relationships, consistent with the new strategy, are built.

The choice of a pure area form of organization represents a similar unidimensional strategic choice on the part of management. While such a structure allows managers to become locally responsive, the ability to coordinate strategies (leveraging the global integration needs of the business) is sacrificed.

Such choices as worldwide product division structures or area structures—the unidimensional and pure forms shown in Figure 8.4—

are extremely limiting in executing complex strategies. Even when the businesses are not very complex, they do not necessarily allow for strategic flexibility or ease of strategic redirection.

## REORGANIZATION IS NOT THE ANSWER

Often firms lose competitiveness in businesses because they cannot respond flexibly to problems and opportunities. For example, a business organized as a worldwide product organization is likely to miss opportunities in markets where product adaptation is a must or where a level of local manufacturing would help politically. Either action is unlikely, given the logic of low-cost, global standards, and uniform policies across markets, a hallmark of a pure product organization. Managers who perceive organizational choices in "pure" form—either product or area—are likely to respond to the loss of competitiveness by reorganizing the business as an area organization. While that allows them to focus on local opportunities, over time it reduces the ability of the organization to coordinate strategies around the world. Further, such drastic shifts in structure are traumatic in terms of human cost. Conceiving organizational choices in pure structural terms, and as a binary choice—product or area organization—is often a self-inflicted restriction.

As the complexity of the businesses increases because of the nature of competition as well as the pressures imposed by customers and governments, managers have to learn to develop and implement complex strategies. At the same time, managers must explicitly examine the tradeoffs between local needs and global integration demands on an ongoing basis. Explicit considerations of the tradeoffs has become a necessity.

A variety of hybrid organizational arrangements is possible between the "pure" form and a multifocal or a matrix organization, where the perspectives of both the area and the product are explicitly and continuously examined. We can discern at least three intermediate steps between a "pure" form and a global matrix:[4]

1. When the businesses are not very complex or when the tradeoffs between area and global product management perspectives are not often an issue, senior management can take on the role of actively managing the substance of the decisions requiring such a tradeoff. For example, in a business operating with an area structure, senior managers could, on specific issues, request staff groups to present

an alternative solution to those proposed by the area managers. Typically, issues like location of manufacturing, product launch strategies, structuring of marketing and sales forces, and choice of technology provide opportunities for substantive arbitration by top management. Essentially, the approach assumes that the organization will operate with the "pure" form, with the provision that any time an important issue is identified and there is a disagreement among managers representing various interests, top managers will make the decision based on the presentations of the interested groups. That allows top managers to exercise control over critical issues. The mechanism is activated only on an "exception" basis, when the interested groups cannot resolve the issue within the framework of the organization. However, if not carefully managed, this can lead to top management overload. Further, top managers can become overly reliant on groups that are advocating fairly parochial views.

2. When the complexity of decisions or the frequency with which they have to be resolved increases, top managers can delegate the responsibility to trusted aides who are responsible for decision arbitration. Those trusted aides act as "integrators"—sensitive to the needs and perspectives of the various groups and at the same time to the overall strategic vision of the firm and its businesses. Geographical units (area managers), product groups (headquarters), and functional groups (manufacturing, R&D) must depend on the arbitrators for some aspect of their operations if the arbitrators are to be effective. Further, a lot of the arbitrator's power comes from proximity to the top management of the firm. LM Ericsson, a Swedish manufacturer of telecommunications equipment, used that approach extensively. The company had operations in more than forty countries. The key product divisions—transmissions, switching, telephones, and accessories—were all located in Sweden, as was the R&D group. The area groups had no direct contact with the production division in Sweden, and vice versa. Contact was managed through the offices of the area marketing vice presidents, who controlled all the traffic of information between the various groups. Since each group, while autonomous, depended on the area marketing vice president for product and market access, he was able to arbitrate and establish priorities. He provided the first-level screening of all the critical issues for top management. LM Ericsson succeeded by using that approach, because it operated in a single industry environment where governments were the primary customers, resulting in a complex and relatively slow decision environment, and where product de-

velopment cycles were long. The approach also is likely to suffer from an overload.

3. When the complexity of decisions and the frequency with which they have to be made increase, top managers have no choice but to withdraw from direct intervention and find other mechanisms, such as temporary coalition management. This approach is based on the assumption that the role of top managers in such situations can be only that of influencing the decision process rather than the decision itself, as in a "substantive decision management" approach. Top managers can influence the decision processes by selectively including and excluding individuals in *ad hoc* teams organized to recommend specific key decisions. Task forces, committees, project teams, and working parties are but a few of the common variations of this approach. Firms like Brown Boveri, whose basic management structure was totally oriented to area management, used this approach frequently to focus the attention of the organization on issues that transcended area concerns. Decisions regarding product development priorities, design, and technology choices were subjects that lent themselves to the approach. Paradoxically, for this approach to work, the management systems and the focus of managers must be broad. If the management systems overwhelmingly reinforce the area or the product perspective, task forces intended to resolve issues that require a careful balancing of both perspectives are unlikely to be successful. In other words, we have in effect moved away from a "pure" organizational form at this stage.

When the businesses become extremely complex, and when the tradeoffs have to be made constantly, senior managers must ensure that the two perspectives of area and product are constantly and explicitly balanced. That leads to a matrix or a multifocal organization, meaning that the two focal points of gaining strategic advantage—local responsiveness and global integration—are explicitly examined and balanced.

Except in very simple businesses, a "pure" organizational choice, be it area or product, is unlikely to be appropriate. In order to consider both local responsiveness and global integration needs, top managers can apply a series of "Band-Aids" to the "pure" form (as shown in Figure 8.5), moving from personal involvement in key decisions based on information provided by groups in contention over the issue (substantive decision mode), to delegating the job to a trusted aide and using that person as a screening device (substantive decision arbitration), to the use of *ad hoc* groups to study a specific

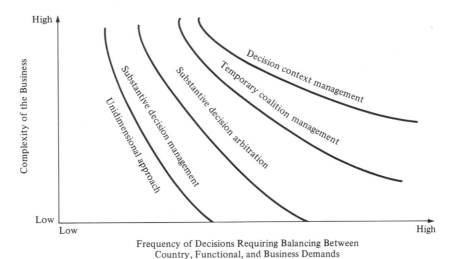

*Figure 8.5.*   Evolution of Organizational Complexity

Source: Y. Doz, C. Bartlett, and C. K. Prahalad, "Global Competitive Pressures and Host Country Demands: Managing Tensions in MNCs," *California Management Review,* Spring 1981, Vol. XXIII, No. 3, pp. 63–74.

issue (creating temporary coalitions). While the formal structure may remain the same, the decision-making process, with each one of these "Band-Aids," takes on a different color. The perspective in decision-making moves from one of leveraging a single perspective (unidimensional "pure" organizations) to adding increasingly heavy doses of multiple and often conflicting perspectives. Further, these "band-aids" provide increasingly sophisticated mechanisms for resolving those conflicts. As business complexity increases, managers have no choice but to move to a complex organizational arrangement, such as a global matrix.

## Managing in the Global Matrix

Most often, managers tend to resist the idea of moving to a global matrix organization, even if the nature of the business decisions—the complexity and frequency with which the tradeoffs between global and local issues have to be explicitly resolved—demand such an approach. Trained to think in terms of "pure" organizational models— the area and the product forms—managers find it difficult to think of organizational forms where "responsibilities are not clearly defined" or "it is not clear who reports to whom or who is boss."

Managers often complain about the inefficiencies of the matrix such as delays in decision-making. However, if we evaluate the appropriateness of an organizational arrangement using the criteria we have developed in this chapter—a balance among ease of strategic control, efficiency of strategic redirection, and capacity for flexible response—no pure form of organization will meet the test.

## A CONCEPT OF COMPLEX ORGANIZATIONS

In our experience, most of the difficulty that managers face in coping with the demands of a complex organization like a global matrix stems from the fact that the concepts managers use to manage such organizations are derived from their experience of simpler forms. A new approach to organizations may be needed before we understand and exploit the opportunities provided by a global matrix.

It is interesting to listen to managers who have had little or no experience with complex organizational arrangements describe a global matrix. They tend to use language like this: "I have a solid line relationship to the area manager and a dotted line relationship with the product manager." Or "I have responsibility for marketing decisions, but I have to consult with the product manager in deciding pricing levels." If we carefully analyze the concepts that go into formulating such statements, they are derived from experiences in a "pure line organization." There is an inbuilt desire to "fix" clearly the responsibilities and authority for decisions on a one-time basis.

A matrix is not a structure. It is a decision-making culture where multiple and often conflicting points of view are explicitly examined. Conflicts are resolved, ideally, through a process of analysis and on a basis of better problem definition. The relative roles and responsibilities of individuals and groups (e.g. area managers and product managers) may vary, depending on the problem at hand. The matrix is an attempt to track a "moving competitive target." Why, then, is there a significant discomfort with complex organizations among managers?

### Organizational Subprocesses

We can start by asking the following questions: Why do managers feel comfortable with a "pure" organization—be it area or product organization—as shown in Figure 8.4? What is the information content of the organization chart? How do managers interpret the chart? Why do managers change the organization chart, almost as a routine, as soon as they take over a new operation? The organization chart is a powerful tool in that it represents the following:

1. *The locus of power to allocate critical resources.* For example, in a pure product organization the power to allocate resources is vested in product managers. On the other hand, in an area organization the country managers are likely to be powerful in resource allocation. Managers also recognize intuitively that the pattern of resource allocation in the area organization will follow a logic quite different from the pattern in the product organization. In the product organization, the manager in charge of a business is likely to look at the various country markets as his portfolio and to assess his risks and opportunities accordingly. On the other hand, the country manager is likely to think of the collection of businesses in his country as his portfolio and assess risks and opportunities accordingly. The two dramatically different bases of power to allocate resources is shown in Figure 8.6.

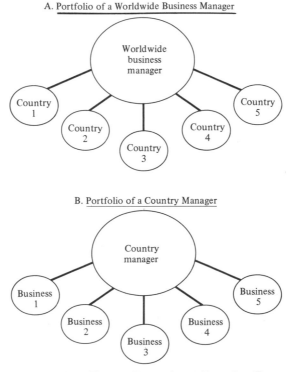

*Figure 8.6.* Two Power Bases for Allocating Resources

2. *A consensus on a strategic posture.* In a product organization, managers at all levels are likely to be concerned about global competition. Their orientation is to compete and defend their businesses worldwide. On the other hand, an area organization fosters a primarily local strategic posture. It is unlikely that a pure area-oriented organization will ever develop a global strategy for a business. A pure organization is a clear statement of the strategic orientation.

3. *A determinant of the mind sets of managers.* The nature of data collected and interpreted in the product-oriented organization is very different from that in the area organization. In the product organization, managers are likely to have product profitability data from around the world, to follow a uniform costing and accounting system, to track competitors globally, and to manage the movement of people and products across country borders. The mind sets of managers are conditioned by the nature of the information available in the organization. The information infrastructure—the sum total of the effects of the budgeting, planning, accounting, marketing, and human resource management systems—is oriented toward making managers think globally. In a pure area organization, on the other hand, the mind sets of managers are likely to be local. The information infrastructure in such an organization is primarily oriented toward local needs.

Undoubtedly no real organization exists in pure form—be it area or product. The three subprocesses described here are thus never totally oriented in any one direction. However, it is useful to examine the "pure" organization as an approach to identifying the essential underlying organizational subprocesses. We can conclude from the analysis above that an organization chart *is a shorthand way of describing the three organizational subprocesses*—the mind sets of key managers, the strategic posture of the group, and the locus of power to allocate critical resources, as shown in Figure 8.7.[5] Every time managers change the organization chart from a product to an area organization, they are in fact fundamentally changing the three subprocesses.

The frustration managers have with the global matrix becomes obvious when we think of the information content of a matrix organizational structure. The lines of the organization do not impart the same clarity to the orientation of the underlying organizational subprocesses. The mind sets of managers, by design, are expected to reflect global *and* local perspectives. The emerging strategic consensus—local or global—cannot be predicted by looking at the orga-

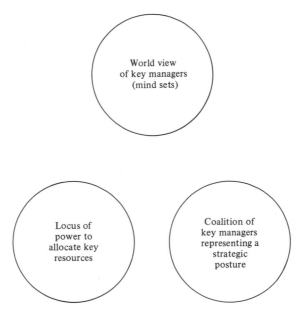

*Figure 8.7.*   A Concept of Complex Organizations

nizational chart. The power to allocate resources is also quite dif-
fused. Further, the three orientations cannot be changed by changing
the lines of organization. Irrespective of which relationships are
termed "solid line" and "dotted line," a matrix structure does not
give clarity to the nature and dynamics of the subprocesses.

## An Approach to Managing Complex Organizations

It is a futile exercise for managers to use the language system and the
concepts derived from "pure" organizational forms to manage a
complex multinational matrix. It is important that they start thinking
of a complex organization as essentially a collection of individuals,
a managerial constellation representing key business and country
managers. It is the mind sets of those key executives, or their world
views, that shape the quality of strategy. Strategy can be conceived
of as the dominant world view among that group of managers,
an implicit or explicit statement of the nature of competition, the
critical success factors for gaining and sustaining a competitive advantage, the nature of risk, and the resource base. Strategy represents the dominant coalition. The dominant coalition of managers

also represents the base of power to allocate human and financial resources.

### Role of Senior Management in Complex Organizations

We can reinterpret the role of senior management in complex organizations using this framework. The three tasks of strategic control, strategic change, and strategic flexibility shown schematically in Figure 8.1 imply managing the orientation of the three organizational subprocesses differently.

#### Strategic Control

Strategic control or efficiency in the implementation of a strategy suggests that all key managers understand and accept the basic strategic posture. For that to happen, key managers must share a common world view as well as a view of the critical tasks that flow from that strategy. The power to allocate resources must be vested in managers in such a way that it reinforces the strategic posture and hence the world view (e.g. relative power to allocate resources to reside with product managers, if a global orientation is desired, and with area managers if a locally responsive strategy is desired). Efficiency in implementation is accomplished when there is consistency among the three subprocesses as well as a shared view of the world. An efficiency orientation, if carried to its limit, will lead to the danger that all the key managers will think alike, causing rigidity with respect to strategy. It will also lead to a consolidation of power in one group. The dominant coalition can drive out "dissenters" and alternative points of view in the organization. There is a need for caution here. A single-minded pursuit of strategic control may compromise the ability of mangers to change strategy.

#### Strategic Change

Changing strategy for a business implies that the three organizational subprocesses be reoriented. Strategic change of the types described in this book—changing the orientation of a business from local responsiveness to global integration or vice versa—requires that the mind sets of key managers, as well as the nature of the dominant coalition, be changed. Ultimately, strategic change implies a different pattern of resource allocation. That calls for a shift in the balance of power among managers. It is easy to see why a preoccupation with efficiency may create problems in changing direction. The more rigid the power structure and the greater the commitment to a strategic posture, the more difficult it is to change.

The difficulties inherent in changing the mind sets of key managers, creating a new strategic consensus, and creating a new balance of power on a proactive basis are such that senior managers do not undertake substantial strategic redirections unless there is a profit crisis. A profit crisis provides legitimacy for change. A profit crisis implies that the current strategy failed its market test. As strategy is derived from the world view of key managers, it also implies that their world views need updating. Since the strategy failed, the dominant coalition of managers who represent that strategy and the power structure also failed. As a result, a crisis affords managers the opportunity to make sweeping changes in the constellation of key managers (we refer to the ritual of firing and hiring of managers that so often accompanies a profit crisis). The new management team represents not only a new power structure, but a new and varied mind set that can lead to a new strategic consensus. In other words, strategic change that follows a crisis appears easy, as senior managers can make shifts in the three organizational subprocesses by changing the constellation of managers. The sequence of change in the organizational subprocesses accompanying a strategic change brought about by a crisis is represented in Figure 8.8. For example, in Chrysler, when Mr. Iaccocca walked in the door, the balance of power changed first. The new constellation of key managers who came in with Mr. Iaccocca represented a new mind set and a different world view, and they were able to forge a new strategy. Those managers from the "old Chrysler" who survived changed their "world views." Chrysler represents a dramatic change—an extreme case that illustrates the underlying process. It also highlights the limitations of such an approach to strategic change.

While cases like Chrysler make the business press—*Fortune, Business Week* and *Wall Street Journal* articles—it is a painful process. It represents an approach to management where senior managers, confronted with the need for strategic redirection, are unwilling to make proactive changes in the power structure. The old dictum "If it ain't broke, don't fix it" says it all. When it gets "broke," fixing is both expensive and traumatic. During a crisis,

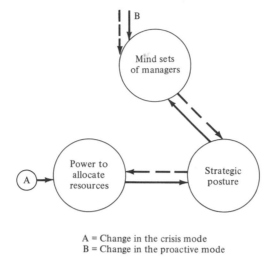

A = Change in the crisis mode
B = Change in the proactive mode

***Figure 8.8.*** Organizational Change: Crisis
Versus Proactive Change

while strategic change appears to be swift, managers are constrained
in their choices by the availability of resources.

Proactive change in strategy means that managers must start with
the mind sets of key managers rather than the power structure. The
role of senior management becomes a matter of alerting the key managers to both the potential opportunities and threats, providing
them with an alternate set of world views, and challenging their current perspectives. The *role of senior management is to create variety.*
In addition, managers must allow for the emergence of a new strategic consensus, based on an active debate of the alternative world
views. Shifts in the balance of power follow. The case of IBM illustrates that approach to change. When Mr. Akers became the CEO
of IBM, he inherited a company that was highly successful. The approach that worked at Chrysler would not have succeeded at IBM.
Creating a sense of urgency and the need for change in a successful
firm like IBM required that Mr. Akers start with changing the mind
sets of managers. He challenged the organization to grow at least as
fast as the industry, which meant doubling itself in less than six years
and becoming a $100 billion corporation. He also challenged the or-
ganization to become the lowest-cost producer in the world. Those
challenges forced managers to reconsider their basic approaches, examine orthodoxies, and rethink their own recipes for success. An
active debate to reconsider alternatives and forge a new strategy for
the various businesses followed. The balance of power shifted at the

very top as well as at other levels in the organization. IBM accomplished a shift in strategic posture as dramatic as that at Chrysler, but with no fanfare or media attention.

Proactive change, as shown in Figure 8.8 (mode B), starts with recognizing the dominant mind sets of managers and their world views and challenging them. It *starts with an educational process.* As a second step, senior managers must create the climate and the organizational mechanisms for an active debate and forge a new consensus on strategy. Shifts in the balance of power follow. The process appears to be slow. The process of change allows the participation of managers, captures their inventiveness, and ensures careful consideration of alternatives. A crisis-motivated change may appear "efficient" and "quick," but changes in strategy undertaken during a crisis often ignore the "quality of strategy." Few alternatives are considered in picking a new direction. Efficiency must be measured by several criteria—quality of the new strategy, commitment and participation of key people in its development, the human costs associated with change, and the time it takes for the change to take place.

*Strategic Flexibility*

Strategic flexibility assumes, unlike strategic change, not great shifts accomplished over long periods of time (for example, a shift from a local responsiveness strategy to a global integration strategy, accomplished over a two- to three-year time span) but continuous adjustments and fine-tuning. Managers must therefore be alert at all times to alternate views of the world and must seek and interpret alternate sources of information for strategy. They should have the capacity to make minor changes in aspects of strategy without great difficulty. That approach means the power structure be not too rigid and there is adequate diffusion of power to challenge the "current wisdom." Strategic flexibility requires *a significant tolerance for ambiguity and variety.* We shall consider this aspect in greater detail in Chapter 9.

## CONCLUSION

It is obvious that the nature of organizational change takes on a different color if we move away from a dependence on formal hierarchies as a way of introducing change (that is, move from a product to an area organization) or think of changing people every time a change is called for. The concept of a complex organization as a collection of three subprocesses suggests greater degrees of freedom for managers to manage and fine-tune their organizations. The "pure" form of organization is a special case where the three subprocesses are aligned with the lines of organization. In a complex matrix, the formal structure does not provide clues to the underlying processes. Further, the tasks of control, change, and flexibility impose different demands on the organization. Senior managers must balance their concerns for flexibility with efficiency of implementation and ability to change. The mechanisms that managers can use to accomplish those complex and often conflicting goals will be outlined in the next chapter.

# 9

## Tools for Strategic Control, Flexibility, and Change

To exercise strategic control, to manage strategic redirection, and to provide for flexibility in global strategies, top management has to go beyond a formalistic view of management authority and corporate structure to shape the world view of key executives, to achieve agreed-upon strategic direction (or redirection), and to align the relative power of key managers to their desired roles in developing and implementing strategies. In Chapter 8, we established the need for managing world views, strategic direction, and relative power jointly in order to be able to achieve coordinated purposive strategic action for the firm's various businesses. In this chapter we focus on the practical aspects of how to shape the mind sets (cognitive), strategic, or power processes underlying the evolution of world views, the development of strategic consensus (or at least of a coalition) to allow action, and the distribution of power within the firm.

To achieve this, a wide array of management tools can be used in a coordinated fashion by top management and by business management. In keeping with our focus on individual businesses as a unit of analysis, we shall first analyze the use of these tools at the level of individual businesses and defer a full treatment of how to manage interdependencies across businesses until Chapter 11.

In this chapter we shall first identify and review the available tools and their use. We shall discuss which of the three processes—

cognitive, strategic, and power—are most directly impacted by which tools, how strongly, selectively, and quickly. More important than the consideration of individual tools, one by one, is the analysis of their overall combined configuration and impact in providing for strategic control, redirection, or flexibility. In a second section, we will introduce the notion of a tool configuration map, both as a diagnostic method to analyze the current explicit or implicit strategic priorities of a business and as a way to help develop an action agenda to improve strategic control, manage redirection, or increase flexibility. The approach, however, would remain rather dry and abstract without concrete illustrations. We shall therefore borrow detailed examples from our research work and use them in the second half of this chapter as illustrations of the use—or misuse—of management tools. In sequence, we shall provide examples of stable strategic control configurations, of the dynamic use of tools to achieve strategic redirection, and of the provision of strategic flexibility.

## MANAGEMENT TOOLS

The top management of most companies—or of individual divisions and subsidiaries within large MNCs—has available a broad repertoire of management tools, such as planning systems, accounting and budgeting systems, management development systems, measurement and evaluation systems, management control systems, and, usually, a plethora of committees for coordination, business reviews, new product introduction signoffs, managers' evaluation and compensation policies, and so forth. Those widely diverse tools provide a rich infrastructure for top management to put to active use in managing global businesses.

For strategic management purposes, the tools can be grouped into three categories: data management, managing manager motivation, and conflict management. Data management tools are those providing and structuring the data pertinent to critical strategic decisions and to the global and local performance of the company. By structuring such data and focusing the attention of executives on specific aspects, these tools transform raw data into useful information for decision-making and strategic control. Managers' management tools shape executive perceptions of self-interest and their expectations by defining "rules of the game" within the firm. Promotion and appointment processes, individual evaluations, rewards and punishment, and management development processes, for instance, all contribute to communicate rules of the game to the various senior- and middle-level executives within the firm. Finally, conflict management tools provide channels and structures for contentious decisions to be made, in particular, decisions for which the priorities of global integration and of national responsiveness have to be traded off carefully. Table 9.1 provides a list of the typical management tools clustered into the three categories.[1]

A first concern in using the tools purposefully is to delineate the scope of their use: Which of the three processes—cognitive, strategic or power—do they principally affect, with what strength, with what selectivity, and with what speed? Although those questions have no single answer applicable across companies—and to seek one would only reflect an overly mechanistic desire for simplicity—a few generalizations can be made.

### General Characteristics of Management Tools

*Critical Process Most Directly Influenced
and Direction of the Influence*

Not all available tools affect all three processes similarly. As an example, key managers' appointments affect power distribution most directly. Appointing individuals who are stronger-willed, more enterprising, or more skillful at eliciting personal commitments as sub-

**TABLE 9.1**  A Typical Repertoire of Management Tools

| *I. Data Management Tools* | *II. Managers' Management Tools* | *III. Conflict Resolution Tools* |
|---|---|---|
| 1. Information systems | 1. Choice of key managers | 1. Assignment of responsibility for decisions |
| 2. Measurement systems | 2. Career paths | 2. Integrators |
| 3. Resource allocation procedures | 3. Reward and punishment systems | 3. Business teams |
| 4. Strategic planning | 4. Management development | 4. Coordination committees |
| 5. Budgeting planning | 5. Patterns of socializations | 5. Task forces |
| | | 6. Issue resolution processes |

sidiary general managers results in greater subsidiary autonomy and higher national responsiveness. Conversely, appointing such individuals to worldwide product or business management responsibilities would result in greater coordination and integration, provided those individuals bring or develop a perspective on global competition that allows them to assess the need for integration and coordination.

Accounting and information systems, by the kind of data they provide, may facilitate or impede the development of one world view or another. In the absence of comparable product-oriented performance data across countries, it is difficult to develop, sustain, and defend a clear worldwide perspective on a product line, and integration opportunities—and even needs—are likely to be overlooked until the evidence becomes overwhelming. Conversely, in a diversified MNC, where each product group pursues its own worldwide strategy independently through its own subsidiaries, opportunities for fruitful coordination at the national level in various countries may not even be seen. Worse, units may work at cross-purposes, for instance, with one business group trying to sell electronics to a country's navy, which calls for offsets, and another business group deciding to close a plant in the same country.

Management development policies, explicit or implicit, beyond their obvious impact on power distribution also have induced influences on world view. A business whose senior managers' careers have included such positions as marketing manager for government electronics in France or managing director in India is likely to be run with a world view quite different from one whose background consisted of consumer product marketing in Belgium or competitive and technologic intelligence in Silicon Valley or marketing in Japan. In sum, individual world views are also shaped by past career achievements.

A complete rundown on all the management tools would be long and cumbersome. It is sufficient to argue, along the lines merely outlined above on a few individual tools, that the top management of a global business should first review the perspective of existing tools and analyze, given their current structure and setting, which of the three processes—cognitive, strategic, or power—they influence most directly, and what induced effect each tool may have on other processes. Second, top management can then analyze whether the current setting of each tool favors global integration or national responsiveness, or provides for a balanced perspective. To be useful, this must involve not only considering the usually recognized explicit management tools but also focusing on some tools often left implicit. Management appointment decisions in the past may have been made under the urgency of filling important vacant jobs, and aggregate patterns may not have been given much consideration, yet a global company whose top management all came up through national subsidiary managing director's positions is likely to be deeply different from one in which top management was drawn from the ranks of worldwide product division managers.

### Strength

Obviously, not all management tools are of equal strength, nor is the strength of a given tool necessarily stable over time. That offers both an opportunity and a threat to top management: the opportunity to allow for a careful management of strategic control by blending tools of various strength and by modulating the strength of individual tools; the threat from the risk of undermanagement of the tools with the danger of loss of control.

Differences of strength between tools are clear. Key executive promotions are a strong tool. For instance, appointing a highly respected and well-regarded senior corporate executive to worldwide product line coordination is a very strong action. First, it modifies the distribution of power through the leadership the new executive can exercise. Second, it is highly visible throughout the organization, and carefully watched, making it a powerful signal with strong symbolic value. Middle managers will look at it for clues about winners and losers. Such an appointment also helps convey a sense of urgency: New senior executives are likely to initiate actions quickly. If they remain strategically inactive for a long period (a year or more) change is then more difficult to initiate. People with new ideas for change are also more likely to come into the open early. In fact, all the successful strategic reorientations observed started with such an appointment.

Significant changes in career patterns at the middle management level are even more powerful, not so much by their immediate results (their impact takes years to be felt through the organization) as by their symbolic value: Their long time frame and their relative irreversibility after a while make them strong signals of top management commitment. Significant hirings from outside, with particular profiles, have a similar impact. The strength of the signals derives mainly from the sense of direction that is usually embedded in top executive choices and in career path. They usually reflect an orientation toward integration or toward responsiveness, or at least they are interpreted as such. The sense of direction is, in turn, reinforced by the relative irreversibility of key appointments. Quick reversals have high costs: wastage of managerial talent, power struggles, resignations, high emotional costs to the managers involved, and loss of credibility and "face" on the part of top management.

Unlike the examples just given, the creation of an intersubsidiary coordinating committee is, by itself, a relatively weak tool. It does not signal direction, it has no necessary permanency, the cost of discontinuing its meetings is low, and the visibility to the organization may remain slight. Yet top management can use such a committee in very different fashions. If it is just a meeting ground, it may be helpful to share information and to understand better what the perspectives and priorities of the participants may be. A skillful top management, by varying the composition and the charter of such committees and by signaling more or less interest in their work, can modulate the strength of their impact almost continuously from the trivial "debating society" to initiating a full-scale strategic redirection. Such mechanisms are of variable strength according to the way they are used and controlled. They provide great opportunity for fine-tuning strategic control or for the management of strategic redirection by top management.

Conversely, if they are not carefully managed they can lead to serious problems. Xerox, for instance, in mid-1973 planned a worldwide senior management conference to be held in the spring of 1974. The conference was to discuss the future of the company's strategy and organization to face growing competition as the original xerography patents expired and new competitors entered the reproduction field. Various study groups were formed to prepare the conference, including one for planning and control, under the chairmanship of the French subsidiary's managing director. Predictably, that study group, left on its own, advocated more entrepreneurial growth, more closeness to customers, and better local service—a whole program calling for more subsidiary autonomy and more responsiveness to national conditions. Yet when the conference was held, after the oil crisis, corporate management was preoccupied more with asset management, excessive inventories, and tighter strategic control over the subsidiaries. By then, though, the message of subsidiary autonomy had been propagated, unchecked, by the various study groups, and considerable confusion followed both at the conference itself and in its aftermath. Further, in a lease-based business like that involving large copiers, with a lot of servicing, it was not clear whether the proper answer to a crisis was more integration and centralization or more autonomy and national responsiveness. Both were in fact needed, but the mishandling of the conference had polarized world views and strategic priorities into conflicting positions between headquarters and subsidiaries.

## Selectivity

Management tools differ in how broad or narrow their impact may be. Key management appointments, for example, are by their very nature quite broad: They directly affect a whole range of decision-making responsibilities, and the tasks of key executives cannot be narrowly constrained. Formal procedures can usually be much more finely tuned. Capital appropriation or contracting procedures may have clearly spelled-out threshold amounts over which the procedures shift from being delegated to subsidiaries to also involving headquarters approvals. Sales to different types of customers can also be handled differently; for instance, car component suppliers often differentiate "global accounts" (e.g. Ford) from regional ones (Daimler Benz) and national ones (Jaguar) and differentiate the respective roles of subsidiaries and headquarters according to the various types of accounts.

More generally, many DMNCs have gone, at one point or repeatedly, through the exercise of developing "decision grids" as a way to make explicit the respective roles of various managers in specific categories of decisions (Figure 9.1). While such detailed specification can seldom become a permanent guide for action—it is too cumbersome and constraining for management action—it can be a useful diagnostic exercise to show whether the actual distribution of decision-making authority in the organization matches the one that the nature of the business on the IR grid and the competitive and governmental demands affecting it would require. It can also show whether the actual political decision-making process, given the personal leadership exercised and the critical resources controlled by key

**Legend:**

| | |
|---|---|
| D — Decides | TC — Technical concurrence |
| A — Approves | C — Concurs |
| R — Recommends | I — Initiates |
| BC — Business concurrence | IP — Inputs |
| [*] Joint decision only | [**] for U.S. decisions only |

## Worldwide Resource Allocation

| | U.S. Electrical Products Division | | | | | European Area — Sovirel | | | | | | | CEE | CGISA | | | | | | | Worldwide Management | | | | Finance | | | | Corporate Staffs | | | | | | | |
|---|---|---|---|---|---|---|---|---|---|---|---|---|---|---|---|---|---|---|---|---|---|---|---|---|---|---|---|---|---|---|---|---|---|---|---|---|
| | Liscomb (Bus. Dev.) | Russell (Controller) | Galloy (Bus. Mgr TV) | Fraley (Mgr Mfg) | Dawson (Gen. Mgr) | Hollack (Div/Plant Controller) | Timbal (TV Prod.) | Presta (TV Sales & Mktg) | Picot (Div. Mgr TV) | Ayotte (Tech. Dir.) | Maurice (Head of Staff) | Regis (President) | McCann (Gen. Mgr CEE) | Winkler (Planning) | Roederer (Licensing) | Roederer (Socialist Countries) | Hamer (Fin. Mgr) | Stoff (Gen. Sales Mgr) | Wunsch (Dep. Area Mgr) | Duluth (Gen. Mgr) | Staff Mktg & Bus. Dev. | Staff Mfg & Eng. | Control & Planning | Dawson (Worldwide Mgr) | Treasury | Control | Bus. & Fin. Planning | Mfg & Eng. | Technical Staffs | Purchasing | Mfg Services | Industrial Relations | Manpower Development | Public Relations | Legal | Government Affairs |
|---|---|---|---|---|---|---|---|---|---|---|---|---|---|---|---|---|---|---|---|---|---|---|---|---|---|---|---|---|---|---|---|---|---|---|---|---|
| 1. Recommend allocation of resources to major new product development programs | $R_1$ | IP | IP | $R_1$ | $R_2$ | IP | $R_1$ | $R_1$ | $R_2$ | IP | IP | BC | | | | C | | IP | | BC | BC | $R_3$ | IP | D | | TC | IP | R/TC | R/TC | | | | IP/TC | | TC | |
| 2. Recommend allocation of resources to major process development programs | IP | IP | IP | $R_1$ | $R_2$ | IP | $R_1$ | IP | $R_2$ | IP | IP | BC | | | | C | | IP | | BC | IP | $R_3$ | IP | D | | TC | IP | R/TC | R/TC | | | | IP/TC | | C | |
| 3. Recommend allocation of resources for major cost reduction programs | IP | IP | IP | $R_1$ | $R_2$ | IP | $R_1$ | IP | $R_2$ | $R_1$ | IP | BC | | | | C | | IP | C | BC | IP | $R_3$ | IP | D | | TC | IP | R/TC | R/TC | | | C | IP/TC | | | |
| 4. Determine need, location, and timing for adding or reducing plant capacity | IP | IP | IP | $R_1$ | D[*] | IP | $R_1$ | IP | $R_2$ | IP | $R_2$ | D[*] | | | R | R | R | IP | | D[*] | IP | R | IP | D[*] | | TC | R | R | | | | IP/TC | | | TC | C[**] |
| 5. Decide management of production work force (expansion, contraction, assignment) | | | | D | C | | | | D | | $R_2$ | D | D | | | | | | | C | | | | C | | | | | | | | TC[**] | | | TC[**] | C[**] |
| 6. Decide on interarea sourcing | IP | IP | IP | $R_1$ | $R_2$ | IP | IP | IP | $R_2$ | $R_1$ | $R_1$ | BC | $R_2$ | | | $R_2$ | IP | IP | | BC | BC | IP | $R_3$ | D | TC | TC | IP | | | | | | | IP | C | C |
| 7. Decide who maintains existing technologies (e.g., black-and-white, spinning) | | | IP | R | R | R | R | IP | R | IP | $R_1$ | BC | | | | R | | | | BC | IP | R | IP | D | | | | R/TC | | | | | | | | |
| 8. Assign specialized people resources to temporary assignments (e.g., to implement special three month project) | | | | | | | | | | | | | | | | | | | | | | | | | | | | | | | | | | | | |
| a. Assign operating personnel (e.g., marketing, manufacturing) to another area | | R | R | R | D/BC | R | R | R | D/BC | D | C | R | R | | R | R | | | | BC | C | C | | BC | | | | D | D | | | | R | | | |
| b. Assign technical staff and M&E personnel | R | R | R | R | R | R | R | R | R | | C | BC | | | R | R | | | IP | BC | C | R | | BC | | | | D | D | | | | R | | | |

*Figure 9.1.* Managerial Grid: Corning Glass Works, TV Business

SOURCE: McKinsey-prepared form as filled out during a decision grid meeting.

managers, is functional or dysfunctional vis-à-vis the requirements of the business. Using such grids as a reference for the structure of collective decision-making processes provides top management with a way to make management appointments more selective by giving a more precise contour to the job and authority of various managers.

### Time Horizon and Continuity

Different tools can have an impact more or less quickly and can be changed or redirected more or less rapidly. We already contrasted the quick impact of single key executive changes with the slower reshaping of patterns of career paths for middle-level executives. The former usually has an impact in less than a year, whereas the latter takes several years to reach critical mass. Individuals also adjust slowly and require a long time to shift world views, develop new strategic perspectives, and accommodate redistributions of power. By itself, a new appointment is not sufficient.

Data management tools also have a relatively long lead time. A new planning and control system takes a few years to take hold, from initial design, introduction, and evolution to becoming a widely accepted and trusted tool for senior and middle executives alike. Typically, it takes three to four years, at least, to reach that stage.

In most companies we analyzed, individual managers' adjustment to newly reset managers' management tools and the lead times involved in building reliable data management tools, or in restructuring them, were the key pacing factors in the development of strategic control or in the management of strategic redirection.

Managers ought to be sensitive to those delays and to the dangers of being impatient. Many tools may give the appearance of change and may create a false sense of security. Views held by individual managers that lead them to support specific resource allocation proposals and discard others, for instance, are shaped over a period of time by perceptions of benefits and risks, by the development of their own careers, and by the building of personal track records. Though the formal criteria and procedures for resource allocation can be changed easily and quickly, as can the format of capital appropriation proposals, the personal views that actually kill a proposal or propel it toward corporate approval cannot. Therefore, it is critical for top management to acknowledge and consider carefully the lead time required for any mechanism to bear results.

*Opportunity for Fine-Tuning and Need*
*for Top Management Involvement*

The discussion so far suggests that various tools give different opportunities to, and put different demands on, top management. First, the quality with which a tool is used usually depends on top management's discipline in making sure it is used effectively; most management tools degenerate or fall into disarray unless explicitly used with determination by top management. Second, tools such as committees and task forces are constantly evolving; group composition, charter, mission, and use of their outputs must all be set, monitored, and modified by top management. They both give much opportunity for fine-tuning and require much ongoing top management involvement. Formal accounting and control systems, on the other hand, do not offer much room for *ad hoc* top management fine-tuning, but they do not require much attention from top management, except to rely on their disciplined use.

Table 9.2 summarizes the main characteristics of the usual management tools along the considerations outlined above: the process they most directly influence, how they influence it, their strength, their selectivity, their time horizon and needed continuity in use, the opportunities they offer to top managers for fine tuning, and the ongoing attention they demand.

## Configurations of Management Tools

So far we have considered management tools one by one. That is obviously an overly simplistic approach. As tools are not independent from one another, what really matters is the total configuration of tools. Also, the impact of one or another tool depends on how it is related to others. Strategic planning can have an impact principally on the cognitive process if it is mainly a broad, intellectual, scenario-planning exercise. If, on the other hand, it is closely linked to operating plans and budgets, and if measurement and evaluation systems are also tightly linked to them, strategic planning becomes the first step of a substantial commitment process, and as such it will influence power distribution very directly. The relative strength of various tools also depends on their conjoint use. For example, the reward and punishment process may look very tough on paper, but if at the same time the setting of performance criteria is quite loose

**TABLE 9.2** Management Tools and Their Attributes

| Tools | Organizational Orientations Affected | Strength and Symbolic Value of Mechanisms | Selectivity | Speed/ Continuity | Need for Top Management's Ongoing Support |
|---|---|---|---|---|---|
| I. Data management | | | | | |
| 1. Information systems | Cognitive, strategic, power | Variable[a] | High | Low | Low |
| 2. Measurement systems | | | | | |
| —Business performance | Cognitive, power | Medium | Medium | Medium | Low |
| —Managers' performance | | High | Medium | Medium | Low |
| 3. Resource allocation procedures | | | | | |
| —Content | Strategic, power | Low | High | Low | Low |
| —Impetus | | High | High | High | Medium |
| —Approval | | High | High | Low | High |
| 4. Strategic planning | Strategic | Variable[a] | Low | High | Medium |
| 5. Budgeting process | Strategic, power | High | Low | Low | Low |

II. Managers' management

| | | | | | |
|---|---|---|---|---|---|
| 1. Choice of key managers | Power | Strong | Low | High | Medium |
| 2. Career plans | Power | Strong | Low | High | High |
| 3. Reward and punishment systems | Power | Strong | Low | Medium | High |
| 4. Management development | Strategic, cognitive | Variable[a] | High | Medium | Medium |
| 5. Patterns of socialization | Cognitive | Low | Low | High | High |

III. Conflict resolution

| | | | | | |
|---|---|---|---|---|---|
| 1. Decision, responsibility assignments | Power | High | High | Medium | High |
| 2. Integrators | Cognitive | Low | High | Low | High |
| 3. Business teams | Cognitive | Low | Low | Medium | High |
| 4. Coordination committees | Cognitive | Low | High | Low | High |
| 5. Task forces | Strategic | Variable[a] | High | Low | High |
| 6. Issue resolution processes | Stratetic | Variable[a] | High | Low | High |

[a]Variable means that the strength and symbolic value of the tool rest mainly on how the tool is set and managed.

SOURCE: Reprinted from "Headquarter Influence and Strategic Control in MNC," by Y. Doz and C. K. Prahalad, *Sloan Management Review*, Fall 1981, p. 19, by permission of the publisher.

and does not stretch current performance much, the toughness of the reward and punishment process is unlikely to be experienced often, and the perceived strength of the tool will decline. In summary, the total tool configuration can be more or less tightly knit, and the interdependencies between tools can be more or less recognized.

The overall configuration can also be more or less consistent. Planning may be oriented toward global competition and recognize fully the global nature of a business, yet if individual managers' career paths are purely local, with their rewards based on national subsidiary performance, and if subsidiary managing directors are seen as the key managers, the recognition of global competition—although intellectually achieved through planning—is unlikely to lead to strategies and actions appropriate for facing global competitors.

A second step for top management, beyond identifying the perspective supported by the tools used and analyzing each tool's impact one by one, is to assess the quality of the overall configuration of tools along several key dimensions.

1. *Consistency.* Do the various tools being used provide a consistent sense of direction to middle-level executives, or do they give mixed and ambiguous signals? Ambiguity, as we shall discuss later, is not necessarily bad and may even be necessary to maintain strategic flexibility in a business. There may therefore be deliberate inconsistencies that top management wants to maintain; more frequent, however, are the unintended dysfunctional inconsistencies that weaken a strategic control configuration.

2. *Tightness versus loosensess.* Are the various tools used in a disjointed fashion, or do they provide an integrated strategic management infrastructure? Tools may have evolved and may be used more or less as a motley collection of disjointed intervention means, or they may be sufficiently coordinated to provide top management with a capability to modify the strategic direction of a business systematically. In other words, is there an explicit integrated organization design and evolution capability or a less integrated "local fix" perspective? Few companies among those we studied had a top management able to comprehend the whole range of tools as an integrated set of interdependent parts, to play conceptually with alternative models of organizational processes, and to recognize the tradeoffs involved. Most companies had a segmented view and attributed problems to the poor use of specific tools, not to the unintended interactions among tools. Those with a more integrated

view, such as IBM, could consider, for instance, the impact a change in transfer pricing policies (from "cost plus" to negotiated or market prices) might have on the mix of cooperative–competitive attitudes that such a change requires from managers. It was feared that such a shift would lead to excessive competition and jeopardize the existing cooperative culture.

3. *Parsimony versus completeness.* How many tools are really needed? Is the corporation over- or undermanaged? Too narrow a repertoire of tools does not facilitate top management intervention, except in a direct personal way, by treating the issues in substance. While that is feasible in a lot of relatively simple companies, with few businesses and few subsidiaries, the demand on top management time and attention becomes overwhelming as the diversity and geographic scope of the company's businesses grow. Too broad a repertoire of tools may just add unneeded complexity and cost to the administration of the company, with little marginal contribution. It is not possible to specify in the abstract what an ideal range of tools would be, as that depends both on the diversity and complexity of the corporate portfolio, as discussed in Chapter 7, and on the specific skills and preferred mode of action of corporate management. The list presented in Tables 9.1 and 9.2 is typical, however.

4. *Discipline in use.* Are the management tools used by all, including senior management, in a disciplined way, which lends credibility to the tools, or are they by-passed or ignored by top management? Discipline starts at the top: Middle managers will not use management tools and abide by the results of their use (for instance for resource allocation or appointments) unless they see top management using the tools. While some decisions will outstretch the management tools—for example, the top few positions in a company cannot be filled by a systematic human resource management process—if most decisions become personalized and overly idiosyncratic, the credibility of management tools will quickly erode, and management processes are likely to become totally politicized. In other words, discipline in the use of management tools is also a safeguard against the personal idiosyncrasies of senior executives.

The four aspects outlined above allow top management to evaluate the quality of the management process within their companies and to assess its potential for strategic control, redirection, and flexibility. Because a description of how tools are used concretely is always more useful and more revealing than a description of the tools themselves, we now proceed to that task.

# THE MANAGEMENT TOOLS IN USE

## Ensuring Strategic Control: The Consistency Between Desired Strategic Direction and Management Tool Configuration

Let us start with two contrasting examples, one of a nationally responsive business and one of a more global one. The Swiss electrical equipment multinational group Brown Boveri (BBC) provides a clear example of a management tool configuration oriented toward national responsiveness (Figure 9.2). In the early 1970s, BBC had been reorganized into five geographic groups. The three principal national companies (in Switzerland, Germany, and France) each constituted a group. A fourth regrouped middle-size subsidiaries in half a dozen countries (Austria, Norway, India, and others). The fifth group originally comprised the international sales network but as time went on included an increasing number of manufacturing operations as they were established in developing countries. The three main affiliates were organized in a field of product divisions, each product division being set up as an independent profit center. The medium-size and smaller affiliates also each constituted a profit center. Thus, if we consider data management tools, they were all oriented toward national responsiveness: Information systems focused on national con-

| Changes | Changes Reinforce | |
| | Local Responsiveness | Global Integration |
| --- | --- | --- |
| I Reorganization<br>profit centers | * | |
| II Corporate staff<br>    marketing<br>    planning<br>    finance<br>    legal | *?<br>*<br>*<br>* | *? |
| III Management committees<br>    KST<br>    KPT | *?<br>*? | *?<br>*? |
| IV Capital appropriation<br>    Career paths<br>    Incentive compensation<br>    Control system | *<br>*<br>*<br>* | |
| V Corporate beliefs | * | |

*Figure 9.2.*    BBC: Organizational Context

ditions, measurement considered national profit performance as the key criterion, and even resource allocation sustained a local more than a global view. First, affiliates were not fully owned, and their management showed a strong concern for local minority shareholders. Second, the company operated in such businesses as heavy electrical equipment, where local state-owned customers, national sources of export credit, and national R&D financing were often important sources of funds. Third, the main affiliates were substantially bigger than the Swiss company, were quoted on their national stock markets, and were hardly dependent upon Switzerland for financing. Resource allocation processes reflected that independence: With the exception of R&D projects and key contracts, which were discussed in the corporate management committee by the heads of the five geographical groups and the chairman (collectively they constituted the top management of the company), resource allocation decisions were made mainly at the level of each group, with little overall coordination. While a corporate strategic planning group existed in Switzerland, planning took place mainly within geographic units and their various divisions. Only in 1976 was some coordination of planning among the three main European affiliates suggested.

Similarly, managers' management tools may strongly reinforce the national responsiveness perspective. Career paths were local, and only in developing countries was there an exchange of Swiss expatriates. Key managers in subsidiaries were all local nationals and in many cases were very prominent in the local environment (e.g. chairmen of local trade and industry associations). That had a strong influence on perceived power allocation. Reward and punishment systems were also, obviously, based on local subsidiary performance, with no element of overall group performance. No joint management development took place across subsidiaries, and informal socialization across subsidiaries was weak. Representatives of the French and German operations went to Baden, where the headquarters were located (except for the home office in Zurich), more as "ambassadors" from their respective affiliates than as members of a common corporation.

While conflict resolution tools existed and were oriented toward cooperation, they remained weak. Corporate marketing staff, for instance, were in charge of allocating exports among affiliates, in principle a powerful integration tool in a company heavily dependent on exports. Yet it worked only part of the time, and for only part of the product range. When capacity exceeded demand, in a cyclical business, affiliates became dependent on headquarter allocations, but when demand outstripped supply, the dependency was reversed. Export allocations thus provided no stable basis for marketing to contribute to central strategic control. Marketing staff had a strong say on only part of the product range: Very large contracts were discussed directly by the corporate managing committee and were allocated to one or another of the affiliates according to those discussions and a bit of horse trading. Mass-produced products required a permanent distribution infrastructure, and geographic markets for them were usually permanently allocated to one large affiliate or another, based on trade agreements, language, and cultural affiliations. Turkey was permanently assigned to Germany, West Africa to France, and so forth. That took power away from central staffs; while intersubsidiary product teams, business committees, and steering groups abounded (called KST and KPT at BBC), their role in coordination was made impossible by the strong orientation of data management and managers' management tools toward national responsiveness alone. As a result, such committees were confined to the cognitive process: They could share information and develop a world view in favor of integration, but no individual manager would see it sufficiently in his interest to pursue such a view in action, except on mundane matters.

In the case of Brown Boveri, the overriding priority for national responsiveness was historically quite appropriate, given the fragmented nature of its markets and the extent of government influence over them. Only when free trade came to prevail, at least for industrial goods, was the national responsiveness approach challenged, and the organizational commitment to that approach became a serious problem, as we shall discuss in the next section.

Among the companies studied in our research, we found no polar opposite to BBC. No business was run with an exclusively worldwide priority, with a strategy ignoring national responsiveness, and with power belonging to worldwide product executives, while subsidiary management was reduced to a caretaker's role. Yet some companies put a strong emphasis on global or at least regional integration—IBM and Ford, for example. We can contrast salient features of the management tools of a globally integrated business to those of Brown Boveri.

In such a business, data management tools would support a primarily global view. Information systems, instead of focusing on national environments, would provide data to develop a single perspective across markets, to provide a comprehensive view of the actions of global competitors, and to compare the performance of subunits producing similar products. Measurement would be oriented toward contributions to global results, not toward local performance. Resource allocation would be managed centrally, with tradeoffs made between countries—for both marketing and sourcing—as a function of their contribution to the global competitiveness of a business. That is the opposite of BBC, where the management in each country ran a portfolio of businesses to maximize national results. Consistent with information systems and with resource allocation procedures, planning and budgeting systems would emphasize a global view of individual businesses and would be aggregated along worldwide product lines rather than geographic multiproduct entities.

Managers' management tools would also be used to emphasize a global orientation. Typically, those tools are used to establish a dominant loyalty to headquarters and to bring individual actions in line with headquarters' priorities. Career paths, for instance, would emphasize moves between countries within the same business and relatively frequent rotation both to increase the commitment of managers toward the company as a whole—which becomes their only stable social reference group—and to prevent the development of local loyalty or even in-depth acculturation of managers in any national environment. While national managers would be recruited and developed, their careers would quickly reach a plateau if they stayed in their country of origin, for they would have to move to other subsidiaries or to headquarters. Management training, meetings, workshops, and so on would mix managers of various nationalities responsible for the same business in various national subsidiaries but would discourage subsidiary-specific efforts varying across businesses. Individual performance would be assessed on the basis of contribution to the group performance, not mainly to an individual subsidiary, and rewards would also be based mainly on some measure of contribution to global performance.

Finally, conflict resolution tools would also favor a global perspective by multiplying communication channels like business teams across subsidiaries. To some extent, though, such conflicts would be minimized by the primary goal of worldwide product and business management over local managers.

The fact that among the large, relatively mature MNCs we studied in detail we could not identify an archetype of the globally run business is an important observation. Probably only a few businesses allow for such a clear-cut approach, mainly businesses that supply engineered commodities, for which the integration pressures totally dwarf local responsiveness needs. Global market leaders, as we discussed in Chapter 3 and 4, are also more likely to take such an approach. In fact, companies that have remained primarily exporters and are not yet true multinationals can operate most easily in this mode; as argued in Chapter 8, their subsidiaries are strongly dependent on headquarters, and their management may not yet have learned to appreciate and exploit needs for local responsiveness. Finally, companies that are clear technological leaders may also find it easier to adopt the global approach, although the available empirical evidence suggests that a worldwide product division approach may ultimately be detrimental to the quick transfer of new products and technologies to overseas operations. Although we did not collect detailed data on them, it seems that in the 1970s Texas Instruments and Boeing fit the pattern of strategic control described above. Some of the fledgling Japanese multinationals also seem to fit the pattern, with very centralized headquarters control over foreign operations.

Yet in most integrated multinational businesses we studied in depth, top management bent over backward to ensure that national responsiveness issues were not ignored. In particular, top management took great care that national subsidiary management views are effectively represented at headquarters rather than ignored, overlooked, or denied. Top management also took care that such views not be confined to primarily local issues, such as employment terms and conditions, but that they also involve strategic aspects of the global business. The premise of top management was that effective representation of national responsiveness was needed to avoid extremes in global integration.

More generally, extremely tight, unidimensional management tool configurations—be they consistent with national responsiveness or with global integration—seriously hampered the ability of an MNC to respond to change in its environment. In the next section we shall contrast the responses of Brown Boveri and of a corporation we shall call "Delta," a large chemical group, to increasing needs for integration and see how BBC's exclusive concern for responsiveness described above made change extremely difficult.

## Managing Strategic Redirection: Successful and Unsuccessful Change Processes

### *Two Examples*

In the 1970s, several of Brown Boveri's businesses, particularly mass-producing standard items for which neither technological exclusivity nor government protection had much importance, came under severe competitive attack. Let us take small electrical motors as an example.[2] Brown Boveri produced small motors in France, Germany, Italy, and Switzerland. Competition came both from within Western Europe, where a growing competitor, Leroy-Somer, was considerably more productive than BBC, and from cheap imports from Eastern Europe. In 1972 the corporate planning group, in collaboration with product and business teams from the five involved national companies, formulated a rationalization plan according to which plants would be specialized among the five countries and a coordinated common product development program undertaken. Italy, where unit costs were lower than in Northern European countries, was to play a significant role in manufacturing, while France, where the development groups were located, would lead the coordinated product development effort. In principle all managers involved agreed that the plan was relatively balanced with no major loser or gainer, and everyone was intellectually in agreement with the need to integrate manufacturing across Europe rather than to leave each country to produce a full product range independently. A marketing manager was appointed as coordinator.

Four years later, in 1976, the plan was far from implemented. While joint development had proceeded reasonably well, but slowly, manufacturing remained largely national. Germany had considerably expanded its manufacturing and exports and still produced a fairly complete product range. The Italian plant had faced difficulty in modernization and expansion and was operating in the red. The French plant was barely breaking even and still produced a full product range.

An analysis of what happened in the meantime shows that the

original understanding was not sufficient to trigger collaboration and integration in the absence of changes that would much more strongly affect the power of managers. Division managers in Germany and France were still measured and evaluated on their own short-term results and had little incentive to help their Italian colleagues. To the contrary, the difficulties in Italy gave the German managers an ability to turn around their business on their own and ignore the joint integration plan. A short-lived capital goods boom in 1973 also gave them the opportunity to succeed in developing their exports without having to rely on the help of the central marketing staff. The way in which the managers' management tools were set and the paucity of tools encouraging more than intellectual lip service to integration caused the integration plan to abort. Despite renewed efforts in 1976, little could be accomplished without a full-scale reorganization of the management tools toward integration.

By the late 1970s, the small motor business, faced with even tougher price competition from the Eastern bloc, was failing. As part of a broader electrical equipment industry rationalization plan, BBC divested its French operations, which were merged with a French national company (CGE-Alsthom). The small motor business was the only part of BBC's French affiliate, Compagnie ElectroMécanique, that Alsthom was not willing to take over. Ultimately, after heavy financial and employment losses, it was merged with Leroy-Somer; its competitor.

We can contrast the change process in Delta's chemical business with the difficulties faced in initiating change at Brown Boveri.[3] Delta is a large chemical and pharmaceutical multinational with significant manufacturing in Europe and the United States and with worldwide markets. Up to 1973, Delta's operations in the petrochemical group we are concerned with here were organized into largely independent national units. While Delta was organized in a matrix organization, with functional, product, and geographic responsibilities mixed and apportioned among members of the executive committee, power within the matrix remained mainly with the area and national managers.

Faced with increasing cost competition and pressure and with growing economies of scale in production, as we discussed in Chapter 2, a newly appointed vice president for worldwide petrochemical operations set out to reorient the business from being locally responsive to being globally integrated. While his broad intent was to compete globally and to use economies of scale to integrate and achieve lower costs, his intent was not conveyed to others, and he had no precise plan to realize that goal.

Over a three-year period he undertook a series of steps.

• Initially, he created a new product planning team, with representatives from the various geographic operations, with the explicit aim of sharing product and market information. The team held several meetings over a period of a few months. It discussed how to improve products and processes, and thus how to obtain better manufacturing yields. The meetings also provided the team with an opportunity to compare the technical performance and economic performance of various plants.

• As a result of the deliberations of the worldwide product planning team, it was decided to rationalize the product specifications across the various plants, making it easier to exchange process innovation without change among Delta's various chemical complexes in Europe, the United States, and Latin America.

• After almost two years of discussion, once the products had been standardized, the new vice president decided to modify the patterns of exports among the various geographic locations. Where Latin American markets had traditionally been served mainly through exports from United States, he decided to substitute European exports partly for U.S. exports. That decreased the overall short-term profitability of the business, but it allowed substantially increased capacity utilization rates in Western Europe and decreased the losses suffered from overcapacity there. It also made the profitability of the European operations directly dependent upon a flow of exports, which was centrally decided by the vice president.

• To establish "fair" transfer prices it became necessary to revise the budgeting and accounting procedures so that they would allow easier comparison between the operations in various countries and better separate operational performance from uncontrollable fluctuations (e.g. exchange rates).

• Similar measurement and budgeting procedures, across national borders, then allowed revision of the management information systems to permit comparison of the economic performance of various operations.

• In the meantime, the work of the worldwide product planning team had been completed and yielded standard technology transfer procedures, while the business group staff, at headquarters, became the node of information about process innovations and new technology. That allowed the control engineering group to take a much more active role in helping the foreign operations use new technologies.

• Three years into the process, the central staff received an added mission in their assessment of new investments. Up to that time their assessment had been purely technical. That is, they examined whether a plant improvement was technically sound, would lead to better yields, was safe, and other such questions. They were now to give not only a technical appraisal but also an economic and competitive one: Was the new investment economically justified in the perspective of its impact on worldwide business results, or should investments be made elsewhere, or could the same result be achieved by a different plant location and systemwide optimization? Investments were no longer approved unless they passed those tests, and resource allocation became much more centralized.

• Finally, more than three years after his appointment, the new vice president was influential in promoting some managers from one subsidiary to another in his business. He also moved some young aspiring managers from the subsidiaries to business group headquarters. Previously, promotions in subsidiaries had involved moves from one business to another within the same country, and only in rare cases moves from one country to another.

There are several important characteristics to the sequence of changes outlined above. First, it did not involve reorganization: In 1977 the formal structure was no different from what it had been in 1973. There were no tangible differences. Yet the way in which the business was run had shifted from national responsiveness to global integration. Second, such a change had been accomplished by a series of seemingly minor steps, at least when seen one at a time. None of the steps created much trauma within the organization. Indeed, some were hardly noticed at their inception. Further, each step was a logical next move after the preceeding one—not the *only* possible move, but one whose logic would be difficult to dispute. In particular, managers of national operations had little to complain about, at least initially: The new vice president brought them improved technological and higher plant capacity utilization rates (at least in Europe). By the time they realized that power was taken away from them, the logic for global integration was prevalent—and it represented not only a common abstract perspective but a concrete strategy on which action had already been taken. It thus became very difficult to disagree with, and local managers no longer had the power to oppose it.

In our research, the strategic transition we observed at Delta was not an isolated instance. The successful transitions we observed all shared a common pattern that abortive or stalled transitions lacked.

### Toward a Framework for Strategic Change

The successful transitions all started with the appointment of a key executive (who was respected and who enjoyed a high level of legitimacy within the organization) to a new position with a broad charter to improve performance through integration. Tough competitive pressures made that approach legitimate.

The appointment was followed by a phase (during which the new executive acted on the cognitive orientation of managers abroad) that led to the explicit consideration of strategic issues from a regional or a global perspective, where the perspective so far had been mostly national. That was done by creating business teams and various types of coordinating or planning committees. In one case (General Motors and its European components business in 1971–73), this was achieved by intensive personal contacts between the new executive and operating managers. That made it legitimate to consider possible strategic changes. The precise explicit consideration of a strategic shift and the establishment of some logical legitimacy for it required new data, which, in turn, often triggered changes in the information systems.

At least a year into the process, minor changes in assignments of responsibility started to be made in favor of headquarters. At first, they were changes that the subsidiaries could easily agree to, such as central export coordination at Delta or the relocation of GM overseas operations staff to Detroit from New York.

At Delta, export coordination was useful in establishing national production programs and improving plant utilization. At GM, subsidiaries had been complaining that the relatively ineffective "overseas" central staffs were a barrier between them and corporate headquarters or U.S. divisions. Both changes were welcomed by subsidiary managers. Those changes in assignment of responsibility consolidated the position of the new executive. Other apparently minor changes were made—for example, technology transfer coordination or joint R&D programs between subsidiaries.

Only late in the change process were strong power or authority changes made; that is, changes in resource allocation procedures, shifts in career paths, and significant status changes (e.g. the move of GM's main foreign subsidiaries to full divisional status). The change process can be divided into three broad stages:

*Stage I: Variety Generation.* Broad cognitive and strategic variety is developed, and subsidiary managers are closely involved in the process. Strategic questions are raised and explicit consideration of strategic change becomes legitimate. The stage closes with changes in the data management mechanisms. Those changes provide for multiple cognitive and strategic orientations and generate precise business or product data across subsidiaries so that alternative strategies may be analyzed. Yet complete strategies are seldom elaborated. Integration strategies are proposed in a functional operation context (manufacturing, for example).

*Stage II: Power Shift.* When skillfully managed, this stage consists of a series of relatively minor reallocations of decision and implementation authority. Each reallocation is made legitimate by the cognitive and strategic shifts explored in Stage I. Individually, no stage is very portentous, and subsidiary managers are unlikely to make a stand against it. Cumulatively, however, the minor changes increase the power of the new executive. At the end, he or she exercises substantive control on exports, technology transfers, plant specification, capacity utilization, and raw material procurement. The new executive now manages many key dependencies of the national subsidiaries.

*Stage III: Refocusing.* Some of the benefits of headquarters control begin to materialize. The shift has acquired legitimacy, and the executive has attained the power to implement substantial changes. Only at this stage are strong tools used, such as sweeping changes in patterns of responsibility or decision-making or visible changes in career paths. Finally, some of the variety introduced in the data management tools early in the change process may be eliminated. Those tools may be refocused and narrowed down to areas critical to headquarters control and integration strategies. The process is summarized in Figure 9.3.[4]

It is important to recognize the time needed for such changes. In the cases we studied, the development and use of conflict resolution tools to bring about a cognitive change and the explicit consideration of strategic changes took about a year. Minor changes in assign-

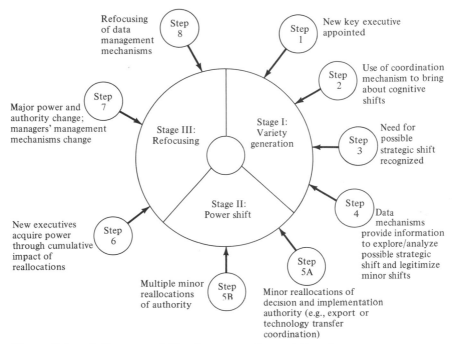

*Figure 9.3.*    A Process of Headquarters Control Development

ments of responsibility took another year. Managers' management change mechanisms were used only in the third year or later. Shifts took about three years, on the average, to be completed.

Why such slow progress? Each tool required some time to become effective. The mere communication of changes in the scheduling of meetings was not enough. Top managers above all had to maintain the credibility of the changes for operating managers to respond.

Top managers approached the change incrementally. New tools were used, or existing tools were reset, one at a time, and feedback was obtained on their effectiveness before further ones were added or reset. As many of the tools have a relatively long time horizon—both the time it takes to set them and the time they need to have an impact—the process was necessarily slow. Considering those difficulties, the change at Delta proceeded remarkably fast.

## Proactive Change

Typically, strategic changes are accomplished through structural change (e.g. from a geographic unidimensional structure to a worldwide product division structure). Such abrupt reorganizations are traumatic for members of the organization and are difficult to implement in the absence of a crisis. It is difficult to justify changes to the members of the organization unless there is a financial crisis for all to see. A shared perception of immediate crisis makes legitimate a variety of changes in managers, systems, and organizational structure.

The experience of Delta and of several other companies we studied suggests, however, that it is possible to spare the organization both the cost of waiting for an obvious crisis and the trauma of responding to it suddenly.

In a multifocal matrix organization, managers may gradually introduce a sequence of changes rather than suddenly reorganizing. In designing such a sequence, managers have to pay attention to the set of management tools they have assembled and to their impact on the evolution of world views, the emergence of a new strategic consensus, and reallocation of power between product and national executives. Typically, they have to change in sequence: a new strategy is unlikely to elicit any commitment, or even to emerge from within the organization, if it is not rooted in a consistent supportive world view. Yet, as Brown Boveri's small motor business illustrates, intellectual agreement on a new world view and a new strategy is likely to have no consequence unless the managers' self-interests and the balance of power among them are modified. While a change in relative power is necessary to implement durable change, to try to change relative power first would not work: In the absence of a legitimate and shared view of the need for change, managers will not accept having their power reduced or their priorities shifted. World views, strategic consensus, and relative power thus change in sequence.

The process of change described above, while less traumatic than sudden reorganization, is very slow, taking three to seven years, and cannot be easily reversed. Such a process requires steadiness of purpose and stability in management. While that may be quite appropriate in mature businesses, where the balance between responsiveness and integration is clear for the foreseeable future, it does not allow for adjustments that are required in intensely competitive, fast-changing businesses where constant tradeoffs between integration and responsiveness have to be made. In such businesses greater flexibility is needed.


## Providing for Strategic Flexibility

Management tools can be used to achieve flexibility in two ways. First, a given tool may be set so that it forces the managers using it to consider both integration and responsiveness priorities in ways that provide for flexibility. Second, the overall tool configuration can create enough ambiguity to allow for flexibility in trading off responsiveness and integration.

An example of a single tool inducing flexibility is provided by human resource management at Ciba-Geigy.[5] Ciba-Geigy was organized, in the early 1980s, as a matrix organization with product divisions, national subsidiaries, and functional groups. Management appointments were decided jointly by divisions and subsidiaries. Subsidiary managing directors could have a strong say in the appointment of their subordinates, relative to the influence of the central product division headquarters, insofar as they knew the various candidates and their supporters well. Potential candidates for a job opening were drawn both from within the subsidiary and from various other operations. A list was established by the divisional management development staff. In order to accept or to oppose appointment to his subsidiary of managers proposed by headquarters, a subsidiary managing director had to know headquarters well and also had to have some knowledge of the potential candidates. Conversely, in order to discuss appointments with the subsidiary manager, headquarter managers had to understand the various priorities involved in the job and in the selection of its holder. Before they ever came to discuss the choice of a candidate for a position, both sides thus had to consider tradeoffs between responsiveness and integration related to the requirements of the job and the profile of the candidates—particularly when potential candidates included both managers to be promoted locally within the subsidiary and Swiss (home-country) or third-country nationals to be rotated to the subsidiary.

Further, management selection decisions also provided a leverage point for top management intervention. Members of both the executive committee and the supervisory board were closely involved in such decisions and met weekly to discuss management succession planning and top management appointments. While in most cases top managers delegated the selection process to intermediate levels, they were nonetheless able to intervene selectively on whatever appointment decision they chose. Senior executives saw that as the main channel through which to exercise influence.

Many of the management tools at Ciba-Geigy reflected the duality of needs for integration and responsiveness. Key resource allocation decisions—for instance, for research labs or for new product launches—received strong inputs both from the divisions and from the national subsidiaries. Those tools were deliberately left ambiguous: They ensured adequate representation of both subsidiary and headquarters views without prejudging the results. Their design is based on promoting different perspectives, not only in dialogues between various types of managers but also in each manager's consideration of an issue.

Beyond each tool's providing for flexibility by forcing explicitly debated tradeoffs between responsiveness and integration, the overall tool configuration can be constructed to force such debate. The configuration must both encourage diversity in world views and provide for a way to arbitrate between these world views or to reconcile them.

To create cognitive variety, LM Ericsson's top management allowed widely different perceptions to develop in the organization. That was achieved by isolating foreign subsidiaries from domestic product divisions and letting managers in each category (multiproduct subsidiaries and world-oriented divisions) develop their own perspectives independently. There were differences in the data used as well as in accounting and budgeting systems. Central divisions were truncated; because some key functional areas (such as manufacturing) were under the central jurisdiction of corporate functional managers, divisions were more product-management groups than full-fledged autonomous strategic or operating units. Communications between divisions and subdivisions usually took place via those corporate functional managers. Subsidiaries' boards of directors included numerous corporate managers, who provided another channel of communication. Both corporate functional managers and subsidiary board members also constituted leverage points for direct top management arbitration. Those managers controlled nodes in the flow of information where detailed subsidiary data and division data met. That, plus direct access to top management, enabled functional corporate managers to effect strategic convergence from different well-represented and strongly argued cognitive maps. Strategic convergence could be kept relatively simple, since most subsidiaries catered only to their domestic markets. Product flows and other aspects of integration were managed through regional functional managers for marketing and through a central "overseas production office," which functioned as a worldwide logistic unit. Tradeoffs for strategic decisions between integration and responsiveness were managed via subsidiary boards, which included, besides corporate executives, prominent local nationals who effectively represented needs for responsiveness. Overall, the boards maintained a balance between subsidiary interests and corporate priorities.

Managers' management tools played a key role in allowing the interaction process described above to succeed. The management was strongly inbred and developed from within the ranks, being composed mainly of Swedish telecommunication engineers trained in the same school. Almost all senior managers had spent their entire careers within the company. The development of individual careers was very clearly managed, and a trusting culture developed among middle managers. Much attention was devoted to selecting, developing, and training high-potential managers. Foreign experience was acquired by successive appointments to bigger and bigger subsidiaries. Conversely, foreign managers in subsidiaries had usually rotated at least once through a position in Sweden, mostly at headquarters. Many Swedes had developed a long-term international career; others had shorter-term international assignments. Management evaluation was multinational and had strong informal aspects. Both subsidiary and headquarters contributed to the evaluation of managers in individual countries. Fear of failure was not very strong. Managers were compensated not according to performance-based incentives but rather on the basis of a broad appraisal of their contribution to the company. Instances of discharge from the company were very few. Local managers running subsidiaries usually had a lifetime job, and only managers fully trusted at headquarters were assigned to such key positions. Those various aspects of managers' management allowed for high levels of cognitive differentiation, healthy conflict between alternate perspectives, and yet an overriding sense of commitment to the corporation as a whole.

All that, added to the relative infrequency of key decisions, diminished the need for structuring decision processes. Rather than formal procedures, informal networks guided decision-making. Direct top management arbitration remained frequent and made formal decision-making processes at lower levels less critical, provided that alternate views strongly supported by data were effectively represented to top management. The relative power of subsidiaries and divisions could be directly arbitrated by top management. The corporate culture—fostered by the use over the long term of the managers' management tools just described—supported such central power by building high commitment to the company among its managers and a sense of top management fairness and leadership. Further, the dependence of both subsidiaries and divisions on central services (for example, manufacturing and research) created substantive dependencies that top management could use to modulate strategic control.

Overall, the blending of management tools at LM Ericsson was highly consistent internally and relied on a small number of high-quality tools. It was also consistent with the requirements of LM Ericsson's industry and of the firm's competitive posture. Alone among major telecommunications companies, LM Ericsson maintained a capacity both to protect its presence in mature markets, where responsiveness was essential, and to manage technology and manufacturing centrally, therefore containing technology-based aspiring multinationals such as Northern Telecom and CIT Alcatel through superior product quality and networking capabilities. Overall, LM Ericsson comes closest to developing a well-balanced capability to use a wide variety of tools to support all key management tasks.

In our research, the companies that achieved a high degree of flexibility combined their use of tools so as to provide stability in the use of a few tools with long time horizons and considerable flexibility in the use of tools with shorter time horizons.

# 10

## Impediments to Change

Chapters 8 and 9 outlined the organizational capabilities required to provide for strategic control, redirection, and flexibility and how those capabilities could be created and maintained with the use of a series of management tools. The examples presented in Chapter 9 also demonstrated that the development of such capabilities is not easy; there are serious barriers to overcome. In this chapter we focus on the analysis of those barriers.

As a starting point, let us consider the pattern of evolution of well-established multinationals, such as Philips, Unilever, and Nestlé, which predated the globalization of industries. Most often those multinationals comprised a series of autonomous, nationally responsive subsidiaries. That was the most prevalent pattern, and it is the one in which issues of strategic control and strategic redirection are most acute. We shall also, however, consider the converse problems of the excessively centralized and too tightly controlled DMNC trying to gain the capability to respond more flexibly to the diversity of its markets.

To succeed in global competition, timeliness is essential, as we discussed in Chapter 3. Merely responding to current competitive situations—and to the existing bases of competitive advantages of obvious competitors—is not sufficient, since competitors are moving targets whose mix of competitive advantages typically shifts over time. Succeeding in global competition thus calls for *anticipation of competitors' moves* and of the underlying conditions that make them possible, and *rapidity in action* throughout the company to counter those moves before they lead to winning positions.

Perception and action lags are important barriers to competitive success. Anticipation in vision and rapidity in action are crucial. In the same way as lead time reduction is an important competitive advantage for innovation, or throughput time for manufacturing efficiency, the reduction of perception and action lags in a complex organization is a critical source of global competitive advantage.

## PERCEPTION LAGS

As we discussed in Chapter 9, the acquisition of strategic control over hitherto independent subsidiaries and the achievement of strategic redirection are slow and long transitions, fraught with difficulties. That makes the reduction of perception lags all the more critical: The earlier change can be initiated, the longer the action time frame for success.

Perception lags arose from several sources in the companies we studied in detail. Quite frequently, they resulted from organizational fragmentation, a consequence of autonomous subsidiaries. Sometimes they were the consequence of misguided and improper use of management methods and tools. Often, perception lags also resulted from the lack of focus on the particular strategic requirements of a specific business in the context of a DMNC with widely different businesses—such as Corning Glass—or in a DMNC where the logic of a single historically dominant business (e.g. power systems) wrongly ruled over the management of all businesses—such as in Brown Boveri in the mid-1970s. Fuzziness in the management of individual businesses resulted from the application of a uniform management system across all businesses.

The rationalization of past successes into "success recipes"—or "how we do things here"—that outlive their usefulness and encourage complacency and competitive myopia also creates perception lags. The organization must unlearn what contributed to its past successes and discover new ways of managing itself.

### Organizational Fragmentation

Strategic vulnerability is difficult to forecast. A latent crisis is hardly ever seen in financial results; in some cases strategic vulnerabilities are completely masked by temporary brilliant financial successes. Yet when a strategic crisis that turns into a financial crisis finally triggers action, it may be too late. Subsidiary autonomy or organizational fragmentation often is the reason for the inability of large DMNCs to perceive strategic crises early.

First, and most obvious, *a strong operational orientation* may divert the attention of managers away from strategic matters. Quarterly bottom line results of individual national profit centers—as in Brown Boveri—do not encourage strategic thinking or behavior and clearly discourage strategic coordination between subsidiaries. While that is a clear example of organizational fragmentation by national markets, an alternate version of the problem may develop in integrated, centrally run companies, where fragmentation is not geographic but functional. In one of the companies we studied, very strong functional headquarters groups reached deep into national subsidiaries. While each function strove for excellence in its own specialty and provided very effective operational support to the subsidiaries it served, the functional managers, either in the subsidiaries or even at headquarters, did not coordinate their actions across functions. Functional fragmentation made consistent strategies in the affiliates, and even at headquarters, impossible.

Second, organizational fragmentation is sometimes encouraged by the well-meaning but *misguided use of management systems.* In many companies, the use of strategic planning processes—around strategic business units—built on product-markets leads to fragmentation, unless balanced by an active management of interdependencies across business units. Portfolios and planning matrices have a similar effect. Such fragmentation negates the very capabilities that multinationality and related diversification provide: the ability to leverage skills and resources in a coordinated fashion across countries and businesses to gain mutually reinforced competitive advantage across a spectrum of related products and markets. Further, customary reliance on an agreed-upon set of planning tools, while useful to create a common language in a corporation, often causes those tools to become "recipes" to be followed rather than mere concepts to help flesh out issues and structure the analyses.

Third, in the nationally responsive MNC, organizational fragmentation is a logical product of *history.* Managers from subsidiaries in different national markets—each market being protected from global competition and facing its own peculiar set of competitive circumstances—had no great reason to cooperate or even to exchange information, except maybe of an operational nature (e.g. tips on machine maintenance).

Organizational fragmentation makes the perception of a strategic crisis difficult. Emerging global patterns in the actions of competitors are not perceived easily. Only piecemeal information is obtained by each subsidiary, and even that is not necessarily shared among them or with headquarters. The sensing capabilities—analysis of competitors and benchmarking them—in MNCs themselves are fragmented, with few central capabilities. That is particularly true when emerging global competitors take highly differentiated approaches to different markets and thus make the identification of any global competitive pattern in their actions difficult to discern, or when they first penetrate peripheral markets where the MNC is not strongly present, or if they attack markets so small that the threatened local subsidiary will not be heard loudly enough at headquarters.

Cognitive changes required to identify the need for increased strategic control or for overall strategic redirection seldom originate within the fragmented operating organization. It often lacks the capability. Often a cognitive shift that will make it possible to overcome the perception lag has to be brought from outside through a new executive who carries with him a different or more open vision, through consulting services, or through some exposure, by senior executives, to different competitors or competitive assumptions. Experiences different from those internal to the existing organization are needed.

The effects of organization fragmentation on perception lags are often worsened, rather than improved, by efforts to end such lags. When Corning Glass appointed, in 1974, international business managers to coordinate product strategies across subsidiaries, their role and mission were not clearly defined—and probably could not be, because the diverse strategic requirements of the various businesses were poorly understood. Yet those critical differences were not recognized by the managers and cost them their credibility in the eyes of subsidiary managers who "knew better" but were not about to share their understanding of their business with business coordinators who had lost their credibility. That further delayed the efforts to gain strategic control over international operations.

Organizational fragmentation may also lead to poor vertical communication. As a result, different perspectives at various levels in the organization are ignored, and there is no opportunity for their confrontation or even comparison, much less compromise. Subsidiary managers, for instance, may have a keen sense of an increased need for national responsiveness but not voice it early enough, before such a need becomes obvious, for fear of being rebuffed as having too partisan a view. Legitimacy of debate, as we shall discuss later, is critical to allow vertical communication and prevent the organization from becoming fragmented into a series of layers with little "real substantive communication" among them.

In sum, organizational fragmentation leads to perceptual lags that may be costly, since the early warning function of the DMNC should not reflect today's operating priorities and principles but rather should be attuned to identifying potential future threats. Since organizational fragmentation usually results from national responsiveness strategies and is of no great cost so long as such strategies are appropriate, the main effort to reduce perception lags should be oriented toward the early identification of different competitors, most often global competitors or nationally responsive MNCs that are shifting to a policy of strategic coordination and operational integration. Strategic scanning ought to go *against* the current dominant strategy and the existing definition of organizational units, *even if* its results only confirm the validity of the current strategic, operational, and organizational priorities.

That is quite difficult to achieve in practice. The simplest approach is to set up a corporate unit for competitive intelligence to monitor markets and competitors and to be on the lookout for changes that would signal the need for strategic redirection. Such units, however, often prove ineffective.[1] While the data they use and the analysis they do may be impeccable, and usually are, their credibility with operational managers is relatively low. They may help stimulate a different cognitive orientation, but that is not enough to allow the new vision to be incorporated. For instance, the corporate strategic analysis group of a major multinational cement company has been quite active for years in "educating" operating managers about the shifts to more active international competition that reductions in sea transportation costs and new competitive concepts—such as floating factories—would bring about. Yet the head of strategic planning admitted that it took a competitor's floating factory sailing up the Saint Lawrence into the Great Lakes for their U.S. operating managers to start believing him! Similarly, in a consumer electronics company it took sophisticated display techniques that visualized competitive threats—as in some kind of a "war map" room—for the competitive intelligence staff to be heard.

Competitive intelligence units also find it difficult to tap into the operating managers' sources of information. Operating managers communicate the information they use selectively—often to gain power and recognition—and see little reason to share it with a corporate staff group, in particular when such information might subsequently be used to challenge their own autonomy and power.

Competitive intelligence thus cannot be delegated to staff units. Yet it is quite difficult to focus the attention of line managers on competitive threats that may or may not exist. While there is no problem in being competitively focused in global industries where the challenge is obvious, as in semiconductors and automobiles, it is much more difficult where the threat is less visible and more distant. European beer manufacturers, for instance, have been concerned over the last decade about a possible shift of their industry to global competition—although not global integration—triggered by U.S. brewers moving into Europe through acquisitions or the development of their own brands. Yet very little happened, and should a move by U.S. companies take place, they might well find their European competitors less ready to respond now than a few years ago: The threat has lost its credibility.

Operating managers can contribute to competitive intelligence through frequent exchanges of information between subsidiaries. Such exchanges make it possible to spot emerging patterns of global competition through the comparison of competitors' activities between countries. Managerial mobility—across businesses in the DMNC and across other firms in single-industry companies—may also help by providing a different cognitive orientation to challenge industry practices and conventional wisdom. Otis Elevators, for example, took bold moves to shift its European operations from a fragmented, nationally responsive setup to a much more integrated one when it appointed as subsidiary head—and subsequently as European head—a French diplomat who had been involved in the creation of the EEC and who brought a fresh Europe-wide view to the management of the company.

Conversely, various approaches can be used to overcome the fragmentation of integrated MNCs. First, horizontal strategies—across businesses—must be managed to prevent the dangers of worldwide product SBU fragmentation, which leads to the neglect of core technologies and of coordinated distribution leverage and market access investments. Core technologies—e.g. microelectronics for a consumer electronics company—and distribution channels must be managed jointly; resources must be allocated to them across business units and independently from the product-market SBU planning, unless the businesses have no common technologies or shared distribution.

Second, information that would challenge the existing pattern of integration should not be screened out. Typically, integration is based on "hard" quantitative data (e.g. a logic of cost reduction and increased efficiency), whereas challenges to integration are based on "soft" data (e.g. the need to build a plant in country X to increase the chances of getting a large public sector order in that country, informally suggested at a dinner party by a senior Ministry of Industry official to the local MNC subsidiary manager). Such "soft" information is often discounted in integrated MNCs, whereas a few points of productivity improvement are given much weight. In a global economy where protectionism and mercantilism are again on the rise, hints about national demands cannot be ignored so easily, although they may still be peripheral to the current operating priorities. They are early warning signals of possible needs for change and redirection or for increased flexibility.

In sum, while organizational fragmentation is unavoidable, and even useful, from the standpoint of the focus and efficiency of current operations in a business—in an existing strategic logic—such fragmentation must be overcome for competitive intelligence purposes if the company is to reduce lags in the perception of new competitive threats (e.g. Komatsu to Caterpillar) or even of different competitive opportunities (e.g. Otis taking the leadership in the elevator industry through Europe-wide integration). The main difficulty is that *cognitive capabilities that run counter to the current operating logic* are hard to implant in the operational organization. Yet by-passing the operating organization to entrust competitive intelligence to a distinct corporate unit also has its limits, both in information gathering capability and in its credibility with line management. In the last section of this chapter we discuss the merits of flexibility and of avoiding a complete operational commitment to a particular strategic approach as a way to minimize perception lags. The maintenance of a dialectic relationship between country managers and product managers, where each side is scurrying for arguments to bolster its views, may be, when actively managed, a guarantee against serious perception lags. Each side keeps on the lookout for signals that would reinforce its position.

## Multiple Business Logics

The presence of businesses with very different strategic requirements in the portfolio of a DMNC may be either an asset or a liability, depending upon how such businesses are managed.

The liability side usually derives from a poor understanding of interbusiness differences and from the mistargeted application of a uniform management system across businesses. That may reflect the historical development of the firm from a dominant business. Usually the management systems used to run that dominant business embody a number of implicit assumptions about such businesses, and those assumptions may be awkwardly transmitted to the management of other businesses, where they do not hold true. Brown Boveri's management system, for instance, was based on heavy generating equipment and national responsiveness and was altogether unsuited to the small motor business, as we discussed in Chapter 9. Similarly, Xerox found it difficult to move from stand-alone copiers and duplicators to an "office automation systems" business. Although a technological innovator in microcomputers, printers, local area networks, and other related office products, it could not translate that technological advantage into a competitive advantage in the office automation market. Similar difficulties were experienced by Olivetti when it moved from typewriters and adding machines to office automation, and by Matsushita and Philips as they move from their consumer electronics base to system products. Even Hewlett-Packard, often cited as an example of excellent management, has had its share of difficulties in refocusing its organization from stand-alone instrumentation divisions to coordinated data processing equipment business groups organized on the basis of broad application fields.

Undifferentiated management approaches do not always result from the historical dominance of a core business around the needs of which management systems were structured and management processes evolved. The intrinsic complexity of businesses and their differences may be hidden by points of relatedness. For instance, Corning's 60,000 products in the 1970s all derived from a common set of core technologies of heat-resistant glass, and from a technology standpoint they all remained somewhat comparable. Organizational fragmentation—Corning over a decade had acquired equity control of many of its licensees and joint ventures with local partners but had not yet succeeded in integrating those operations—also made the recognition of differences between businesses difficult. Most were run through independent multiproduct autonomous subsidiaries in various countries. Headquarters had no access to information to clarify the subtler differences between businesses, in terms of the IR grid outlined in Chapter 2. The lack of cognitive differentiation in the way businesses were seen by Corning's top management led to perception lags. The required level of strategic coordination and operational integration for businesses most exposed to global competition and the required autonomy at the subsidiary level for businesses most exposed to needs for national responsiveness went largely unrecognized.

Third, top management and corporate staff often strive for uniformity and symmetry in management systems and processes. That not only is intellectually satisfying but also simplifies top management's role: The same data and approaches can be used for all businesses, or at least simple categorization schemes can be relied upon. Such simplicity is dangerous; it hides the nuances between businesses and may encourage strategic recipes on the part of line managers.[2] They are driven to fit the categories of management systems and worry about interacting successfully with headquarters in the planning and budgetary games, rather than concerning themselves with competitive success.

The imposition of a uniform management system may also lead managers to demotivation and discouragement. They do not have the tools appropriate to run their business, and they know it. In some of the companies we analyzed, the weight of management systems and the strength of the corporate staff groups who defend them are such that it is very difficult for individual managers to challenge compliance with those systems or to request exemption from them.

On the other hand, well-understood different business logics in the DMNC may be a tremendous source of strength. They provide the corporation with the experience of running multiple businesses and enable it to develop a flexible approach to individual businesses.

That assumes not only that an approach to understanding interbusiness differences is developed—in the first five chapters of this book we suggested one—but also that the management of the company is able to codify its experience in running different businesses and to learn from such differences. That requires a reflective capability in top management, an ability to understand the organization as a tool to be engineered and reengineered as needed, which is not very widespread among action-oriented line managers in most companies. While, again, the task of reflective codification can be delegated to corporate staff groups, those groups are not always effective. First, they need to be genuinely oriented toward learning, rather than drift into defending their past commitments. Their role should be *to challenge the systems, not to be their guardians.* Second, they need to work at a plurality of levels, from broad characteristics of planning processes to the defusing of individual defensive routines. Third, such groups must have credibility with line managers if their learning is going to stand a chance of being transmitted to operating managers. In the companies we studied, patterns differed widely. Some, such as IBM, showed great capability to reflect on themselves and to have the learning systematized and transmitted back to operations.

In IBM, the key seemed to be a blending of *intellectual power* (on the part of a few key permanent staff members) with *credibility derived from business savvy* (the most successful line managers were occasionally rotated to corporate organization and planning staffs to carry out the implementation of important changes) and *power through access to top management* (the planning systems and organization staff reported directly to a senior vice president who had been in charge of management systems for a number of years, and was also the chairman of the "Business Operating Committee," where key operating and strategic issues were debated). In the companies less adept at learning explicitly the management skills to tackle interbusiness diversity, organization and management process staffs were of a lower status, populated with "career staffers" (who sometimes have failed rather than succeeded at line responsibilities) and lacked sufficient respect from top management. Top management decisions often by-passed staff inputs and lacked the crucial link between management systems and business decision-making so evident in IBM.

In sum, while deep interbusiness differences in the DMNC are a challenge to top management capabilities, a lack of explicit recognition of those differences among businesses can lead to fuzziness in management and to downright failure. However, diversity is also a valuable opportunity to learn. When corporate management and its staff have the ability to "reflect on" differences across businesses, adjust their management systems and processes, and codify results, the DMNC gains a competitive advantage over rivals who do not invest in such activities. *Learning to organize* is as critical a skill as learning about technologies and customers.

## Replication of Past Success Recipes

The third important source of perception lags in MNCs—one we have already alluded to—also follows from lack of adaptive learning: the mere repetition of the actions that led to past successes without much concern for adjustments to new and different conditions. Texas Instruments was successful in formalizing into a management system the innovative and entrepreneurial spirit that Pat Haggerty, its chairman after World War II, had imprinted on the company. Yet when conditions changed and the mix of Texas Instruments' businesses evolved toward consumer products and systems, where the requirements were different from semiconductors and geophysical systems, the management systems were not changed. Texas Instruments merely continued to replicate what had led to past success, with increasingly questionable results.[3] Poor financial results prompted top managers to intervene much more directly in day-to-day operations at the business unit level, which negated the innovative and entrepreneurial spirit that had led to the early success of the company. Adherence to the traditional recipe did not help solve the problems of new businesses at Texas Instruments.[4]

Even within a single business, successful strategies may transform themselves into recipes at the very time when changes are called for, as at Caterpillar during 1975–81.

How can top management overcome the tendency toward the mere replication of past successes and toward complacency? It is necessary to create the conditions for "double loop" learning, that is, for changing the norms defining effective behavior rather than merely repeating behaviors that have proved effective in the past.[5] First and foremost, as we mentioned at the end of Chapter 8, there is a strong need for variety and, therefore, a need to avoid too close a "fit" between the business and its environment, to maintain sources of tension with the current conditions of the environment, to challenge the existing "fit." As we suggested in Chapter 8, maintaining an active debate—*"a battle of ideas"* within the company—where various subunits work on different arguments and put them forward, is a basic guarantee against turning past successes into recipes that outlive their usefulness.[6]

Avoiding the "nondiscussability" syndromes that develop around personal defensive routines is equally critical. As Argyris has pointed out, human beings in organizations bring with them defensive routines—for avoiding conflicts and saving face—to make organizational life easier. Those individual processes often have the result that collective problems are not explicitly discussed, and actions are taken as a function of the defensive routines of key players. Often managers do not discuss either the defensive routines or their consequences. A cover-up of mistakes follows. Managers do not learn from their mistakes. While no full guarantee can exist against defensive routines (they are brought by individuals into organizations), their danger can be minimized by an explicit discussion of the "invisible" rules of behavior they represent. Efforts to make the assumptions underlying actions explicit, visible, and testable force a discussion. That is insurance against the risk that past success will be translated into orthodoxies or that defensive routines of individuals will interfere with management processes.

A substantive business language—rather than abstraction—can also hinder the development of orthodoxies. While strategy analysis methods and strategic planning systems are useful tools, they should not be allowed to dominate the process and crowd out thinking in the concrete. Discrepancies between reality and its perception by key executives are usually most visible if *both* very concrete substantive knowledge and abstract conceptualizations exist. The dialogue within the company has to be rich enough not to be reduced to abstractions, which too often become a substitute for actual hard strategic thinking.[7] The substitution of method for reality and the flight into abstract strategic concepts were part of the difficulty at Texas Instruments in the late 1970s.

Taken together, the three propositions just presented—active debate of ideas within the company, explicitness and testability of assumptions underlying actions, and the blending of facts and concepts into a rich corporate language—help reduce the risk of merely replicating past successes and turning them into recipes.

Even more important, strategic change should be seen not as a "grand plan," where outcomes and the paths to reach them are fully planned, but as evolving sequences of steps as described in Chapters 8 and 9, where each step involves a vision—at least of the next step— and action and reflection, or learning and "doing," coexist. Strategic change is an iterative process where "mind set" modifications, concrete changes, and power changes alternate. In the next section we discuss the difficulties faced by action, mainly in terms of modifying the distribution of power within the constellation of managers representing a business.

## ACTION LAGS

Action lags have some of the same causes as perception lags, one of which is organizational fragmentation. They derive more, however, from problems of power than simply from the lack of awareness created by organizational fragmentation itself. Power issues often manifest themselves as inaction in the face of a recognized set of problems, where the problems are known but veto power exceeds the power to initiate, and therefore the situation is allowed to deteriorate. In this section, we shall thus concentrate on power-related issues, first at the operating managers' level and then at top management level.

### Power Fragmentation Among Operational Managers

Organizational fragmentation not only fragments attention but also fragments power. Very autonomous subsidiary managers or SBU heads are accustomed to unrestrained power. While corporate management bestows rights on them and expects them to be accountable for a set of targets, those managers are still able to maintain a large degree of autonomy in their action. The imposition of strategic control or strategic redirection means power is taken away from them, at best in exchange for some shared influence on broader decisions that involve a plurality of subsidiaries or businesses. Such a change is difficult, particularly the reduction of power for a subsidiary. They involve not only cognitive changes, to which individuals can adjust, but much more difficult adjustments in self-image and perceived self worth—emotional rather than cognitive issues for the individuals involved. The changes themselves are also difficult and painful. Integration of operations across borders usually carries with it substantial writeoffs (factory equipment may be replaced to allow efficient focused manufacturing of a narrower range of products than in the past). More traumatic for the local managers are layoffs and the loss of status in the local community that may result, as well as the loss of goodwill toward the company and toward them personally or, even worse, toward their families. Within the firm itself, integration nearly always makes winners and losers of individuals. The loss of prestige can be substantial. In one of the companies we studied, a car component manufacturer, the British subsidiary had always been the leader in technology and in size. In the 1970s and early 1980s, however, the development of the automobile industries of France and Germany spurred the subsidiaries in those two countries not only to grow bigger than the British one but also, in the case of the German subsidiaries, to develop superior design, engineering, and development capabilities to meet the requirements from the most demanding customers (BMW, Audi, and Daimler Benz). In the meantime, the management of the U.K. subsidiary developed excess capacity, had to shed workers and technical specialists, and ultimately had to accept a Europe-wide integration plan in which the British subsidiary did not have the upper hand. That made for a very painful transition, which the U.K. subsidiary management would have been happy to put off.

Indeed, from the standpoint of national subsidiaries, the cost of such transitions—financial, human, and personal—will most often exceed the cost of continuing with a marginal operation. That also helps to explain the partial results achieved by Brown Boveri's small motors rationalization plan. Action lags result from the relative powerlessness of headquarters executives confronted with such situations.

We have observed that cognitive shifts were not sufficient to effect shifts in power; hearts and minds do not necessarily follow each other. Managers were quite able to recognize intellectually their collective interest, and that of their company, in achieving rationalization, but they still would see the process as too difficult managerially to initiate action.

The transition is undertaken only if the cost of transition is made "bearable" to the involved executives. That requires that the loss of power be offset by other visible advantages—e.g. the improvement in business results of Delta's European subsidiaries following the start of their exports to Latin America—and by options offered to the involved individuals, such as a move from a country managing director's to a worldwide product manager's post.

In other words, individual managers have to be co-opted both intellectually and emotionally. They have to adhere to a new vision and must accept the personal costs of turning that new vision into reality. Short of that dual intellectual and emotional conviction, lip service will be paid, but action will not follow.

## Top Management Power

The fragmentation of operating power makes top management tasks all the more difficult. First, in many companies top managers are themselves products of the old system and may not easily initiate or lead a change that reverses their prior actions and positions. Their own past success runs against the change. Second, it takes personal courage to embark on a change process, the steps of which cannot be individually planned at the outset. Planning for the unknown, like complex organizational change processes, is particularly difficult. Beyond courage, it takes a mix of organizational savvy and intellectual distance, the ability to act very concretely and at the same time to learn and reflect. On the part of top management, that calls for the skills of both the entrepreneur and the statesman. Third, each organization has its "givens," accepted beliefs and rules that form its culture, and top management cannot easily change them.

Cognitive shifts have to precede a transition that challenges established norms and rules, and such shifts are relatively slow, as we discussed in Chapter 9. The time horizon of top management, particularly when tenures are limited by mandatory retirement ages, limits the feasibility of change processes. Attempts to accelerate the process may result in top management's losing its grip on the company.

While changing key managers would accelerate the process, that is not usually an available option. In the absence of a drastic crisis, the CEO does not ordinarily have the power to remove other key executives. There is no legitimacy for such a move, and an attempt to change the composition of the management team would lead to infighting. In the traditional and relatively tightly knit business communities of Western Europe, such changes are not well accepted. As a result, the pace of the strategic redirection process may be influenced by the time of retirement of key executives, particularly managing directors of the largest subsidiaries. That provides an opportunity to replace them with younger executives who have an altogether different perspective and who see the need for global integration and/or strategic redirection.

Quite often the power of top management is also limited by "autonomous barons." The CEO can initiate and carry out change only insofar as change is supported by those barons. Further, each baron exercises his own responsibilities over a domain in the firm, which in the DMNC is usually a mix of businesses, regions, and functions that report to him. While that allows collective management of the total company at the level of the management committee, it also complicates strategic change or flexibility. Major shifts in the strategic position of a business or shifts in emphasis between businesses are difficult to accomplish, because they result in shifts in the relative power between key executives who are members of the management committee. In those circumstances each member will adopt a conservative posture, and collective veto power will exceed the power to take initiatives. Strategic paralysis may result.

Fragmentation of power thus creates action lags both at the operating levels and at the top management level. Often fragmentation of power locks the business (or the whole corporation) into a particular strategic position.

One should not conclude, however, that concentration of power is the answer. While it would make action easier—by coercion—it both reduces the quality of action, by enforcing compliance but discouraging commitment, and increases perception lags. Power concentration thus has its own severe drawbacks.

What seems to be needed to limit action lags is not only the existence of several power centers within the corporation but also a relatively fluid power structure, where power can flow between those centers. That makes it possible both to minimize the perception lags, as various sides vie for power and try to support their own perspectives, and action lags, since multiple power centers can be used by management to create dynamic instability conducive to flexibility and change. In Chapter 12, we discuss several concrete characteristics of the management processes and practices that encourage fluidity of power.

### Administrative Infrastructure

As we discussed in Chapter 9, the exercise of strategic control, the management of strategic redirection, or the achievement of strategic flexibility requires a rich set of management tools. The absence of active use of such tools is one of the main barriers to strategic redirection. Developing new management tools takes time. For example, a new accounting and budgeting system may take several years to develop and apply with confidence. As we discussed, managers' management tools take even more time to put in place and to begin making an impact. They are one key barrier to effective control, redirection, and flexibility.

Further, without a smoothly functioning administrative infrastructure middle managers—who bring the drive for change—lack the mechanisms to initiate strategic redirection. Absence of those mechanisms also restricts the ability of top management to accept debate. Open debate without rules to channel it, arenas to voice it, clear milestones to open and close it, arbitration procedures, and guarantees of due process can be threatening both to top management, who can be challenged in uncontrollable ways, and to middle managers, who are exposed to the unstructured politicization of all decisions. A rich administrative infrastructure is thus a necessary condition for an active and healthy internal debate, at least in the large complex DMNC, where debate is not confined to a small group sharing the same views and based on the same premises. In other words, dissent is easier and less threatening when the integrity of decision-making processes is protected than when dissent becomes a free-for-all internal competition.

A rich management infrastructure also provides safeguards against idiosyncrasies at the top management level. It encourages a view of the organization as a tool to accomplish strategic purpose, a tool that can be adjusted to respond to new needs. It discourages a view of the organization as a given immutable framework—particularly when line and staff positions alternate in one's career—or a view of the organization as merely a way to obtain a *modus vivendi* among key executives.

### The Meaning of Failure

Defensive routines are also a barrier to action, or at least to corrective action. Norms of consistency and the need to avoid visible failures may lead to the continuation or escalation of misguided courses of action against all logic. How the company handles personal failure thus has a strong impact on its capacity for strategic redirection and flexibility. Tolerance for failure enhances the strategic action capabilities, provided that the causes of failure are analyzed and understood and that a clear effort is made to learn explicitly from failure. Tolerance for failure should not be confused with the acceptance of continuous substandard performance. What we try to avoid here is the activation of defense routines which usually result in cover-ups and escalation to unwise commitments that perpetuate mistakes and failures, make their consequences dearer, and prevent learning from taking place.

## CONCLUSION

In this chapter we have focused on the specific barriers faced by the exercise of strategic control, by the management of strategic redirection, and by the achievement of strategic flexibility. Those barriers manifest themselves as perception and action lags that may be fatal in the context of dynamic global competition. While we limited our prescriptions here to pointing to a few approaches to overcoming those barriers, in the last two chapters we shall deal with the development of organizational capability for global competitiveness in greater detail.

# *11*

---

# Managing Interdependencies
# Across Businesses

## INTRODUCTION

In Chapter 6 we outlined both the benefits derived from actively managing interdependencies and the difficulties faced and costs incurred in doing so. That led us to advocate balance and selectivity, which means to avoid trying to manage too many or too few interdependencies.

It is a difficult balance to achieve in practice. Few companies seem to have found an approach to manage the evolving interdependencies across businesses successfully. In this chapter we review the underlying organizational capabilities that facilitate the management of interdependencies.

In the DMNC, interdependencies flow both across product groups—worldwide or within specific countries—and across countries within the same product group. Logistical interdependencies, as they result from integration strategies in a business, clearly link distinct countries in a business. Government-driven interdependencies, or distribution leverage, clearly impose interdependencies across products in a country. In taking the individual business as a unit of analysis in the preceding chapters, we have addressed interdependencies between countries in a business. Indeed, much of our discussion of strategic control, change, and flexibility derived directly from the strategic advantages of managing such interdependencies. But we have not treated interdependencies between businesses explicitly, except in the broadest sense of interbusiness variety and diversity of experience within the corporation. That is the purpose of this chapter, which picks up the discussion of interdependencies across businesses where we left it in Chapter 6.

To a large extent, the capabilities for managing interdependencies selectively and effectively rest with the same management tools that we found useful in providing for control, redirection, and flexibility.

In most companies we observed, interbusiness interdependencies are not actively managed. The barriers discussed in Chapter 10 are even stronger against the management of interdependencies between businesses than against global strategic management within a business. Interfunctional interdependencies within a business are rather obvious, and a lack of attention to their management results in rapid performance deterioration. International interdependencies within a business are driven by clear globalization forces, and, despite perception and action lags, the impact of such forces usually becomes clear, at least after a few years. The need for intersubsidiary interdependencies within a business thus becomes very visible. Interbusiness interdependencies are often less clear. When selectively managed, they may offer strategic and operational opportunities. However, they do not represent clear problems or threats when not managed, as interfunctional and intercountry interdependencies within a business usually do.

The natural tendency of most business managers is thus to ignore interdependencies with other businesses. While the costs of not managing interdependencies actively are not conspicuous, the active management of interbusiness interdependencies significantly adds to the complexity of the managerial tasks.

To be exploited, interdependencies across businesses have to be managed explicitly. Yet, once explicit attention is paid to interdependencies, managers may be tempted to manage interdependencies too completely: The strategic and operational benefits from managing interdependencies are compelling—from an analytical standpoint—while the usual costs (such as the danger of a loss of focus in managing the business, the risk of slower competitive responses, the reduced visibility of business performance, and the costs of coordination) are difficult to pin down, are not measurable, and may be discovered, at one's expense, only through experience.

The difficulty is thus to strike an approximate balance, in the context of the DMNC business portfolio between letting operating managers ignore interdependencies and, conversely, trying to exploit all possible interdependencies for strategic and operational effectiveness, but at the cost of greater managerial flexibility.

Our analysis of the management processes of a few MNCs that tried to manage interdependencies successfully—typically companies with a single industry focus but a broad complete range of products and systems (such as IBM)—suggests the somewhat paradoxical observation that a focus on the management of individual businesses and strong corporate demands for performance at the individual business level are prerequisites for the effective and selective management of interdependencies. Unless the performance of individual businesses and of their managers can be well assessed, and unless pressure is put on them to improve performance, their concern for efficacy and selectivity in managing interdependencies will be slight. Either lack of performance pressure makes ignoring interdependencies easy, or a lack of visibility of individual business performance makes the cost-benefit tradeoffs of managing interdependencies murky and difficult to assess, with the danger that managers will be prompted to consider too few or too many interdependencies, and run the risk of mediocre choices in managing interdependencies.

In this chapter we shall consider how various management tools can be used *both* to improve the visibility of individual business performance *and at the same time* to encourage their managers to cooperate with their counterparts in other businesses to exploit interdependencies to their mutual benefits.

The approach we adopt in this chapter is to revisit the categories of management tools used in Chapter 9—tools to manage information, tools to manage managers, and tools to manage conflict—and to analyze what additional demands the management of interdependencies puts on the setting of those tools. To some extent, those demands are similar to demands stemming from the need for strategic flexibility: horizontal integration paths that can be connected (or disconnected) according to circumstances.

## DATA MANAGEMENT TOOLS

The effective management of interdependencies across businesses depends first on the quality of business performance data. Interdependencies make accounting and control murky, as noted in Chapter

6. Unless the accounting and control systems are set up to cut through such murkiness, interdependencies result in a loss of focus in the management of individual businesses and in a loss of clarity in the assessment of their performance.

## Visibility of the Performance of Individual Businesses

The first requirement interdependencies impose on data management tools is that the visibility of the quality of the business performance not be compromised by the management of interdependencies. Quite to the contrary, as we argued above, the effective management of interdependencies puts additional demands on the visibility of discrete business performance.

That assumes an ability on the part of the accounting and control tools to bundle and unbundle product lines, business units, and interdependent businesses with enough precision to allow the simultaneous assessment of such business units as "stand-alone" (What if the rest of the corporation did not exist?) and as a part of an interdependent set of businesses (What does this product, business unit, or division contribute to the whole corporation?). Assets should therefore be allocated in a realistic fashion to individual businesses to identify their asset-intensity and productivity as stand-alone businesses. Such ability also requires that transfer pricing policies be clear and well defined, and that the impact of internal transfer prices be easily measurable.[1] The issue here is not necessarily to provide a permanent single transfer pricing "solution" but to provide an analytical, measurable basis to the conflicts and tensions that are almost always triggered by interdependencies. In order to resolve the conflicts on the basis of analytical debate, a reliable measurement and accounting system that can isolate the impact of transfer prices is needed. Issues are obviously complicated in the case of the DMNC by exchange rate fluctuations.

## Business's Performance Versus Manager's Performance

An ability to separate managerial from business performance is also needed. While there is no simple way to accomplish such separation, it helps for corporate management to be familiar with both the business and its managers. The ability to calibrate business performance may be enhanced—at least by helping ask the right questions when performance is not up to par—by references to analytical data bases such as PIMS.[2] While such an approach is hardly ideal, it enables managers to identify businesses where performance is lower than could be expected and to start exploring the possible reasons. Calibrating managerial performance is no easier. Only personal knowledge of the managers and an analysis of their actions can help. For that, corporate management must go beyond figures to review courses of action when assessing the performance of individual businesses and managers and must be sufficiently familiar with the substance of the business to evaluate such courses of action.

The two capabilities outlined above—bundling (managing interdependencies) and unbundling businesses (treating them as discrete businesses) for analytical purposes and separating the quality of management from that of the business—are required to provide enough visibility to business performance and to permit an adequate understanding of its quality despite the existence of interdependencies between businesses. The clarity of individual business performance is important in alleviating some of the risks outlined in Chapter 6, in particular the loss of strategic focus on individual businesses and the corresponding loss of responsibility on the part of operating management. Visibility on its own, however, is not sufficient to provide focus.

## Strategic Performance Versus Financial Performance

A third set of requirements is an understanding of strategic performance as separate from financial performance. First, the "stand-alone" strategic performance of a business has to be assessed. Such assessment requires that strategic performance measurement criteria be developed. While some criteria are obvious—relative market share, for example—others are less clear, particularly in global competition. For instance, as discussed in Chapter 3, small positions in the home markets of global competitors may never be profitable, but they may be sufficient to prevent the competitors from turning their home markets into profit sanctuaries. How can performance in such a strategic mission be assessed? Paradoxically, it may not even be identified with certainty, let alone measured accurately!

Strategic performance thus cannot be reduced to a few recipe-oriented indicators such as relative market share. While those indicators are useful to measure the "stand-alone" performance of the business in a given market, they fail to reflect the strategic contribution of a business to competitive advantage for the whole corporation. Further, reliance on such indicators may be misleading, in that they ignore the potential offered by a business for cross-subsidizing others or for strengthening their market presence by sharing distribution or by reconfiguring the business and redefining its markets.

An understanding of the strategic performance of each business (beyond the financially obvious criteria), both as a stand-alone unit and as an interdependent contributor to overall corporate performance, is a prerequisite to focus in managing a business. At the business's level it enables management to take action with an overall strategic perspective. At the corporate level, an understanding of the strategic performance of individual businesses is required to achieve selectivity and focus in resource allocation between businesses. That comprises an ability to invest and divest selectively with an understanding of the likely strategic consequences. In some of the companies we analyzed, the existence of strong, but poorly understood, interdependencies between businesses became a perennial alibi for top management not to exercise leadership in investments and divestitures or in significant reallocation of resources between businesses. Strategic paralysis followed, while more agile competitors usually gained competitive advantage.

## Core Competencies: A Complement
## to Business Measurement and Planning

A final building block to business performance visibility, when businesses are interdependent, is the ability to consider performance and resource allocation choices from standpoints other than those of individual businesses. We have already discussed in Chapter 8 the dangers associated with worldwide product structures and the need in most DMNCs to confront geographic and product line orientations. Beyond that obvious duality, there are other reasons for tempering the supremacy of product line orientations. First, businesses are often centered upon product-market opportunities that may be transient because of market, technological, and competitive changes. The product-market portfolio of a strategically managed firm may thus evolve relatively rapidly, particularly in businesses where life cycles are short. A more enduring view of the company may be that of a set of core technologies and competencies leveraged into transient market opportunities through a stable distribution infrastructure. Exclusive attention, in the strategic management process, to individual businesses may ignore deeper-rooted sources of competitive strength and even unintentionally harm them. Business performance measurement and resource allocation choices must consider those longer-lasting technical competencies and marketing and distribution infrastructure.

The integration of strategic and technological planning and the allocation of resources to core technologies that intersect specific businesses are essential here. Without specific planning processes and resource allocation channels, investment in core technologies is likely to be neglected. In Matsushita, for instance, a tradition of product division autonomy, translated into formal planning, budgeting, and control systems that emphasized product line performance, delayed the attention to developments in microelectronics and made the initial responses ineffective.[3] Each division approached microelectronics in its own way and on too small a scale. As a result, Matsushita became increasingly dependent on outside sources for critical components. Only since 1984 have resources been mustered centrally and a corporate R&D effort in microelectronics launched. The company lags behind its Japanese and European competitors in that critical technological field.

Conversely, General Telephone and Electronics (GTE), among many others, has put in place a formal planning process to link individual businesses' needs for new technologies and resource allocation to core technologies that serve multiple businesses. At GTE, each business unit defines its "Strategic Technical Areas" (STA), and those STAs are then compared across business units to identify which are common to multiple business units, leading to the development of a corporate portfolio of STAs that have applications in multiple business units. The potential impact of STAs on the total business mix and on the competitive technical strength of GTE can thus be evaluated. The corporate R&D budget is then allocated by STA, also considering an assessment of the time horizon of the needs from various business units. The most critical STAs receive priority for corporate resource allocation.[4]

Marketing and distribution investments that serve multiple businesses deserve similar attention. We discussed in Chapter 3 how General Electric faced difficulties in international consumer goods markets for want of sufficient coordination between various product divisions. Lack of attention to distribution channels that could have been common to multiple product divisions weakened the competitive position of GE outside North America in the 1970s. Conversely, whereas Matsushita paid relatively little attention to core technologies (corporate STAs in GTE's parlance), it did pay close attention to establishing and managing distribution channels, in Japan and overseas, in ways that would maximize its joint competitive leverage across business divisions.

In summary, in order to be able to manage interdependencies without losing business focus, we have suggested a set of data management capabilities as a prerequisite. We first suggested that the quality of data management tools be sufficient to preserve the visibility of the quality of business performance despite the existence of strong interdependencies between businesses. We then argued that the strengthening of information management tools along a business orientation must not lead to ignoring the often more permanent competitive strength to be gained from managing interdependencies between businesses, particularly when common core technologies and/or shared distribution channels can be exploited by several businesses. Such tools, however, only provide the infrastructure required to manage interdependencies. They must be complemented by conflict management and managers' management tools.

## MANAGERS' MANAGEMENT TOOLS

For interdependencies to be successfully managed, the natural tendency to fragmentation and autonomy, often reinforced by management cultures that stress individual entrepreneurship and responsibility and nurture a "heroic" view of leadership, must be overcome. Managers must find their interest in working together.

Perceiving potential *joint interest* is a first step, and the use of data management tools suggested in the previous section may facilitate it. As with strategic reorientation, however, a cognitive acknowledgment of the benefits of interdependencies is not sufficient.

Managing interdependencies is a complex task. It requires operating managers to share responsibility, but in so doing they must accept the fact that their responsibility extends beyond their direct authority. Managing interdependencies is also time-consuming. It requires political and organizational savvy to "oil the wheels" of the organization, and it requires an ability to manage complex tradeoffs.

For managers to undertake such tasks and do their best to perform them successfully, they need not only an intellectual recognition of their importance but a more direct fit with self-interest. Managers' management tools should therefore lead managers to pay attention to interdependencies. Several complementary approaches are possible.

First, business line managers may be evaluated not only on their individual results and on those of their business, but also as a function of their contribution to the group. The manager of Mazola Oil in Germany, whose situation we discussed in Chapter 3, must be rewarded, rather than penalized, for achieving less than the best possible results in Germany but helping his Brazilian counterpart by doing so. The same applies across businesses as across countries within a business. Vertically integrated businesses are likely to have divergent priorities; for instance, in the electronics industry third party sales are likely to be a bone of contention, with the upstream component supplier division wishing to have third party sales and the downstream division sometimes wanting to maintain exclusivity of supply to its advantage, sometimes encouraging third party sales for the sake of cost reduction. Unless some way is found jointly to optimize choices for both divisions, such a situation may result in grossly underoptimal choices. Yet the best overall choice may lead to asymmetric results for each division, with one gaining much more than the other. Unless such asymmetry is taken into consideration for measurement and rewards, cooperation is unlikely. Some companies went to great lengths to formalize such systems by creating "quasi-contracts" between product lines and divisions, containing provisions for "side payments" between divisions. Others left the formal accounting, control, and transfer pricing systems unchanged but tied managers' evaluation processes to interdependencies more directly. Often, for instance, managers' evaluation processes included an assessment of their contribution to other units and to the whole group, with managers from other interdependent units providing significant inputs into the evaluation process. Appointments to positions involving the management of significant interdependencies took those into account, and managers with a track record of teamwork and contributions to the whole corporation were selected for such positions. Some other companies, in the development of their key executives, favored an alternation of autonomous line management responsibilities with positions requiring much sensitivity to interdependencies (e.g. special coordination task forces or marketing or engineering staffs). Such mobility favored both an appreciation for interdependencies and the early development of negotiating and relational skills needed to manage them successfully. It may also develop in managers an attitude oriented toward sharing information and joint success, leading them to see relationships with colleagues in other units of the firm in a "win-win" rather than a "win-lose" perspective.

Finally, as will be discussed more fully in Chapter 12, the management of interdependencies is facilitated by ideological and cultural characteristics that allow the individual managers' commitment to the company to transcend particular business circumstances and individual positions.

In summary, managers' management tools can be set to facilitate the effective management of interdependencies, rather than make it more difficult, by creating the appropriate incentives for managers not only to be sensitive to interdependencies but to find it in their own interest to manage them actively.

Again, though, it is all too easy for interdependencies to become an alibi for bad performance. We have seen them result in "passive resource allocation," that is, maintaining the *status quo* and allocating resources to all components without selectivity. That makes the ability to unbundle business performance and to separate managers' from businesses' performance all the more important. To prevent interdependencies from becoming an excuse for poor results and unfocused resource allocation, some companies hold managers jointly responsible for their total results. At IBM, for instance, downstream end product divisions are dependent on internal suppliers of parts, components, and subsystems. Yet delays or poor performance on the part of those supplier divisions is not accepted by top management as an explanation for poor performance of the end product divisions. The resulting peer pressure can be easily imagined! Other companies, such as Matsushita, go to great lengths to disentangle and analyze causes of poor results and identify their sources.

Indeed, as we suggested earlier in this chapter, managing interdependencies on an ongoing basis also requires much performance pressure on business unit managers to seek the help of their colleagues in finding solutions that transcend the parochial interests of each unit. They must jointly consider and develop courses of action that exploit interdependencies between their units to increase their own competitive advantage. Matsushita's top management, again, used that approach, increasing the demand for performance on the individual product divisions in 1984–85 to convince their managers that they could not achieve, overall, the demanded performance improvement without cooperating around core technologies, common components, and shared distribution channels more actively than in the past.

The management of interdependencies thus requires *simultaneously* creating the conditions for managers to cooperate—that is, "win-win" perspectives on relations between units, a team spirit, and strong loyalty to and identification with the corporation—*and also* subjecting managers to enough performance demands to make them seek cooperation in response to the demands. At the same time, though, operating units' managers must have at their disposal the data management tools needed to assess the joint benefits from cooperation around interdependencies and to assess the sharing of those benefits.

Despite clarity in data and incentives for collaboration, interdependencies still have to be channeled, and conflicts are likely to take place around the choices in managing interdependencies. Unless channels are open and procedures to handle conflicts are established, the management of interbusiness interdependencies is likely to stumble on the lack of a structure for making choices. Conflict management tools thus also have a key contribution to make to the management of interdependencies.

## CONFLICT MANAGEMENT TOOLS

Interdependencies are likely to create conflicts between units. Unless such conflicts are acknowledged, accepted, and channeled, managers may shy away from the tensions of managing interdependencies.

While clarity in the use of data management tools and incentives to manage interdependencies provided by managers' management tools are important preconditions, it is also useful to provide explicit channels for the identification, management, and resolution of conflicts created by interdependencies.

Among the companies we studied in our research, IBM had the most fully developed approach to the management of interdependencies.[5] The cornerstone of IBM's system was known as "contention management," a process that took place in planning and budgeting. The many operating units of IBM develop plans, which they then have to send to the various other units with which the plans assume interdependencies and to corporate staff groups whose task it is to review the plans from the standpoint of functional excellence. Any of the units receiving the plan, or other units whose management thinks their own operation may be affected by the plan, can object to one or another aspect of the plan, that is, they voice a "nonconcurrence." That triggers a "contention" process between the involved units, during which a joint solution is sought by a joint working group, often under the chairmanship of a corporate officer not directly involved in the contentious interdependencies. Similarly, corporate staffs could lodge a "nonconcurrence" and trigger the contention process. In both interunit and in unit–staff contention, if the joint work group does not reach a solution acceptable to both units, the "contention" is then escalated for arbitration to a top management committee. In the early 1980s that was the "Corporate Management Committee," which runs the company.

There are, however, strong disincentives to escalating a contention to the Corporate Management Committee, and strong incentives for an amicable resolution between the operating or staff managers directly involved.

The process works well at IBM not only because it provides an explicit channel and a due process in the management of interdependencies, but also because the preconditions of clarity of data and performance-oriented culture and management processes provide the infrastructure and the incentive for managing interdependencies actively. The corporate philosophy and competitive strategies of IBM also stress the benefits from interdependencies quite explicitly.

Interactive planning processes between businesses, such as the one described above, are a first requirement for developing a capability to manage interdependencies. Further, at IBM, as in many other companies, there are also, beyond the business planning process described above, many strategic programs that intersect organizational boundaries along lines of interdependencies and/or specialized units whose task it is to address interdependencies.

General Electric, for instance, had special staff groups involved primarily in managing government imposed interdependencies, such as the sale of jet engines to the Canadian air force or of locomotives to Brazil, both of which required large offset agreements involving a number of other business units unrelated to aeroengines or loco-motives but with the potential to export more from Canada and Bra-zil, respectively, and to contribute to the offset agreement.

Many companies regrouped individual businesses into clusters. Usually the boundaries of those clusters are drawn to contain most strategic and operational interdependencies within each cluster, and "group" or "sector" executives pay attention to interdependencies within the cluster of businesses they oversee.

Some companies, such as Texas Instruments in the 1970s, insisted that individual line managers wear two hats simultaneously: oper-ating manager of an individual business unit *and* program manager for a strategic program intersecting multiple business units.[6] Ex-amples of a strategic program may include new components common to several end products (e.g. microprocessors for appliances), func-tionally oriented programs that apply to many units (e.g. total qual-ity control), and core technology or competency development (e.g. factory automation, consumer marketing, or logistics).

Beyond staff groups and specific action programs intersecting organizational boundaries, most companies also use coordination committees of various kinds. Nippon Electric, for example, had about forty-five interbusiness committees dealing with various types of interdependencies. The committees worked on critical issues cut-ting across the units, some being interbusiness interdependencies, others being corporate-wide programs to improve specific aspects of operations such as quality or software development. In addition, NEC organized its research around "core technologies," but in close interdependence with the operating groups, which could contribute to the technological area or make use of its innovations. That was achieved through joint research conferences and joint programs. Similarly, NEC was organized in marketing groups that intersected product units and managed customer-driven interdependencies.

The efficacy of those groups varied widely according to the fac-tors analyzed in the previous sections: incentives for individual man-agers to find joint solutions and clarity of required information. The approaches used to provide flexibility within a business, discussed in Chapter 8, can also be used to manage interdependencies between businesses in a selective way.

Beyond the horizontal linkages between units discussed above, interdependencies also modify the nature of vertical relationships be-tween subunit and corporate management in DMNCs.

The IBM example shows two critical aspects of the role of top management in managing interdependencies. First, top management sets the rules, allowing for due process to govern the debates and conflicts between subunits; second, top management may be called in to arbitrate should horizontal cooperation fail. Decentralized SBU management approaches, much in favor in the 1970s, are thus not applicable in the face of strong interbusiness interdependencies. Top management has to be much more involved in setting the course for the whole set of interdependent businesses, and arbitrating between business units as needed. In turn, this implies that in DMNCs, corporate and business unit relationships will be quite different between "stand-alone" product divisions that have few interdependencies and "interdependent" product divisions that have many linkages between them.

## STAND-ALONE VERSUS INTERDEPENDENT BUSINESSES

In an electronics company, for instance, instrumentation products may very well be managed through stand-alone units with only distant corporate supervision, while office automation systems may have to be managed with much more intimate top management involvement in setting overall strategies for a cluster of businesses and in managing interdependencies between them.

The differences between stand-alone and interdependent businesses also imply different roles for corporate staffs. The example of IBM shows the extent to which corporate staffs are used in identifying, analyzing, and advising on interdependencies. Corporate staffs can be much more intimately involved in arbitrating interdependencies between businesses than in monitoring stand-alone businesses.

DMNCs thus need to use differentiated concepts of business management according to whether the business can be run as a standalone unit or is heavily interdependent with others.

Yet many of the companies we studied had developed a dominant logic of how to manage businesses. If we just take the example of one single industry—information technology—there were widely different approaches to it, with, for instance, IBM putting much emphasis on managing interdependencies, NEC on leveraging core technologies, and Hewlett-Packard on managing independent entrepreneurial business units. In Europe, Philips saw interdependencies as critical, whereas GEC ignored them, and Bull was striving to find a balance between a product line focus and the management of interdependencies.

No single dominant logic will work well, though, even in the context of a single industry, given the needs of various product lines. Personal computers, for instance, are engineered commodity products, with clear technical standards, that can be treated as standalone, whereas large systems cannot. Those interbusiness differences grow more complex as hitherto independent industries converge, for instance computers, communications, and home electronics. Companies have to develop new patterns of management to cover a spectrum of independent and interdependent business units.

The learning process is made more difficult by the development, over time, in major companies of orthodoxies, which then act as "givens" and even become ideologies about organizations. In the next chapter we shall suggest how top management can establish stable points of commitment or even a competitive ideology that transcends individual business conditions.

# 12

## Creating Strategic Capability: Toward an "Ideal DMNC Organization"

### INTRODUCTION

In the previous chapters, we have outlined the nature of global competition as well as the organizational challenges it imposes. In this chapter we suggest that accepting the challenge of *creating globally competitive organizations* will be the centerpiece of the agenda for managers over the next decade. The challenge manifests itself in a wide variety of forms in a DMNC. At the level of a discrete business, it finds expression in the need for maintaining that difficult balance among strategic control, strategic change, and flexibility. As we saw in the preceding chapter, the need for selectively managing the interdependencies across businesses presents the next challenge. At the corporate level there is a need for recognizing and managing a widely varying set of management orientations at the level of discrete businesses, and at the same time preserving a level of uniformity of management processes and equity across business units. The need for variety at the level of businesses and at the same time a common set of beliefs and processes presents the most difficult challenge to top management. In this chapter we shall first outline the dilemmas faced by managers. We shall then discuss the need for building "strategic capability." Finally, we shall derive from the analysis an agenda for management.

# EMERGING CONCEPTS OF STRATEGY

Traditional concepts of strategy focus attention on competition and the process of gaining and sustaining competitive advantages. Our analysis of businesses in Chapters 2 and 3 started with the same assumption: that the goal of the manager is to understand the underlying structure of the business and to try to leverage that understanding to his advantage. The process of minimizing the total delivered costs (through a continuous process of tradeoffs among factor costs, productivity, and exchange rate fluctuations) as well as maximizing net prices (through selective pricing in various markets and by leveraging a product family and distribution presence) was seen as the essence of global competition. We argued that the key is to understand global cash flows in a business and how they can be coordinated. Assigning different strategic missions to different country managers in a business and to different products and businesses in the same country was suggested as a mechanism to protect global cash flows. We may call that "competitive strategy." It is a view of strategy wherein success is determined by the ability of contestants *to organize and manage variables totally within their control.* Competitive outcomes are determined by the relative abilities of contestants to anticipate changes in the sources of advantage in that business and to organize themselves to exploit them.

In Chapter 4 we started to deviate from that "pure" form of competition and argued that, in a large number of businesses, host governments are active players who can influence competitive outcomes. Through a wide variety of national policy tools, governments can effectively change the competitive dynamics within a market. By allowing privileged access to public sector markets, by insisting on local manufacturing as a precondition to participate in that market, or by providing support and subsidies to national champions, governments influence competitive outcomes. We argued that MNCs can approach strategy as a process of "negotiation" with host governments. The basis for competitive advantage in a specific country market for a business subject to significant government influence may reside in the ability of managers to negotiate with governments. We may call that "negotiated strategies."

Yet another emerging trend is for firms to form strategic alliances with other global firms. In many industries such as computers, communications, biotechnology, and automobiles, global competitors seem to form alliances. Strategy in such a setting is not totally competitive but collaborative as well. Collaboration might be restricted to a market segment or one element of the value-creating activity (e.g. joint research or joint production). While firms continue to compete, within that overall competitive framework they may collaborate. We may want to characterize this as "collaborative strategy."[1]

A diversified MNC like GE may use the competitive model of strategy in the incandescent lamp business, a negotiated strategy in the locomotive business in China, and a collaborative strategy in its "factory with the future" business. Even within the same business, Ford might use the competitive model of strategy in the large car segment, negotiate with the Spanish government before a significant investment in Spain, and collaborate with Mazda in its small car business. Such examples indicate the complexity of the strategic task facing MNC managers.

## Concepts of Strategy and Its Managerial Implications

In outlining the managerial tasks of operational integration, strategic coordination, and strategic redirection in Chapter 8, we assumed that managers have the freedom to make decisions affecting subsidiaries. Decisions regarding products, prices, manufacturing processes, choice of people, priorities in resource allocation, and timing of market strategies were assumed to be within the domain of the organization in question. That is often true in the case of businesses where the primary strategy mode is "competitive." However, in negotiated and collaborative strategies, we cannot assume that managers have the freedom to change elements of strategy unilaterally. Host governments, or partners in the case of a strategic alliance, can significantly reduce the freedom to manage.

Managers must learn to use alternate analytical models in evaluating a decision. For example, most managers are comfortable with using profitability as the basis for evaluating decisions. Host governments, on the other hand, tend to evaluate decisions on the basis of "cost-benefits." Even business managers from different DMNCs who are collaborating may not use the same analytical logic for evaluating decisions. For example, the time horizons for evaluating the strategic worth of an investment may be quite different in a Japanese firm from that of a U.S. firm. In order to coordinate strategies, managers must become adept at understanding alternate paradigms and must learn to work with others whose motivations differ.

Yet another managerial implication of the use of alternate types of strategy is that the boundaries of the business becomes blurred. Under the competitive model, managers have control over most resources they need within their business or within their firm. In the collaborative model, the strategic tasks are shared across organizational boundaries, often with firms that are current or potential competitors (e.g. Toyota and General Motors, Kodak and Canon). The responsibilities for action and the nature of transactions between the partners evolve and can be quite ambiguous.

We suggested in Chapter 11 that visibility of the performance of each subunit is critical for enhancing the performance of that business as well as managing interdependencies across businesses. In other words, the precondition for performance evaluation is that the business boundaries are "contained," and the business should act as a "stand-alone" entity within the DMNC. However, in both negotiated and collaborative strategies, visibility and the accountability for performance can be quite ambiguous. In many cases, the partners may not even agree on what constitutes performance. Return of net assets (RONA), so frequently used by managers, may mean very little to a French bureaucrat who is concerned about enhancing the technological infrastructure of France.

As top managers change, in negotiated and collaborative strategies, the goals of the joint effort may also undergo significant changes. As a result, the ability of managers to control strategies and operations or to change strategic direction becomes problematic.

The emerging patterns of global competition may be forcing managers into an ever more complex web of strategies and organizational relationships. Those impose new demands. Implicit in our discussion of the tools of control, change, and flexibility in Chapters 8, 9, and 10 is the assumption that managers have the power to use those administrative mechanisms as a way of mobilizing the organization. In both negotiated and collaborative strategies, managers may not have unfettered control over administrative tools. Their ability to manage is thus effectively reduced. That managerial impediment may explain the frustration most managers feel in coping with the pressures imposed by joint venture partners.

## MANAGING INTERDEPENDENCIES

As we discussed in Chapters 6 and 11, selectively managing interdependencies imposes the next big challenge to the DMNC. Interdependencies are of several kinds. They are not all equally important to manage. The critical interdependencies are hard to identify. Those imposed by vertical integration, as in the chemical industry, represent a different challenge from those imposed by distribution channels in a country (e.g. consumer electronics). Further, interdependencies relating to common core competencies (e.g. optical recording, which can lead to a wide variety of businesses like compact audio disc to dense storage devices for computers) are different from those imposed by the nature of the emerging markets (e.g. office automation, which includes a wide variety of products like personal computers, mainframes, and local area networks). Each type of interlinkage is qualitatively different. When they are hard to identify and manage, no DMNC can totally ignore them.

In order to manage the linkages effectively, managers must ask the question: When do we treat businesses as if they are "stand-alone" businesses, and when do we treat them as if they are an integral part of an "interdependent set of capabilities" for the firm?

## Managerial Demands of Interdependencies

The organizational demands of interdependencies manifest themselves in a wide variety of managerial tasks, most notably in resource allocation. Managers have to ensure that there is "balance" in the way resources are allocated among business units that are a part of the interdependent chain. Resources allocated to individual businesses as "stand-alone" businesses on the basis of requests made by business unit managers may result in a skewed resource allocation pattern. Mechanisms for establishing "checks and balances" must exist. The approaches used to ensure that such a balance is struck in resource allocation vary widely. Most often, corporate staff groups are assigned the responsibility to coordinate the resource requests from various constituent units.

Interdependencies also lead to conflicts over priorities, timing, and transfer prices. Appropriate conflict resolution mechanisms must be built. The "contention" system at IBM and the system of "committees and task forces" at NEC are examples of mechanisms created for effective resolution of such conflicts. Top managers must ensure that conflict resolution does not become a purely political process and that all players—both the weak and the strong—have a voice in how conflicts are resolved.

Most important of all, top managers have to ensure that business managers, while actively advocating their parochial perspectives, are willing to put on a "corporate hat" as well. Systems of measurement, rewards, and recognition must reinforce behaviors that simultaneously promote "parochial" and "corporate" perspectives. That is no mean accomplishment in most DMNCs.

## MANAGING THE TOTAL CORPORATION

The demands on the top management of a diversified DMNC, as should be obvious by now, are characterized by inherent contradictions. Getting a market focus to a particular business may be at variance with promoting collaboration among business unit managers. While business unit managers must be allowed and encouraged to pursue strategies that are in their "best interest," they have to be concerned at the same time with what is good for the total corporation. While sacrificing visibility of performance at the level of a business unit, top managers must be confident that the overall well-being of the DMNC is enhanced. The dividing line between a portfolio of stand-alone businesses and a monolith that attempts to manage all interdependencies is elusive at best. In fact, all the firms we studied are experimenting with that dilemma. As outlined at the end of Chapter 11, the experiments have met with varying success.

Top managers in a DMNC face other problems as well. While they have to recognize that the differences in the strategic imperatives among different businesses require that they accept different managerial orientations, *simultaneously* they have to be concerned about the need for "uniformity" across businesses in at least some aspects of the management system. For example, if IBM, recognizing the differences between the PC business and its more traditional mainframe business, had allowed the PC business to violate IBM's personnel policies in hiring and firing and in rewards (paying PC managers salaries and bonuses consistent with the PC business rather than IBM's policies), over time it would have established two different IBM cultures. That would have made it difficult for IBM to move people across businesses. Such examples could be multiplied. The key issue is: What policies should be uniform across the DMNC and what policies can be varied? While accepting the need for business-oriented subcultures, should managers pay attention at the same time to a "meta-culture" that transcends businesses and unifies the whole

| | Unit of Analysis | | |
| --- | --- | --- | --- |
| | Stand-alone Business | Interdependent Businesses | The Corporation— A Portfolio of Businesses |
| Key strategic issues | • Blend of competitive negotiated, and collaborative strategies<br>• Balance between global integration and local responsiveness | • Identification of critical interdependencies | • Accepting differences in the strategic imperatives of businesses in the portfolio<br>• Concern over core competencies that need nurturing |
| Managerial focus | • Quality of performance of a specific business | • Quality of performance of an interdependent set of businesses | • Performance of the portfolio of businesses |
| Key organizational issues | • Strategic and operational control of subsidiaries<br>• Strategic redirection<br>• Flexibility<br>• Innovation<br><br>↓ | • Developing checks and balances in resource allocation<br>• Conflict resolution<br>• Strategic worth vs organizational cost<br>↓ | • Creating a broad capability<br>• Providing a "glue" that holds the organization and businesses together<br>• Developing a "metaculture" |
| | Each business is unique; pursue parochial interests | Some linkages are worthwhile managing; Collaboration across businesses | Focus on value added by the portfolio. What is common across diverse businesses? Search for a "glue" |
| | | Strategic capability? | |

*Figure 12.1.*   Managerial Dilemmas in a DMNC

corporation? Should top managers worry as much about a broad range of organizational capabilities that endure?

The dilemmas that managers face in a DMNC at the level of a single business, in managing a set of interdependencies, and in the corporation as a whole is summarized in Figure 12.1. Any agenda for top management must take into account those inherent contradictions in the DMNC.

## ORGANIZATION AS A COMPETITIVE ADVANTAGE

Western managers have run large DMNCs for more than fifty years. Why then haven't these dilemmas surfaced earlier? We believe that since the end of the second world war, U.S. and some European firms enjoyed such a resource advantage over their Japanese and other Asian rivals that that resource asymmetry effectively masked the inefficiencies in the way businesses were organized and run. We believe that the sheer size of Western firms and their technological superiority during the period 1950–75 effectively provided the "slack." Insufficient attention to managerial dilemmas did not result in significant and measurable competitive disadvantages. During the last ten years, global rivals have gained not only comparable size but resource and distribution parity. Figure 12.2 identifies several industries where a new set of competitors have emerged over the last ten years. To be an effective competitor, all firms will have to pay increasing attention not only to their resource base but more importantly to the effectiveness with which those resources are deployed. Effectiveness in resource deployment may take several forms, including a shortened product development cycle or global coordination of strategies. We would like to suggest that effective competitive advantage over the next decade will accrue not to the DMNC

| Key Players in 1975 | | Key Additional Players in 1985 |
|---|---|---|
| | Automotive | |
| General Motors | | Toyota |
| Ford | | Nissan |
| | Semiconductors | |
| Motorola | | NEC |
| TI | | Fujitsu |
| | | Hitachi |
| | | Toshiba |
| | Consumer Electronics | |
| RCA | | Matsushita |
| GE | | Philips |
| | | Sony |
| | Tires | |
| Goodyear | | Michelin |
| | | Bridgestone |
| | Medical Systems | |
| GE | | Siemens |
| | | Philips |
| | Earth Moving Equipment | |
| Caterpillar | | Komatsu |

*Figure 12.2.* The Emerging Resource Parity Among Competitors: The Emergence of New Competitors

with the best resource base but to the one that leverages it best. That explains the emerging interest in the "quality of organization" and the attempts by all Western firms to "restructure" their operations.

Figure 12.3 identifies the resource base of selected global competitors in a few industries as an illustration of the emerging resource parity. (In some industries, like the computer industry, resource disparities still exist. IBM still dominates that industry, even though in personal computers it is challenged by a wide variety of competitors. However, Boeing is being effectively challenged by Airbus Industries.) The emerging resource parity goes beyond technology and financial resources. It includes geographical spread and managerial resources. As managers we have to ask: If resource asymmetries do not provide us with a competitive advantage, what will? We believe the quality of organization will become the source of competitive advantage.

In the next ten years, we believe, managers will have to increasingly shift the debate from resource-based advantages to advantages derived from the strategic capability of an organization—*its ability to conceive and execute complex strategies.*[2] Our thesis in this book has centered on the importance of coping with complexity in strat-

| | | North America | Europe | Japan | Latin America | Rest of the world |
|---|---|---|---|---|---|---|
| Automobiles | | | | | | |
| | General Motors | + + + + | + + + | (+)[1] | + + | + + + |
| | Ford | + + + | + + + | (+)[2] | + + | + + + |
| | Toyota | + + + | + | + + + + | + + | + + + |
| | Nissan | + + | + | + + + | | + + + |
| | Volkswagen | + | + + + + | + | + + + | + + |
| Lamps | | | | | | |
| | Philips | + + | + + + + | (+ +)[3] | + + + | + + + + |
| | General Electric | + + + + | 0 | 0 | + + | 0 |
| | GTE Sylvania | + + | + + | 0 | + | + + |
| Medical imaging systems | | | | | | |
| | Siemens | + + + | + + + + | + + | + + + | + + |
| | General Electric | + + + + | + + | + + | + + + | + + + + |
| | Philips | + + + | + + + + | + | + + | + + + + |
| | Toshiba | + + | + | + + + + | + + | + + |
| Color TV sets | | | | | | |
| | Philips | + + | + + + + | 0 | + + + | + + |
| | Matsushita | + + + | + | + + + + | + | + + + |
| | RCA | + + + + | 0 | 0 | 0 | 0 |

[1] Via equity control of Isuzu.
[2] Via minority position in Toyo Kogyo.
[3] Via agreement with Matsushita.

Key:  + + + +   dominant presence
      + + +   strong presence
      + +   average presence
      +   weak presence
      0   no significant presence

*Figure 12.3.*   Some Examples of Global Market Presence of Leading Competitors

Source: Compiled by authors from various industry sources.

egies and in organization. The organizations that develop this strategic capability are the ones with the best chance of winning.

## DIMENSIONS OF STRATEGIC CAPABILITY

Strategic capability is not the same as strategic planning or strategic management. Strategic capability in a DMNC is the inherent capacity of the organization continuously to learn about its environment, develop appropriate responses (strategies), and mobilize its resources to compete. It represents an underlying management infrastructure that facilitates effective strategy development and implementation. Strategic capability so defined requires that we build organizations with the following infrastructure of capabilities.

### Dimension 1: Information Processing Capability

Global competition requires firms to develop complex strategies, which may include negotiations with several host governments, cooperation with other firms in specific aspects of the business in specific areas of the world, and cooperation with joint venture partners. In order to monitor and direct strategies, managers must have adequate sources of data of both a local and a global nature, as well as the analytical tools to process that data into information meaningful for strategy. Further, the processing must be accomplished in a relatively short time (almost on a real time basis in industries like financial services!). Asymmetry in the availability of data and in the speed of processing varied data into useful information may increasingly separate the most successful global competitors from those least successful. Further, their global network of information gathering may be a particularly strong advantage of MNCs over national firms, which have no firsthand access to overseas data. The information processing capability of an organization comprises several factors:
 • *Availability of different types of data,* ranging from data about costs, technology, customers, and competitors on the one hand to data regarding political changes and bureaucratic processes in various country markets on the other. This calls for a capacity within the organization to collect and process a wide variety of information with varying degrees of verifiability. Moreover, not all data are quantifiable. Among many pitfalls that may limit the usefulness and the

effectiveness of data gathering, three stand out in the MNCs we studied in our research. First, to be effective, information gathering must be a line management responsibility, not the responsibility of some isolated staff group. Country managers, sales managers, research scientists, and the like must all be involved in gathering and circulating information. Second, "soft" data are often more important than "hard" data but tend to be driven out by the design and demands of the management information systems. A country manager's understanding of the nuances of host government policies toward the industry of his firm and his knowledge of how those policies came into being may be critical but cannot be easily communicated via standardized channels. Third, information has to be effectively communicated to top management within the organization and integrated into decision-making.

• *Integrity of the data base.* Most often managers focus attention on the data processing capability of the firm rather than the integrity of the data base. The integrity of the data base requires that managers explicitly recognize the "biases" inherent in the various sources of data. That enables the decision-makers to calibrate both the sources and the types of data used in making important decisions.

• The quality of management depends as much on the *analytical sophistication of managers* as on the availability of information. Most often managers tend to become overly committed to a methodology or an analytical tool, be it discounted cash flow or competitive mapping. The ability of a management team to use alternative analytical tools selectively—from profit and loss analysis to social cost-benefit analysis, for example, to develop a programming model to study optimum plant location taking into account an understanding of the benefits of political accommodation in a given country—is an essential ingredient of the information processing capability. Yet, while analytical competence and conceptual diversity in using information are critical, substantive knowledge is also important. In most of the successful MNCs we researched, top management was knowledgeable about the specifics of individual businesses, their technologies, customers, financial characteristics, and so on. Top managers did not retreat into the abstraction of portfolios and accounting-oriented measurements of managerial performance.

• In addition to the ability to maintain a global data base with widely differing types of data, as well as the analytical sophistication to use it and the knowledge to understand it in substance, managers must evaluate the *response time in the organization.* Response time is a function of the quality of the global communication network that links the various operations of the firms as well as the decision-making processes within the firm. A global communications network provides the infrastructure, but the decision-making process determines the response time. Decreasing the response time requires top management attention not so much to the communication infrastructure itself but to the discipline with which it is used. Many organizations inherit a culture where information is power and where, therefore, it cannot be easily shared. Corporations that can modify that attitude and can learn to process information collectively may acquire a strong advantage over those in which information remains fragmented and does not flow across units. Discipline in bringing information to bear on critical decisions is another key element. Unless top management demands—and also abides by—explicit analytical inference rules in reaching critical decisions, and unless decision implementation checkpoints are carefully set, corporate strategic response may be slow, half-hearted, and murky, an unlikely recipe to define or regain competitive advantage.

Those four elements taken together—availability of different types of data, integrity of the data base, analytical sophistication of managers, and fast response time in the organization—provide the basic capabilities to conceive and articulate complex strategies in the context of a large, diversified multinational company. In exploiting those capabilities, fundamental differences between businesses and countries have to be recognized.

## Dimension 2: Creating a Differentiated Management System

All DMNCs comprise a variety of businesses. However, most often the management systems, formal organizational structure, and decision making processes used by senior management to manage diverse businesses tend to be uniform. They may fit well with the requirements of one or several businesses, but seldom of all. Misguided and suboptimal decisions are likely to follow in businesses in which the uniform management structures, systems, and processes do not fit the underlying economic and competitive demands. Therefore, the ability to create and maintain a highly differentiated management system is an essential ingredient of the quality of management. Differentiation must be developed along several dimensions:

- *Businesses:* A recognition that the unit of analysis for building a management system is not the total firm but a discrete business is necessary. Besides other characteristics that are not specific to global competition, the central distinction is between global businesses and local businesses. Some businesses require extensive adaptation to different local conditions best understood by national subsidiary managers. Those businesses ought to be managed with a national responsiveness priority in mind. Some other businesses may be local from an operational standpoint, but also part of a global competitive game along a few major players. Businesses such as industrial gases and beverages fall into that category. While not global, those businesses may benefit greatly from strategic coordination across borders. Finally, some businesses are global not only from a strategic standpoint but also in their manufacturing and logistic networks, such as consumer electronics and automobiles. While the differences are increasingly obvious to executives, in an intellectual sense they are not always translated into how specific businesses are run and more specifically into how headquarters–subsidiary relationships are structured and managed.

- *Functions, tasks, and segments.* Even within a given business, different aspects of the business may be managed differently. For example, R&D may be totally centralized, manufacturing may be regionalized, and marketing may be handled on a country-by-country basis, with little attempt to impose one approach. In some cases, even within marketing, such aspects as pricing or large global accounts may be managed centrally, and others, such as channel management and promotion, are decentralized. Honda, Canon, and other Japanese competitors have been quite sensitive to the need to differentiate the extent of integration between functions. Typically, they have integrated R&D and manufacturing more than their Western competitors but have given their marketing subsidiaries and their distributors a greater latitude to adapt to national conditions as needed. That flexibility to differentiate across functions has proved to be a significant source of competitive advantage. Finally, market segments within the same business may have to be served differently. In the paint businesses, for instance, OEM car paint and marine paints may be global businesses, while residential paints may have to be nationally responsive and industrial paint coordinated across countries. The important issue is whether the management process recognizes the need for a variety of approaches and whether it is flexible enough to accommodate such variety not only across businesses but across various functions, key decision areas, and segments within a business.

• *Countries.* A differentiated approach must recognize not only differences across businesses but also differences across national markets. We can recognize, in most multinationals, three distinct types of national markets in a given business: (1) large, mature country markets with a significant infrastructure capability—be it in R&D or manufacturing—such as Britain, France, or Germany can provide for most MNCs; (2) countries that are significant manufacturing locations for a business (e.g. export platforms like Singapore or Taiwan) but are not significant markets for that business; and (3) country markets that are neither export platforms nor broad line operations, but essentially small markets best served through imports and some local assembly, if necessary (e.g. Kenya, Zambia). The three types of country markets represent different risks and potentials for the firms and therefore must be assigned different missions. The management process and the nature of headquarters–subsidiary relationships have to be different. While export platforms need to be tightly integrated into a centrally coordinated network, investment in smaller countries aimed at matching import substitution policies may be left autonomous. Managers from subsidiaries in large mature markets may be associated with the definition of global strategies for the business—either through some worldwide "key country" teams (as do an increasing number of Continental European MNCs) or through specific worldwide product management responsibilities (as do some Swedish MNCs).

A management process that does not account for the differences outlined here among businesses, functions, tasks, market segments, and countries is likely to hamper rather than facilitate the development of strategies that can lead to sustained competitive advantage.

## Dimension 3: Managing Strategic Change

In the constantly changing competitive environment in which most multinationals find themselves, the ability to shift strategies and refocus the attention of managers in a given business is of paramount importance. Shifting strategy in a multinational operating within a complex organizational context (resulting from the demands imposed by dimensions 1 and 2 above) is a time-consuming and demanding task. Often it requires a very careful balancing of the relative power of various subunits of the business. The process of managing the relative balance of power requires an understanding of the administrative tools available to the manager and the sequence and timing of changes in the administrative infrastructure of that business. A large number of studies of both successful and unsuccessful strategic shifts in multinationals have given us insights into the difficulties of such change as well as the opportunities open to those firms that can manage such changes with the least organizational cost and trauma.

Almost all the documented cases of strategic shifts required three to five years, and some considerably longer. The strategic benefits that accrue to the firm that can manage faster strategic shifts in a given business is obvious. Faster strategic redirection requires that managers share a common mission and a common set of goals, transcend parochialism in decision-making, ensure that debates are depoliticized, and examine explicitly conflicting perspectives.

## Dimension 4: Managing Innovation

We have so far outlined the problems of managing existing businesses in a multinational as well as managing strategic changes in those businesses. A more significant problem for the multinational is to create new businesses by managing the process of innovation.

Creation of new businesses requires fostering a spirit of entrepreneurship in a complex organization with multiple layers of general management and complex decision-making processes. Managing an existing business in a complex matrix of relationships requires sharing of information, development of a consensus, a fluid power structure, and joint ownership of risks. However, the process of innovation is a more visceral and personal activity. Ownership of the idea, accepting its risks, championing the concept, and marshaling the resources of the organization behind it are less likely to form a widely shared process. Firms have experimented with a variety of operations, from internal venture teams to spinning off new activities as separate business units in order to exempt them from the burden of the complex administrative structure of the ongoing businesses.

Involving subsidiaries requires a capability to use them as sources of information on market and customer requirements and effectively to connect those inputs to the product development process. Both the U.S. and European MNCs we observed often suffer from lack of such market–R&D connectedness. Our research points to a few critical issues, such as the importance of career paths for middle level executives, alternating headquarter product management and product policy tasks with foreign subsidiary management, for both home country and host country executives. Our research also suggests the importance of having "key country" teams play an active role in setting product specifications.

Many new opportunities—home entertainment and interactive systems, corporate private networks, office automation, and factory automation—require that firms be able creatively to pull together products, skills, and services from a variety of formerly discrete businesses to create systems. In other words, an ability to participate in the new opportunities requires that firms be able to cope with business boundaries that are ill-defined and that may change with each class of customers.

Yet internal entrepreneurship and interdependencies are particularly difficult to reconcile. While entrepreneurship works best to promote innovation, it does not recognize interdependencies or manage them easily. Still, too much concern for interdependencies and overall optimization makes entrepreneurship difficult. Our research on those issues points to a few critical capabilities to manage differentiation and interdependence simultaneously. In particular, entrepreneurship seems to require (1) that multiple perspectives be maintained within the organization as new technologies, (2) that multiple resource allocation channels coexist within the firm, (3) that personal risks and rewards be managed explicitly, and (4) that multiple flexible modes of managing people be nurtured and blended as needed. Further, the relative priorities between interdependence and differentiation must be able to fluctuate over time to reflect the changing nature of a new business, of its customers, and of its competitors.

## Dimension 5: Establishing Pivots

So far we have discussed the need for creating administrative variety to manage the strategic variety with which a multinational is confronted. While the ability to create administrative variety is critical for gaining competitive advantages and leveraging the resource infrastructure, constant change in an organization unsupported by some fixed "pivots" will result in confusion and anxiety among managers at all levels. Several approaches may be used to determine and anchor the pivots around which a firm can build its flexible administrative infrastructure. For example:

- Common goals and shared missions can serve as a central pivot for the organization (e.g. "computers and communications" as an overriding goal at NEC).
- Common principles of management across various businesses can help provide the glue (e.g. the importance of the individual, concern for excellence, long term employment at IBM).
- Common culture shared by a significant portion of top managers can contribute to stability in the midst of change (e.g. LM Ericsson, Hewlett-Packard, Philips, and Ciba Geigy).
- Participation in one single industry, even if it contains a very large number of distinct businesses, can help develop a common culture (e.g. Citibank in financial services).

While the approaches of various firms to develop organizational pivots are different, they all have one overriding function: to make constant and rapid change tolerable and to build administrative and strategic variety by providing managers with stable emotional and intellectual "roots" or basic principles that they can go back to. Many firms have further refined their approach with company songs, legends, and myths.

The tools managers use to create administrative variety are quite distinct. Planning, budgeting, measurement, rewards, information systems, people choices, training, task forces, and capital appropriation procedures are some of the tools often used to create administrative variety.

Increasingly, we can conceive of a complex multinational as a combination of some core values or pivots and a constantly changing administrative infrastructure to support a wide and constantly changing product-market mix supported by critical *common* core skills. That conception is shown schematically as follows:

Schematic of the quality of MNC management

## Dimension 6: Quality of Executive Process

Successfully developing the capabilities outlined along dimensions 1 through 5 above puts many demands on top management. Unless the role of top management is clearly understood, and unless the nature of relationships among the top ten or fifteen officers or the executive process is well-defined, such demands may tax top management capabilities. Contrary to past situations, in which competitive advantage resulted from slowly evolving changes in resource configuration, MNCs now face a need for constant adjustment in the configuration of their resources.

What are the properties of the executive process that facilitate configuration adjustments to resource reconfiguration and adjustment of the organization? The executive process is often the result of the formal sharing of authority among the top management group, along with the informal norms of acceptable behavior that have evolved over time. It is influenced by the personal agenda of individuals as well as the personal relationships among the members of the top management group. The formal structure provides only the skeleton around which the executive process evolves. Unwritten rules are equally important. Behavior among the top ten or so executives tends to be influenced by the following:

• *Competition and collaboration among the members of the top management team.* All members of top management—be they in charge of groups of businesses or functions—are competing for the top job. They are measured and rewarded on how well they perform in their businesses or functions. Their performance on their assigned responsibilities gives them their power base. On the other hand, as part of the overall top management team they must collaborate with other managers, often compromising what is in their best short-term interest. Collaboration often loses out. While the dilemma—collaboration versus competition—is an issue at all levels of management, nowhere else are the penalties for not collaborating as severe as among top managers.

• *The quality of collaboration and competition as a function of the succession process.* Often, three to five senior officers are in open competition for the top job, as was the case at General Electric and CitiCorp. In some firms, the senior officer almost automatically assumes the job of president and/or chairman. Some pick a "crown prince" fairly early. In some the guessing game is on till the last minute. Each approach has an impact on the quality of collaboration and competition among the top management group.

- *The role of the chairman.* Whether the chairman prefers to use committee meetings as information sharing mechanisms with bilateral bargains struck prior to the meeting or as true conflict resolution mechanisms will strongly affect the quality of debate and conflict resolution.

The quality of the executive process and its "visibility" constitute an important ingredient in building trust in the system. Lower-level executives take cues from how the top managers deal with issues as well as with each other.

## BUILDING THE IDEAL ORGANIZATION

While we have so far outlined not just the complexity of the strategic management task in a DMNC but its demands on the quality of the organization, we have not yet outlined what it takes to build such an organization. What are the basic principles on which an organization with the capabilities we have outlined can be structured? We move from our orientation so far, one of reporting on our research findings, to informed speculation. We start with the notion of an "ideal organization," recognizing it to be just that, an ideal. All real organizations will be less than perfect but can strive to meet the exacting demands of the ideal organization. We also believe that the ideal organization can be built on fairly simple premises. We outline below what those premises are and how the drive toward that ideal affects the agenda for senior managers.

### Building Blocks of the Ideal Organization

The ideal organization is based on a comprehensive decision-making culture that is not bound by constraints imposed by the formal structure or systems. It uses the formal structure and systems as the skeleton. The "flesh and blood" and the "mind" of the organization are supplied by the building blocks, *the principles that govern the process of management and conflict resolution:*

1. A multiple advocacy process or pluralism that allows multiple perspectives and sources of tension surrounding an issue to be explicitly examined
2. A fluid power structure that allows an opportunity for anyone to challenge the "existing logic" and "current wisdom" in the organization (This implies adequate diffusion of power in

the organization to ensure that current concepts of business and strategy can be effectively challenged without an organizational trauma.)

3. A certain legitimacy to dissent, which implies an organization where responsible disagreement and challenges to the "party line" are seen as legitimate and required behavior, and a system that does not "shoot the messenger"

4. A certain discipline in the organization, for a "due process" cannot work unless each employee feels bound to implement the decisions that come out of the exercise of that due process (Both the exercise of the right to disagree and the obligation to implement what has been agreed to on the basis of a due process are imperatives.)

The principles outlined above, we believe, will build the decision-making capabilities needed by a diversified MNC. They form the basis for developing an agenda for top management. We give below the requirements for each of the basic principles to take root in the organization, as well as the agenda for action to which that leads.

## Multiple Advocacy Process

### Requirements

- The quality of data management is enhanced. Advocacy must be based on alternative analytical interpretations of information.
- Tradeoffs do not result purely from "power plays" or "bargaining" but are based on improved problem definition.
- Various organizational groups do not restrict their approach to advocating a point of view but participate in evolving a joint solution; there is no "win–lose" framework to advocacy. Advocacy is seen as providing explicit attention to a set of perspectives.

### Agenda for Action

The critical tasks to which managers must pay attention are:

- The integrity and comprehensiveness of the data base in the organization must be ensured. While transaction data (e.g. sales data) are relatively well monitored in most organizations, soft data are not. Management's attention should shift from managing the data processing function to data base management.

- Advocacy must be based on analysis. Top managers should promote the use of multiple methodologies. No methodology, however attractive, should be allowed to become dogma. Managers must be trained continuously to keep up with the new analytical tools.
- Top managers must strive to monitor power imbalances among contending groups so that improved problem definition is not thwarted.

## Fluid Power Structure

Relative power in organizations must be dissociated from positions in the hierarchy.

### *Agenda for Action*

- Top managers must actively manage the balance of power among senior managers and groups/organizational subunits. They can use a wide variety of administrative mechanisms to manage power.
- Top managers must restrict the use of relative power shifts to accommodate strategy to two to three levels of organization or subunits. At those levels rewards and recognition should be dissociated from short-term results.
- Top managers must develop a broad concept of managerial performance that includes an assessment of the quality of the business as distinct from the quality of management of the business. The concept should include, at least, an explicit assessment of (1) business performance (strategic and operational) and (2) managerial performance (tasks and people).

Organizations should move away from simple measures of managerial performance like RONA and develop a complex system of measurement.

## Legitimacy of Dissent

Dissent is based on good analysis and not on parochialism or a consideration like "defending turf."

*Agenda for Action*

- If the long-term motives of key players are well understood, dissent is less threatening. That calls for continuity in top management.
- Economic security facilitates the ability to dissent. Long-term employment provides economic security.
- Closer identification of personal growth with the prosperity of the firm allows for dissent. In order to foster such identification, managers should not be moved too often across businesses.

## Discipline in Implementation

*Requirements*

- All employees must have an opportunity to challenge the current wisdom in their businesses and must be protected by due process. The system should allow people to participate in developing a framework for competitive success for their businesses.
- Strategies and policies are determined through an active process of debate. Once a strategy is agreed upon, each employee is informed about the policy and how it relates to his function, and is provided with all help to make it work. Once the organization has gone through the process, all employees have responsibility for ensuring the total implementation of the strategy.

*Agenda for Action*

The critical tasks to which managers must pay attention are:

- The integrity of "due process" in the organization must ensure that no employee is denied the privilege of participating and contributing to competitive success.
- Significant investments must be made in vertical communication among layers of managers and employees to ensure that policies and strategies are well communicated and that all employees understand how they can contribute to the competitive success of their business and the firm.
- Stringent performance criteria should reward people who actively participate in decision-making processes and contribute

to the implementation of decisions. Those who "drag their feet," after they have had their opportunity to contribute and are clear how the final decision was arrived at, should be penalized.

At a minimum, an agenda for top managers would involve a reexamination of the concept of managerial performance, a continuous drive for better information and analysis, less dependence on formal structures and hierarchies, an emphasis on long-term employment and economic security, a reliance on individuals, a concern for their development, and a capacity for recognizing individual differences and using them selectively.

## CONCLUSION

Our ongoing dialog and debate with managers of large DMNCs over the last ten years, the research reported in this book, have led us to conclude that the work of managers in DMNCs represents one of the most difficult intellectual and administrative challenges. The sheer complexity of businesses, the competitive dynamics, host and home government demands, and internal interdependencies of various kinds impose a set of demands that challenge the very best. Management is no longer, if it ever was, just for the "doer." It is as much for the "thinker." Successful managers will be "half yogis and half commissars." We hope that this book has captured some of the excitement of managing today's large corporations.

# Notes

## 1. Introduction (pp. 1-9)

1. C. K. Prahalad, "The Strategic Process in a Multinational Corporation," doctoral dissertation, Harvard Business School, 1975, and *idem,* "Strategic Choices in Diversified MNCs," *Harvard Business Review,* July–August 1976, pp. 67-78.

   Altogether about a score of major multinational companies were studied in depth, with particular emphasis on one or several of their businesses. The companies studied include "Delta" (disguised U.S. petrochemical company), Hewlett-Packard (medical electronics business), "Nippon" (disguised major diversified electrical and electronic equipment Japanese group), Brown Boveri (small motors and heavy generating equipment businesses), General Telephone & Electronics (telecommunication equipment business), LM Ericsson, IBM, Ford, General Motors, Philips (several businesses), Ciba Geigy (pharmaceuticals business), and several other companies who wish to remain anonymous (two European chemical companies, one European pharmaceutical group, and one American automotive components maker). In total more than twenty businesses were studied in depth by the authors and others following a similar research method, jointly or separately. While a number of the individual company studies had to remain confidential, several cases have been published about the companies. These include "Hewlett-Packard," Harvard Business School Case, 1983; "Brown Boveri," Harvard Business School Case No. 9-378-115, 1983; "Ford in Spain (A)", "Ford in Spain (B1)", "Ford in Spain (B2)", Harvard Business School Cases Nos. 9-380-091, 9-380-098, 9-380-092, 1979–80; "Ford Bobcat (A1)," "Ford

Bobcat (A2)," "Ford Bobcat (B)," "Ford Bobcat (C)," "Ford Bobcat (D)," Harvard Business School Cases Nos. 9-380-093, 9-380-099, 9-380-100, 9-380-101, 9-380-102, 1979; "General Telephone and Electronics: International Telecommunications Division," Harvard Business School Case No. 2-379-061, 1978; "Philips MIG Audio (A)," "Philips MIG Audio (B)," "Philips MIG Audio (C)," Harvard Business School Cases Nos. 1-377-195, 1-377-196, 1-377-197, 1977; "Ciba-Geigy—Management Development (A)," INSEAD-CEDEP Case, 1983; "BOK Finishes," INSEAD Case, 1986; "Kolbe Chemicals (A) and (B)," INSEAD Cases, 1986.

2. Further studies were carried out by doctoral students or colleagues using a methodology similar to ours. In particular, Christopher Bartlett and Peter Mathias made significant contributions. See Christopher E. Bartlett, "Multinational Structural Evolution: The Changing Decision Environment in International Divisions," doctoral dissertation, Harvard Business School, 1979, and Peter F. Mathias, "The Role of the Logistics System in Strategic Change: The Case of the Multinational Corporation," doctoral dissertation, Harvard Business School, 1978.

   The research on strategic realignment is summarized in Yves Doz and C. K. Prahalad, "A Process Model of Strategic Redirection in Large Complex Firms: The Case of Multinational Corporations," in Andrew Pettigrew, ed., *The Management of Strategic Change* (Oxford: Basil Blackwell, forthcoming).

3. Although we have for long criticized the false dichotomy to which separating strategy "formulation" and "implementation" too often leads (see, for example, Joseph Bower and Y. Doz, "Strategy Formulation: A Social and Political Process," in D. Schendel and C. Hofer, eds., *Strategic Management; A New View of Business Policy and Planning* [Boston: Little, Brown, 1979] pp. 152–66 and 180–88), we recognize the value of this distinction for clarity of exposition and have thus organized the book in this way. There is direct parallelism, though, between the analytical argument developed in Part I and the managerial argument developed in Part II. For instance, Chapter 6 and Chapter 11 both deal with managing interdependencies, but from complementary standpoints.

## 2. Mapping the Characteristics of a Business (pp. 13–37)

1. See Thomas Hout, Michael E. Porter, and Eileen Rudden, "How Global Companies Win Out," *Harvard Business Review,* September–October 1982, pp. 98–108.

2. C. K. Prahalad, "The Strategic Process in a Multinational Corporation," doctoral dissertation, Harvard Business School, 1975.

3. For a detailed analysis, see Christopher Bartlett, "Multinational Struc-

tural Evolution: The Changing Decision Environment in International Divisions," doctoral dissertation, Harvard Business School, 1979.

4. See "The European Paint Industry—1977," "BOK Finishes," "BOK Finishes—Decorative/Do It Yourself," "BOK Finishes—Car Refinishes," "BOK Finishes—Automotive," INSEAD Cases, 1986.

5. Bartlett, "Multinational Structural Evolution."

6. *Ibid.*

7. See C. K. Prahalad, "The Strategic Process in a Multinational Corporation," doctoral dissertation, Harvard Business School, 1975.

## 3. The Dynamics of Global Competition (pp. 38–66)

1. Gary Hamel and C. K. Prahalad, "Emerging Patterns of Global Competition," in N. Hood and J.-E. Vahlne, eds., *Strategies in Global Competition* (London: John Wiley & Sons, forthcoming, 1987).

2. Kenichi Ohmae, *Triad Power: The Coming Shape of Global Competition* (New York: Free Press, 1985).

3. Yves L. Doz, C. K. Prahalad, and Gary Hamel, "Competitive Collaboration," in Farok Contractor and Peter Lorange, eds., *Cooperative Strategies in International Business* (forthcoming, Fall 1987).

4. C. K. Prahalad and Gary Hamel, "Unexplored Routes to Competitive Revitalization," working paper, London Business School, 1986.

5. For detailed data, see "Komatsu Limited," Harvard Business School Case Services, No. 0-385-277, 1985.

6. For historical information on the color television industry, see Michael Radnor *et al., The U.S. Consumer Electronics Industry and Foreign Competition* (Washington, D.C.: U.S. Department of Commerce, May 1980). See also Yasunori Baba, "Japanese Colour Television Firms' Decision-Making From the 1950s to the 1980s: Oligopolistic Corporate Strategy in the Age of Microelectronics," doctoral dissertation, University of Sussex, 1985.

## 4. Responding to Host Government Policies (pp. 67–100)

1. For instance, see Richard D. Robinson, *National Control of Foreign Business Entry: A Survey of Fifteen Countries* (New York: Praeger, 1976).

2. See, for instance, Louis T. Wells, Jr., and David N. Smith, *Negotiating Third World Mineral Agreements* (Cambridge, Mass.: Ballinger, 1975).

3. For a summary, see Organisation for Economic Cooperation and Development, Special Group of the Economic Policy Committee on Pos-

itive Adjustment Policies, "Positive Adjustment Policies Final Report," mimeo, Paris, 1982.

4. See R. A. Caves, "Causes of Direct Investment: Foreign Firms' Shares in Canadian and United Kingdom Manufacturing Industries," *Review of Economic and Statistics* 56 (August 1974): 273–93, and *idem,* "Multinational Firms, Competition and Productivity in Host Country Industries," *Economica* 41 (May 1974): 176–93.

5. Raymond Vernon, *Sovereignty at Bay* (New York: Basic Books, 1971).

6. See Raymond Vernon, *Storm over the Multinationals* (Cambridge: Harvard University Press, 1977), and Detlev F. Vagts, "The Host Country Faces the Multinational Enterprise," *Boston University Law Review* 53, No. 2 (March 1973): 261–77.

7. For a detailed critical analysis, see Sanjaya Lall, *Foreign Investment, Transnationals and Developing Countries* (Boulder Colo.: Westview Press, 1977).

8. See W. Warren, *Imperialism: Pioneer of Capitalism* (London: NLB, Verso Editions, 1980), esp. Chapter 7, and Albert Fishlow, Carlos F. Diaz-Alejandro, Richard R. Fagen, and Roger D. Hansen, *Rich and Poor Nations in the World Economy* (Washington, D.C.: Council on Foreign Relations, 1978). See also Jack N. Behrman and William A. Fischer, "The Coordination of Foreign R&D Activities by Transnational Corporations," *Journal of International Business Studies* 10, No. 3 (Winter 1979): 28–35.

9. See Nathan Fagre and Louis T. Wells, Jr., "Bargaining Power of Multinationals and Host Governments," *Journal of International Business Studies* 13, No. 2 (Fall 1982): 9–24.

10. See Yves L. Doz, "Ford in Spain (A)," Harvard Business School Case Services, HBSCS 4-380-091, 1979.

11. See Steven Guysinger *et al.,* "Investment Incentives and Performance Requirements," unpublished monograph, World Bank, Washington, D.C., 1984.

12. See Ministry of International Trade and Industry, *The Vision of MITI Policies in the 1980s* (Tokyo: MITI, March 1980); Chalmers Johnson, *MITI and the Japanese Miracle* (Stanford, Calif.: Stanford University Press, 1982); and G. C. Allen, *The Japanese Economy* (London: Weidenfeld & Nicolson, 1981). See also Ira C. Magaziner and Thomas M. Hout, *Japanese Industrial Policy* (London: Policy Study Institute, 1980).

13. See José de la Torre, "Airbus Industrie," INSEAD case study, 1980, and Yves Doz, "Compagnie Internationale pour l'Informatique–Honeywell Bull," Harvard Business School Case No. 9-380-156, 1980.

14. See James Abheglen, *Kaisha: The Japanese Corporation* (New York: Basic Books, 1985).

15. See John Zysman, *Political Strategies for Industrial Order: The French Electronics Industry Between the Market and the State* (Berkeley: University of California Press, 1976).

16. Gary Hamel and C. K. Prahalad, "Creating Global Strategic Capability," in N. Hood, D. Schendel, and J.-E. Vahlne, eds., *Strategies in Global Competition* (London: John Wiley & Sons, forthcoming, 1987).

17. J. Fred Bucy on "Strategic Technology Transfer to the Soviet Union" (1977).

18. See Michael J. Piore and Charles F. Sabel, "Italian Small Business Development: Lessons for U.S. Industrial Policy" in J. Zysman and L. Tyson, eds., *American Industry in International Competition* (Ithaca, N.Y.: Cornell University Press, 1983).

19. See Steven Young and Neil Hood, *Dynamic Aspects of U.S. Multinational Operations in Europe* (Farnborough, Eng.: Saxon House, 1981).

20. See Yves Doz, *Strategic Management in Multinational Companies* (Oxford: Pergamon Press, 1986), ch. 8, pp. 199–200.

21. See Young and Hood, *Dynamic Aspects.*

22. See Yves Doz, *Government Control and Multinational Management: Power Systems and Telecommunication Equipment* (New York: Praeger Special Studies, 1979), chapter 3.

23. See Charles-Albert Michalet and Michel Delapierre, "Impact of Multinational Enterprises on National Scientific and Technical Capacities: Computer and Data Processing Industries" (Paris: OECD, 1977), and *idem,* "European Aerospace Industry: Competitiveness and Market Share," *Interavia,* No. 6, 1977, pp. 587–94.

24. See Yves L. Doz, Landis Gabel, José de la Torre, *et al.* "Competition in the European Information Technology Industry: The Role of the Foreign Multinationals," discussion paper, *INSEAD,* 1984.

25. *Ibid.*

26. See Louis T. Wells, "Social Cost-Benefit Analysis for MNCs," *Harvard Business Review* 53, No. 2 (March–April 1975): 40–50.

## 5. The Impact of Organized Labor (pp. 101–121)

1. For a good summary, see Roy B. Helgott, "American Unions and Multinational Companies: A Case of Misplaced Emphasis," *Columbia Journal of World Business* 18, No. 2 (Summer 1983): 81–86.

2. For a thorough analysis, see Jacques Rojot, *International Collective Bargaining* (Deventer, Netherlands: Kluwer, 1978).

3. *Ibid.*

4. See Jacques Rojot, "Sociétés Multinationales et Relations de Travail," *Analyse Financière* 2 (1984): pp. 41–47.

5. See Organization for Economic Cooperation and Development, "Positive Adjustment Policies," Final Report, mimeo (Paris, 1983).

6. For a concise but complete argument, see Peter Enderwick, "The Labour Utlisation Practices of Multinationals and Obstacles to Multinational Collective Bargaining," *Journal of Industrial Relations,* September 1984, pp. 345–63.

7. See Roger Blanpain, *The OECD Guidelines* (Deventer, Netherlands: Kluwer, 1982).

8. For details on these cases, see Richard L. Rowan and Duncan C. Campbell, "The Attempt to Regulate Industrial Relations Through International Codes of Conduct," *The Columbia Journal of World Business* 18, No. 2 (Summer 1983): 64–72.

9. See Jacques Rojot, "The 1984 Revision of the OECD Guidelines for Multinational Enterprises," *British Journal of Industrial Relations* 22, No. 3 (September 1985): 375–93.

10. See Gary Busch, "The Shifting Balance of Power in the International Labour Movement," *Multinational Business Quarterly,* No. 3, 1983, pp. 18–25.

### 6. Evaluating Interdependencies Across Businesses (pp. 122–138)

1. Interdependencies have been discussed mostly as a sharing of costs between businesses based on common elements in their value chain; see Michael Porter, *Competitive Advantage* (New York: Free Press, 1984). While the economic and technological benefits of interdependencies are in principle relatively clear, their organizational costs are seldom fully appreciated. Among works that touch upon the organizational aspects are Porter, *Competitive Advantage,* chapter 11, and Bruce Kogut, "Designing Global Strategies: Profiting From Operational Flexibility," *Sloan Management Review* 27, No. 1 (Fall 1985): 27–38.

2. This section draws on data published in Yves Doz, "Background Note on Hi-Fi: Western European Markets and Industry (revised by Kenneth Winslow), Harvard Business School, No. 4-377-193, 1977. See also Yves Doz, "Philips M.I.G. Audio (A), (B) and (C)," Harvard Business School Cases Nos. 1-377-195, 1-377-196, and 1-377-197, 1977.

3. Jay Forrester, *Industrial Dynamics* (Cambridge, Mass.: MIT Press, 1961).

4. The interpretation of IBM's evolution is based on "IBM Corporation: Background Note," and "IBM: The Bubble Memory Incident," Harvard Business School Cases Nos. 180-034 and 180-042; Abraham Katz, "Planning in the IBM Corporation," 1983, "Personal Computers: And

the Winner Is IBM," *Business Week,* October 3, 1983; "The Coming Shakeout in Personal Computers," *Business Week,* November 22, 1982; and the authors' series of interviews with senior executives at IBM in 1979 and in 1984–85.

5. The interpretation of Hewlett-Packard's evolution is based on "Hewlett-Packard: Challenging the Entrepreneurial Culture," Harvard Business School Case No. 9-384-035, 1983.

6. See Yves Doz, Reinhard Angelmar, and C. K. Prahalad, "Technological Innovation and Interdependence: A Challenge for the Large, Complex Firm," *Technology in Society* 7, Nos. 2–3 (1985): 105–125.

## 7. Building the Corporate Portfolio of Businesses (pp. 139–153)

1. Organizational variety must exceed strategic variety in order to allow the company to maintain the possibility of strategic choice. For a theoretical introduction to the concepts of "requisite variety," see W. Ross Ashby, *An Introduction to Cybernetics* (London: Chapman & Hall, 1956). For an application to corporate management, see Eric Rhenman, *Organization Theory for Long Range Planning* (New York: John Wiley & Sons, 1973). For an elaboration of some of the ideas presented in this chapter, see Christopher A. Bartlett, "MNCs: Get Off The Reorganization Merry-Go-Round," *Harvard Business Review,* March–April, 1983, pp. 138–46, and Gary Hamel and C. K. Prahalad, "Managing Responsibility in the MNC," *Strategic Management Journal* 4 (1983): 341–51. The way in which Corning's management processes evolved over time between 1975 and 1982 (as described in the series of Harvard Business School case studies) reflects a learning process on how to cope with diversity within the IR grid, followed by a phase of redirection in the variety of the businesses, as the costs of differentiating the management processes across businesses in turn become more apparent. By the early 1980s, Corning's international management processes were increasingly polarized into only two categories, one for businesses that remained nationally responsive (mainly consumer cookware) and one for businesses that had shifted toward more globally conducted and integrated management (the bulk of the other businesses).

## 8. Control, Change, and Flexibility (pp. 157–185)

1. See Yves Doz, *Government Control and Multinational Strategic Management* (New York: Praeger, 1979), chapters 6 and 9.

2. For detailed evidence, see R. A. Bettis, "Dresser Industries and the Pipeline," Edwin L. Cox School of Business, 1984.

3. For a more detailed discussion, see C. K. Prahalad and Yves Doz, "An Approach to Strategic Control in MNCs," *Sloan Management Review,* 22, No. 4, Summer 1981.

4. This distinction is based on the work of Christopher Bartlett and our own research. For a more detailed argument, see Yves Doz, Christopher A. Bartlett, and C. K. Prahalad, "Global Competitive Pressures and Host Country Demands: Managing Tensions in MNCs," *California Management Review,* Vol. 23, No. 3, Spring 1981.

5. Earlier versions of this argument have been presented in C. K. Prahalad, "The Concept and Potential of Multidimensional Organizations," in F. Stevens, ed., *Managing Managers* (Eindhoven: NV Philips, 1980), and in C. K. Prahalad and Y. Doz, "Managing Managers: The Work of Top Management," in J. G. Hunt, D. M. Hosking, C. Schreisheim, and R. Steward, eds., *Leaders and Managers* (New York: Pergamon Press, 1984).

## 9. Tools for Strategic Control, Flexibility, and Change (pp. 186–216)

1. A fuller discussion of these management tools can be found in Yves Doz and C. K. Prahalad, "Headquarter Influence and Strategic Control in Multinational Companies," *Sloan Management Review,* Fall 1981, pp. 15–29.

2. For details, see Yves Doz, "Brown Boveri & Cie," Harvard Business School Case No. 9-378-115, 1983.

3. For details see C. K. Prahalad, "The Strategic Process in a Multinational Corporation," doctoral dissertation, Harvard Business School, 1975.

4. For a systematic comparison of the various companies in our research sample, see Yves Doz and C. K. Prahalad, "A Process Model of Strategic Redirection in Large Complex Firms: The Case of Multinational Corporations," in Andrew Pettigrew, ed., *The Management of Strategic Change* (Oxford: Basil Blackwell, forthcoming).

5. For details, see Yves Doz, "Ciba-Geigy—Management Development (A)", INSEAD-CEDEP Case, 1983.

6. See Yves Doz, *Government and Multinational Management: Power Systems and Telecommunication Equipment* (New York: Praeger Special Studies, 1979), chapter 7.

## 10. Impediments to Change (pp. 217–234)

1. Sumantra Ghoshal, "Environmental Scanning in Korean Multinationals," doctoral dissertation, MIT, 1985.

2. For a detailed discussion, see C. K. Prahalad and Richard A. Bettis,

"The Dominant Logic: A New Linkage Between Diversity and Performance," *Strategic Management Journal* 7 (1986): 485–501.

3. For a detailed discussion, see Mariann S. Jelinek, *Institutionalizing Innovation* (New York: Praeger, 1979).

4. See "When Marketing Failed at Texas Instruments," *Business Week,* June 22, 1981, pp. 91–94; "Texas Instruments Shows U.S. Business How to Survive in the 1980s," *Business Week,* September 18, 1978, pp. 66–90; "Texas Instruments Wrestles with the Consumer Market," *Fortune,* December 3, 1979, pp. 50–57.

5. Chris Argyris and Donald Schön, *Organizational Learning* (Reading, Mass.: Addison-Wesley, 1978).

6. Chris Argyris, *Strategy, Change, and Defensive Routines* (Marshfield, Mass.: Pitman, 1985).

7. Richard Normann, "Business Logics for Innovators: Competitiveness Rethought" (research in progress).

## 11. Managing Interdependencies Across Businesses (pp. 235–249)

1. For a thorough discussion of these issues, see Robert G. Eccles, *The Transfer Pricing Problem* (Lexington, Mass.: Lexington Books, 1985).

2. See B. S. Chakravarthy, "Measuring Strategic Performance," *Strategic Management Journal* 7, No. 3 (September–October 1986): pp. 437–458.

3. See K. Takahashi, "The Matsushita Electric Industrial Co. Ltd.—Management Control Systems," Harvard Business School Case No. 9-373-922.

4. For a detailed description, see Graham R. Mitchell, "New Approaches to the Strategic Management of Technology," in *Technology in Society* 7, Nos. 2/3 (1985): 227–40.

5. See A. Bhambri, J. L. Wilson, and R. F. Vancil, "IBM Corporation: Background Note," Harvard Business School Case No. 180-034, 1979.

6. See R. F. Vancil, "Texas Instruments Incorporated—Management Systems," Harvard Business School Case No. 9-172-054, 1972.

## 12. Creating Strategic Capability: Toward an "Ideal DMNC Organization" (pp. 250–272)

1. For a more detailed discussion of these strategies, see C. K. Prahalad, "Creating Strategic Capability: An Agenda for Top Management," *Human Resource Management* 22, No. 3 (Fall 1983): 237–55.

2. This argument is more fully developed in Yves Doz and C. K. Prahalad, "Quality of Management: An Emerging Source of Global Competitive Advantage?" in N. Hood and J. E. Vahlne, eds., *Strategies in Global Competition* (London: John Wiley & Sons, forthcoming, 1987).

# Index

Accumulated volume, 59–60
Action lags, 229–230, 232
Administrative infrastructure, 232–233
Administrative variety, 143, 144, 256, 266
  containment of, 148
Airbus, 82, 83
Area organization, 171–172, 173, 178, 179
Automobile industry, 27–28, 73n, 102, 230
  Japanese, 76, 77
Autonomous barons, 232
Autonomous (national) development, 76, 80–81

Bargaining leverage, 134–135
Bargaining structures, 110
Beatrice Foods, 142
Belgium, 125
Boundaries, business, 253
Brand presence, 46, 47, 48, 53, 137
Brown Boveri, 175, 200, 202–206, 212, 218, 224, 230
Business and Industry Advisory Committee (BIAC), 114
Business logics, multiple, 224–225
Businesses, 262
  characteristics of, 15
  classification of, 22
  definition of, 13
  diversity of, 2
  functions within, 35–36
  global, 18
  mapping characteristics of, 16, 22, 24–25
  mapping dynamics of, 26–30
  multidomestic, 18
  resegmenting, 28

Cash flows, 163–164
  global, 39–40, 41, 48
Chairman, role of, 268

Change, 35, 158, 159, 160, 165, 184–185
  proactive, 182–184
  rate of, 145
Change process, 212, 231
  stages in, 210
Chemical industry, 26–27, 167
Chrysler, 87, 182
Ciba-Geigy, 213–214
Citizenship costs, 91, 106
Codes of conduct, 114, 116, 117
Co-determination, 119
Cognitive process, 186, 202
Cognitive variety, 214
Collaborative strategy, 252, 253
Color television (CTV) industry, case study of, 53–58, 61
Committee on International Investment and Multinational Enterprise (CIME), 114–115
Competition
  dynamics of, 65–66
  essence of, 40
  global, 36–37, 39
  multinational, 19
  nature of, 134
Competitive advantage, 2, 4, 15, 44, 45, 54, 58, 158, 171, 251, 256–257, 265
  layers of, 52–54
  net, 43
Competitive intelligence, 221–223
Competitive strategy, 251, 252, 253
Competitiveness, 77
  country's level of, 76
Competitor, multimarket, 61, 72, 75
Complex organization
  concept of, 177, 185
  managing, 180
  senior management role in, 181
Complexity, 174, 175, 176
  dimensions of, 145–148
Computer industry, 36, 38, 258
Conflict management tools, 188, 201, 203, 210, 245